Inspiration and Innovation

The Western History Series
SERIES EDITORS

Carol L. Higham and William H. Katerberg

The Western History Series

Inspiration and Innovation

Religion in the American West

Todd M. Kerstetter

WILEY Blackwell

This edition first published 2015
© 2015 John Wiley & Sons, Inc.

Registered Office
John Wiley & Sons, Ltd, The Atrium, Southern Gate, Chichester, West Sussex, PO19 8SQ, UK

Editorial Offices
350 Main Street, Malden, MA 02148-5020, USA
9600 Garsington Road, Oxford, OX4 2DQ, UK
The Atrium, Southern Gate, Chichester, West Sussex, PO19 8SQ, UK

For details of our global editorial offices, for customer services, and for information about how to apply for permission to reuse the copyright material in this book please see our website at www.wiley.com/wiley-blackwell.

The right of Todd M. Kerstetter to be identified as the author of this work has been asserted in accordance with the UK Copyright, Designs and Patents Act 1988.

Library of Congress Cataloging-in-Publication Data

Kerstetter, Todd M., 1963–
    Inspiration and innovation : religion in the American West / Todd M. Kerstetter.
        pages cm – (Western history series)
    Includes bibliographical references and index.
    ISBN 978-1-118-84833-3 (hardback) – ISBN 978-1-118-84838-8 (paper)
1. West (U.S.)–Religion.   I. Title.
    BL2527.W47K47 2015
    200.978–dc23

                                                    2014032714

A catalogue record for this book is available from the British Library.

Cover image: George Caleb Bingham, *Daniel Boone escorting settlers through the Cumberland Gap*, 1851–52, oil on canvas. Washington University, St. Louis, USA / The Bridgeman Art Library

Set in 10.5/12pt Minion by SPi Publisher Services, Pondicherry, India
Printed and bound in Malaysia by Vivar Printing Sdn Bhd

1   2015

Contents

List of Illustrations

Acknowledgements

Thanks to Carol Higham and Will Katerberg for inviting me to write this book. Thanks to both of them, also, for teaching me about writing and for devoting considerable time to helping develop the manuscript. Their expert guidance made this book much better than it would have been. Carol gets an extra measure of thanks for extracting this book from me. Without her encouragement and good humor, this thing might still be floating around in the space between my ears. I appreciate Andrew Davidson's support as well as considerable help from Georgina Coleby, the project's editor at Wiley Blackwell.

Colleagues at Texas Christian University helped this project in several ways. Peter Worthing, chair of the Department of History and Geography, provided course releases to compensate for the burdens of the graduate program. Becca Sharpless kindly and good-naturedly asked after my progress, which motivated me to work so I would have something to report in the hallways. Charlotte Hogg in the Department of English organized a faculty writing boot camp in the summer of 2013 that helped me do much of the work on Chapter 5. Her follow-up program during the 2013–2014 school year helped keep me on task. Thanks to Andrew Schoolmaster, dean of AddRan College of Liberal Arts, for supporting the boot camp and for supporting scholarship in general. TCU's Mary Coutts Burnett Library generously provided me with a faculty research office where I could escape distractions to read, think, and write with immediate access to the library's excellent resources. Thank you June Koelker, dean of the library! I consider myself profoundly fortunate to have had the manuscript reviewed by a Roman Catholic, a Mormon, and two ordained ministers (Presbyterian, Disciples of Christ), all of whom are very smart and who happened to be advanced doctoral students in history at TCU when I finally finished a complete draft. In alphabetical order, they are Lisa Barnett, Amanda Bresie, Brett Dowdle, and Beth Hessel. Their religious and historical expertise saved me from making several errors and improved the writing.

Elsewhere, I appreciate everything John Wunder taught me in graduate school at the University of Nebraska. His fingerprints appear throughout, sometimes conspicuously. Three anonymous reviewers wrote the best (thorough, thoughtful, and helpful) batch of reader reports I've ever received. I appreciate their support and excellent suggestions. I couldn't make all of them work, but I tried. Despite my best efforts and all the help I received, some problems will probably surface in the final work. Those are my fault.

Closer to home, thanks to my parents, Ned and Joyce Kerstetter, teachers who instilled in me a love of learning and gave me so much more that I'll just let it go at that. My brother, Chad, helped keep me on track with his wicked sense of humor. At home, I could not have done this without the patient love and support of my wife, Holly McFarland, and the energy, wonder, and love brought to our home by Nora and Leah.

Introduction

This book examines the religious history of the trans-Mississippi United States for its own sake and to supplement topics neglected or only briefly mentioned by most textbook histories of the American West. As I worked on this project, two discoveries surprised me and inspired me. First, many histories of the West say little about religion's roles in the region. This situation afflicts much of what has been written about US history. Two historians concluded in 2010 that, "Religion is everywhere in history, but nowhere in mainstream historiography." Second, many surveys of US religious history say next to nothing about what happened in the West. A reader who relied on only those books for knowledge of US religious history might conclude the United States extended from the Atlantic Ocean all the way to the Appalachian Mountains or, in expansive passages, to Chicago. People have lived west of the Appalachians (and west of Chicago) for thousands of years. Those people held religious beliefs and they participated in important events that touched the history of religion on regional, national, and transnational stages. This book delivers some of those stories and enriches our understanding of the American West by placing religion at center stage.

Inspiration and Innovation: Religion in the American West,
First Edition. Todd M. Kerstetter.
© 2015 John Wiley & Sons, Inc. Published 2015 by John Wiley & Sons, Inc.

Religion plays a major role in many people's lives. It defines who they are, how they fit into the world, and how they view the world. It can motivate or shape their behavior. The trans-Mississippi West, likewise, played, and plays, an important role in US and world history. Before the United States existed, numerous human groups settled in the region. Before the United States existed, trans-Mississippi North America drew diverse settlers from Europe and Africa who interacted with the indigenous population. Shortly after the United States came into existence, the nation set its eyes on the western two-thirds of North America and in short order conquered those lands and the people living there and incorporated both into the nation. People from around the world rushed in. The best-known versions of these stories focus on secular matters and in so doing exclude matters of vital concern. This book asks: What roles did religion and the West play in each other's histories?

"The West" is both an idea and a place. The idea has meant many things to many people. It has moved over time and even historians of the region disagree about precisely where to draw its boundaries. Before I became a western historian I encountered the region's ethereal nature on a cross-country bicycle trip from Myrtle Beach, South Carolina, to Vancouver, British Columbia. When my cycling buddy and I crossed the Mississippi River at St. Louis we visited the famous Arch and the Jefferson National Expansion Monument, landmarks that announced we had entered the West. Despite crossing a line on a map and a psychic threshold marked by the national monument, the landscape did not seem dramatically different and I did not sense I had moved into a new or different region. Later we pedaled across the Missouri River into Nebraska. Again we had crossed a boundary and had entered a state that I considered western. Things felt a little different, but not particularly western. Within days, though, somewhere not too far west of Norfolk, Nebraska, the landscape, the vegetation, the sky, the very air seemed different and at last I thought to myself, "*Now* we're in the West." Near Valentine, Nebraska, I saw a tumbleweed (and made an ill-advised attempt to catch it while riding) and that banished any lingering doubt that we had reached *The West*. The landscape shifted time and again from there to the conclusion of our ride in Vancouver, but we remained within the West as far as I was concerned. My professional colleagues have a similarly murky idea of where the West begins and ends. A survey of western historians that asked them to define the region's boundaries showed widespread disagreement. A map of the territory they all agreed upon as "the West," which the survey called "the unambiguous West," depicted a surprisingly narrow swath of land between the Mississippi River and the Pacific Ocean. Only Idaho, Utah, Arizona, and Nevada among current states had their boundaries entirely within this unambiguous West. Every other state west of the Mississippi was open for debate as far as its "Western-ness" was concerned. This does not fit well with many narratives or popular conceptions about the region, which often include everything from St. Louis to San Francisco.

This book focuses on the United States west of the Mississippi River. That region, ethereal as it might be, holds an iconic place in the nation's history and mythology. It has also stirred the imaginations of people around the world. For historian Frederick Jackson Turner, these western states represent a region where a line of settlement, the frontier, progressed westward and explained American development. For historian Patricia Nelson Limerick, western states represent a place of conquest that yields a different understanding of American history. In that vein, I argue that the region's acquisition by the United States and the nature and timing of its incorporation into the United States distinguish it from regions east of the Mississippi. People's religious impulses motivated as well as aided and abetted conquest. Many of the conquered turned to religion for solace and strength to face the disruption and turmoil of conquest. This book argues a two-pronged thesis. First, religion inspired people who lived in and who came to the West. Second, the region's historical development shaped religious innovations.

This book emphasizes the period during which the United States acquired and asserted control over the area west of the Mississippi, but it also discusses the time before the United States conquered the region. The region's story and the United States' story cannot be appreciated fully without understanding the people who lived there before US conquest, how that process unfolded, and how it influenced both conquerors and conquered. Several central questions shape this book. How have diverse societies and empires shaped and reshaped the region over the centuries? In the US era, has the West been more of a colony or a region and when and how did it change? Does it today act as a national and international center of power in its own right? Most important and most pervasive, what did religion have to do with the West? This book puts religion at the center of a familiar narrative that usually ignores it.

What exactly do I mean by religion? I was surprised to find that many of the religious history books I consulted for this project jumped right into the subject without defining terms. Having written this book, I know why: it's very difficult. One scholar offered this definition: "Religions are confluences of organic-cultural flow that intensify joy and confront suffering by drawing on human and suprahuman forces to make homes and cross boundaries."[1] That's blessedly short and to the point, but it calls for some unpacking. Religions might intensify joy in the process of being grateful or giving thanks or in the act of welcoming a newborn infant or recognizing a marriage. Religions help people confront sorrow in the face of tragedy or death. Humans, of course, occupy center stage in those events and as they intensify joy or confront suffering they engage in some kind of relationship, prayer perhaps, with one or more suprahuman forces, God for example. That action helps the people be at peace or at home and it might also help them cross some type of boundary be it geographic or spiritual, such as a soul moving to an afterlife. The beginning of that definition, "confluences of organic-cultural flow," might be the toughest part to understand. I read that as arguing that religions emerge from the interplay of environment and intellect. This robust and relatively abstract definition might be particularly useful for students interested in religious studies.

 Other students might prefer this more grounded definition, which combines insights from various sources: Religion is a set of practices and beliefs through which people find meaning, order their lives, and understand their place and purpose in the universe, especially when they view the universe and themselves as the creation of a supernatural agency or agencies. More importantly, religion is about the human relationship with the divine, or spirits. People express this relationship in many ways including worship, expressing awe about God or spirits, in thanks for their existence and the world that is their home, and in supplication for their needs. Worship usually involves devotional practices and rituals, sometimes personal, often communal. Finally, religion typically contains a moral code governing the

---

[1] Thomas Tweed, *Crossing and Dwelling: A Theory of Religion* (Cambridge: Harvard University Press, 2006), 54.

conduct of human affairs. This is important stuff. It applies to just about everybody who dwells in the pages that follow. Some people paid very close attention to religion and recognized that it played through every aspect of their lives. Others paid less attention and probably lost sight of religion in their daily lives at least on occasion. Still others paid no attention to religion, yet even for them it would be almost impossible to live a life not touched in some way or ways by the religious beliefs of others.

In this book I try to portray all religious traditions and the people who practiced them with respect and impartiality. The book does not offer an exhaustive treatment of religion in the West, but I have attempted to be as inclusive and thorough as possible given the confines of this series. I focus on people, places, and events where religion played a particularly important role. I include organized religion, unorganized religion, spirituality, easily recognized denominations, and groups some would label cults. Writing about religion presents challenges because of its supernatural character and because it can be very difficult to discern people's motives, especially when one motive among many might involve religion. Further complicating this task, mainstream American culture tends to isolate religion as distinct from economics, politics, and personal relationships even though religious beliefs might influence people's thoughts and actions in one or more of those realms. The separation of church and state provides an excellent example and in several chapters I probe the issue of whether religion and state really can be separated. For some groups discussed in this book, religion *cannot* be separated from *any* aspect of their lives because it informs and is intimately involved in *every* aspect of their lives and the day-to-day working of the world. As if that didn't complicate matters enough, even mainstream histories of the United States that would celebrate the separation of church and state include and acknowledge the significance of Manifest Destiny, which identifies the United States, its people, and its institutions as God's chosen instruments. Of course, Manifest Destiny's role in history and the American mind has for many citizens of the United States explained and justified expansion across North America, which makes it central to the history of the American West.

With few exceptions this book moves chronologically through the human history of the trans-Mississippi West. Chapter 1 samples indigenous religions in the region that came to be known as the

American West. The concept of "the West" as we know it meant
nothing to these people or their religions, but place meant everything
and because of that place had remarkable significance. The region's
first occupants had religions, but those who subsequently conquered
the region usually considered those religions inferior to Christianity.
Indigenous religions endured and changed in the face of conquest
despite attempts to eradicate them. These interactions surface regularly through the rest of the book. Chapter 2 discusses expansion into
the West by colonial powers from outside North America and the religious component of that expansion through 1867 when Russia sold
Alaska to the United States. Catholicism, Orthodox Christianity, and
Protestantism all rode in the van of conquest and this chapter examines their roles in the colonial development of the West by Spain,
France, and Russia. The United States enters the book in Chapter 3,
which covers religion's influence and religious developments from the
Louisiana Purchase in 1803 through 1860 when the United States
stood at the brink of the Civil War. Chapter 4 explores the roles religion played in the West during the tumultuous years of the Civil War
and Reconstruction and carries its discussion and analysis through
the Wounded Knee tragedy of 1890. After 1890 Frederick Jackson
Turner and others would argue the West entered a post-frontier
period. The years 1890 through 1945 hold together as the "Modern
West." Chapter 5 maps religion's role during those years when the
West still functioned, more or less, as a colony of the rest of the nation
even as World War II spurred the nation into a total war footing that
transformed the West into a more developed or mature region. The
nation and the West boomed after World War II, and Chapter 6
explores relationships between religion and region from 1945 through
1965, which I've labeled the "Cold War West." Chapter 7 examines
the West's religious life in the years since 1965, when changes to US
immigration law dramatically shifted immigration from Europe to
Latin America and Asia. The period also witnessed a boom in new
religious movements with significant consequences for the nation
and the region.

   What role did religion play in the West's history? What role did the
West play in religious history? The answers are as complicated as the
people who made this history and pursuing them enriches our understanding of ideas and places dear to many of us.

Suggested Reading

Gaustad, Edwin and Leigh Schmidt. 2004. *The Religious History of America: The Heart of the American Story from Colonial Times to Today*, revised edition. New York: HarperSanFrancisco.

Guarneri, Carl and David Alvarez, eds. 1987. *Religion and Society in the American West: Historical Essays*. New York: University Press of America.

Higham, Carol L. and William H. Katerberg. 2009. *Conquests and Consequences: The American West from Frontier to Region*. Wheeling, IL: Harlan Davidson.

Hudson, Winthrop S. and John Corrigan. 1999. *Religion in America: An Historical Account of the Development of American Religious Life*, 6th ed. Upper Saddle River, NJ: Prentice Hall.

Limerick, Patricia Nelson. 1987. *The Legacy of Conquest: The Unbroken Past of the American West*. New York: Norton.

Limerick, Patricia Nelson. 2000. *Something in the Soil: Legacies and Reckonings in the New West*. New York: Norton.

Schultz, Kevin M. and Paul Harvey. 2010. "Everywhere and Nowhere: Recent Trends in American Religious History and Historiography." *Journal of the American Academy of Religion* 78: 129–162.

Szasz, Ferenc M. 2000. *Religion in the Modern American West*. Tucson, AZ: University of Arizona Press.

Turner, Frederick Jackson. 1920. *The Frontier in American History*. New York: Henry Holt.

Williams, Peter W. 2002. *America's Religions: From Their Origins to the Twenty-First Century*. Urbana and Chicago, IL: University of Illinois Press.

Wynn, Mark. 2008. "Phenomenology of Religion," *The Stanford Encyclopedia of Philosophy* (Winter Edition), Edward N. Zalta (ed.) Available at: http://plato.stanford.edu/archives/win2008/entries/phenomenology-religion/ (accessed 27 June 2014).

1

Indigenous Religions in the West

All the earth was covered with water, and everything was dark in the beginning. There was no sun, no moon, no stars. Then one day a raft appeared, floating on the water. In it was Turtle. Down from the sky a rope of feathers came and dangled near the bow of the raft, and then a being, who shone like the sun, descended. He was Earth Initiate. When he reached the end of the rope he tied it to the bow of the raft, and stepped in. His face was covered, so that Turtle was not able to see it. In fact, no one has ever seen his face uncovered. Earth Initiate sat down and for a long time said nothing.

"Where do you come from?" Turtle asked at last.
"I come from above," Earth Initiate said.
Then Turtle asked: "Brother, can you not make for me some good dry land, so that I may sometimes come up out of the water?"
Earth Initiate did not answer at once, and Turtle asked, "Are there going to be any people in the world?"
After thinking for a while, Earth Initiate said, "Yes."
"How long before you are going to make people?" Turtle asked.

Inspiration and Innovation: Religion in the American West,
First Edition. Todd M. Kerstetter.
© 2015 John Wiley & Sons, Inc. Published 2015 by John Wiley & Sons, Inc.

"I don't know," Earth Initiate answered. "You want to have some dry
  land: well, how am I going to get any earth to make it of?"
"If you will tie a stone about my left arm I will dive for some," Turtle
  answered.

Turtle was gone for six years, and when he came up he was covered
with green slime, he had been down so long. He returned with only a
very little earth under his nails. The rest had all washed away.

Earth Initiate scraped the earth out from under Turtle's nails, and
put it in the palm of his hand and rolled it about until it was round
and about the size of a small pebble. This he laid on the stern of the
raft, and went away and left it. Three times he returned to look at it,
and the third time found that it had grown very large. The fourth time
he looked at it, it was as big as the world, the raft was on ground, and
all around were mountains.

When Turtle knew the raft was on ground he said: "I cannot stay in
  the dark all the time. Can't you make a light so that I can see?"
As they got out of the raft, Earth Initiate said: "Look that way, to the
  east! I am going to tell my sister to come up."
Then it began to grow light, and day began to break, and the sun
  came up.
"Which way is the sun going to travel?" Turtle asked.
"I will tell her to go this way, and go down there," Earth Initiate
  answered.
After the sun went down it grew very dark.
"I will tell my brother to come up," said Earth Initiate.
Then the moon rose.
"How do you like it?" Earth Initiate asked Turtle.
"It is very good," Turtle answered. "Is that all you are going to do for us?"
"No, I am going to do more yet."
Then he called the stars each by name and they came out.
Some time after this he said: "I am going to make people."
So he took dark red earth and mixed it with water, and made two figures,
  one a man and one a woman.

This account of the origins of the world and human beings comes
from the Maidu people of what is now California. It is one example
from a countless number of ways the first human inhabitants of North
America organized and made sense of their lives through what this
chapter calls indigenous religions.

Each tribe that lives in North America has its own rich history explaining its origins and how it came to reside in its particular location. Many tribes continue to maintain those accounts. Europeans have long held tribal accounts in low esteem for reasons that have a lot to do with this book and the history of the American West. For one thing, Europeans considered Indians pagans and, therefore, unreliable. Tribal accounts of creation and migration frequently did not correspond with anything that could be found in Christianity and the Bible. That led Europeans to label Indian creation stories as myths, folk tales, and legends, which demeaned them in comparison to European Christian accounts of human origins. For their part, the Maidu recognized the similarities between their creation story and that in the Bible (the step-by-step creation of heavenly bodies, day and night, and eventually human beings), which they considered evidence of *their* story's accuracy. Later, many Europeans and Americans rejected tribal accounts as being unscientific. Some Indian intellectuals questioned this science, arguing that it reflected an ethnocentrism not unlike Christian views of tribal "paganism."

Many tribal creation and migration stories have another important link to this book. Most say the people in question migrated from the "land of the setting sun." Some tribal accounts reference other compass points, but many indicate the west as the point of origin. On the one hand, that places great importance on "the West," although it is not "the West" in the sense it is used in US history and in most of this book. On the other hand, such a western origin story followed by a human migration to the *east*, turns the best-known story of westward expansion (that told from the European or Atlantic perspective) on its head and demonstrates that from the time of first human occupation, the history of the American West is much more complicated and nuanced than is typically thought.

The ancestors of American Indians lived in the Americas for thousands of years before Christopher Columbus arrived and initiated sustained contact with the rest of the world. Accounts of how the first human residents of the Americas arrived vary. Archeologists and anthropologists cite evidence that indicates people migrated into North America from Asia. Many tribal histories such as the Maidu story above say their ancestors were created there and have occupied their homelands since time immemorial.

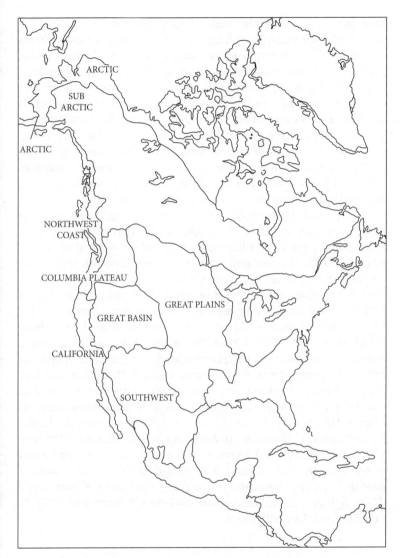

Figure 1.1 This map shows the geographical location of the major cultural groups who inhabited the West in pre-Columbian North America.

The area west of the Mississippi River, which is the focus of most of this book, contains a variety of culture areas (see Figure 1.1). Culture areas are zones defined by geography in which climate and resources have influenced the development of distinctive human cultures. The Great Plains, for example, with its vast treeless expanses, massive herds of bison, and relatively sparse precipitation shaped the development of particular human economies and societies. Within each culture area, one can find many tribes and some variation in how people lived. This chapter does not offer an exhaustive list. It samples the religious beliefs of one tribe from each of eight North American culture areas west of the Mississippi to give a sense of the diversity of religious beliefs that existed among American Indians in the region that came to be known as the American West. While similarities exist among American Indian religions, it would be misleading to try to generalize any one tribe's religious system to American Indians as a group.

Timing and transmission also complicate the discussion of indigenous religions here. The chapter aims to give a sense of what indigenous religions were like before non-Indians showed up. This is extremely difficult to accomplish. For one thing, dynamic indigenous religions changed over time both before non-Indians showed up and after. For another, much of what we know about indigenous religions as they existed hundreds of years ago comes to us in words recorded by European Christians. Whatever their intentions might have been (much more on this later), those European Christians left a written record from an outsider's perspective clouded by their own religiously influenced perspectives. Furthermore, much of this discussion uses the past tense as it refers to events or people in the past. It should be noted that Indian people are still very much with us as are some of the religions and beliefs discussed here. So, this chapter provides both a limited sample of the variety of American Indian religions of the West and a particularly vivid lesson in the messiness of writing history across vast distances of time and culture. It shows some areas of overlap, but it also shows how widely American Indian religions could differ. Spirits roamed everywhere and people lived religiously to maintain harmony with them.

Arctic

The Inuit, culturally similar peoples who inhabit the Arctic coastal regions of what is now the United States (Alaska), Canada, Russia, and Greenland, lived in a world populated by an indeterminate number of spirits that lived in animals, objects, and places, and that the Inuit sought to manipulate through rituals and the aid of shamans. The Inuit identified three different kinds of human souls. The immortal spirit left the body at death to dwell in a spiritual world. Another, a person's breath and bodily warmth, died with the body. A third, the name soul, lived in a spirit world before inhabiting a human form. Typically this soul entered a baby, but an ill adult might change names with the hope that a new name soul might bring restored health. The Inuit believed most disease resulted from breaking a taboo, which offended spirits, or from the loss of part of their soul. They enlisted shamans to help them rectify the taboo violation or to recover the lost part of their soul. In a variation on shamanic belief, the Inuit believed a soul or spirit would enter a shaman's body and take control of it. The Inuit also believed in "soul flight," that a shaman could send his soul to the spirit world where it could recover another person's lost soul or consult other spirits regarding an issue that had arisen on earth.

In addition to rank and file spirits, the Inuit believed in several more powerful spirit figures known to all. Sedna, a goddess who lived in the sea and controlled marine mammals, ranked as the most important. The Inuit believed Sedna had run away from her husband to live with another man. This angered her father, who captured her and set out to return her to her husband, which involved a boat trip. While at sea, a storm arose and threatened their boat. Sedna's father figured the storm resulted from spirits angered by his daughter abandoning her husband. He threw Sedna overboard to calm the spirits, but she clutched the side of the boat. He chopped at her fingers joint by joint until Sedna lost her grip and drowned. Sedna's finger joints transformed into sea mammals, which is why the Inuit seek to appease her before hunting sea mammals. The story of Sedna demonstrates the interconnectedness of the natural and the supernatural worlds that exists in many American Indian religions and how spirits play important roles in everyday tasks and events. The story, which depends on the sea and reflects the importance of hunting marine mammals, also shows the critical importance of place to the religion of the Inuit.

Sub-Arctic

A more detailed example of how American Indians view religion comes from the Koyukon Indians. The Koyukon people, Athapascan-speakers who live in the interior part of what is now known as Alaska, can stand in for many other American Indian peoples in the broad outlines of their spirituality and how it permeates every facet of life. The particulars vary from tribe to tribe because American Indian spirituality depends heavily upon the land, plants, animals, and spirits of a tribe's homeland.

For the Koyukon people, in Distant Time it is said animals were human. They had human form, lived in human society, and spoke with humans. Raven created this ancient world and controlled it. When Raven first created the earth, rivers flowed both ways – upstream along one bank and downstream along the other. Raven decided this made things too easy for humans, though, as their boats could drift in either direction without paddling. So, Raven changed rivers so they flowed in only one direction and that is how they are today. Distant Time ended when a catastrophic flood covered the earth. Raven arranged for a pair of each species to board a raft. These plants and animals survived, but after the flood they could no longer behave as humans. All the humans from Distant Time died, so Raven recreated people in their present form.

This much-abbreviated story gives a sense of how one group of American Indians considered the origins of the world and the interconnectedness of people with plants, animals, and spirits. The Koyukon people knew well the biblical parallels (once they learned of the Bible). They did not consider this story a reinterpretation of Christianity. In fact, they saw it as evidence supporting the accuracy of their traditions.

The Koyukon people have hundreds of Distant Time stories, which collectively explain the behavior and appearance of living things, the cosmos, even the weather, and they suggest proper relationships in the world. Some stories are short and can be told by children. Others are long and might take weeks of evening-time tellings to complete. Usually older people who have memorized the epics and have expertise in interpreting their meanings tell them.

Distant Time stories served (and serve) many functions for the Koyukon people. They help pass the long, dark winter months as a form of entertainment. They explain the world and how it functions. They provide a code of behavior toward nature and natural resources. Most important in that code is a set of taboos. A person who violates a taboo might suffer any number of consequences ranging from bad luck on a hunt to clumsiness, illness, or even death.

Distant Time stories shape the Koyukon people's outlook on life and help explain certain animal and human behaviors and how they relate.

A Koyukon wanting to know about someone's character might ask, "What kind of animal is he?" For example, in Distant Time the sucker fish was a thief and the Koyukon people hold them in disdain to this day. One Koyukon man told an anthropologist he could not bring himself to eat a sucker fish because he feared it would turn *him* into a thief. A known thief might be described as "just like a sucker fish."

Ravens provide a more complex example. On one hand, the Koyukon people recognize Raven as creator and have great respect for the bird's spirit power. On the other hand, Distant Time stories often portray Raven as a lazy trickster who bedevils people and often finds a way to get ahead through the work of others. A boastful person who makes big promises but delivers small results or who gets ahead by trickery might be described as "just like a raven." In other words, ravens have awesome power, but annoying personalities.

Humans and animals enjoy close relationships in other ways explained by Distant Time stories. The Koyukon people believe animals have many human characteristics. Animals have emotions and personalities and communicate with each other. They understand human language and behavior. They constantly monitor human actions and their spirits are offended by disrespectful behavior such as breaking of taboos. In fact, animals behave in ways that can be interpreted as religious, following their own sets of taboos. A brown bear that killed and ate a ground squirrel, except for the heart, lungs, and windpipe, which it left on a rock, was believed to be observing a dietary taboo. To avoid offending animals, the Koyukon people avoid pointing at them and they speak carefully about them. They avoid boasting about their hunting or trapping skills, for example, for fear of offending their prey. They consider bears so spiritually powerful that they carefully choose every word when speaking of them. They rarely keep wild animals as pets, except those whose personality traits they value. A child who keeps a hawk owl, for instance, might do so with the hope of acquiring the owl's hunting skill. Overall, the Koyukon people aim to treat all animals with respect. They will end the suffering of animals they find injured or starving, and the animals they kill to eat they hunt and butcher according to rules meant to demonstrate respect and gratitude.

The Koyukon people see themselves living in a world where natural and supernatural are unified in ways most of us would not recognize. *Everything* has power and awareness and the Koyukon people live with great sensitivity to and consideration of that. Animals, plants, the earth, landforms, air, sky, stars – everything – has a spiritual component and exists in a seamless web of which humans constitute one part. Furthermore, the importance of the raven, a bird with a limited habitat, shows again the significance of place to American Indian religion, in this case that of the Koyukon. Koyukon raven stories, for example, would not make sense in Florida, where ravens don't live.

Northwest Coast

The Tlingit Indians occupy the fjords and islands of southeastern Alaska. Tlingits lived in villages of wooden houses during the winter. During summers, they typically left the villages to live in hunting or fishing camps. As this pattern suggests, Tlingits followed a seasonal cycle of hunting, fishing, gathering berries, and harvesting crops. The Tlingit diet centered on salmon, and the seasonal salmon runs drove the Tlingit economic cycle. Tlingit religion shared some characteristics with other animistic (the belief that everything from plants to animals to landforms has a spiritual essence) tribes, particularly those of the Koyukon people, but had distinctive elements as well. This discussion shows how the raven as an element of the local environment played an important role in Tlingit religion, but in a significantly different way. It also discusses Tlingit shamans as an example of American Indian religious leadership.

Tlingits considered all living things, natural features, and even celestial bodies to have spirits or souls. To ensure harmonious relations with others, the Tlingits followed carefully established customs to show respect. Maintaining proper relationships could bring favor or help from spirits, while violating taboos could lead to suffering or calamity. As did the Koyukon people and other tribes in the region, Tlingits held Raven in awe. Tlingits did not recognize Raven as creator, but they did credit Raven with playing important roles in shaping the world as they knew it. Tlingits saw Raven motivated often by base motives and in that sense probably considered him a relatively more malevolent creature than did a group such as the Koyukons. Given their heavy reliance upon salmon, Tlingits were careful not to offend the fish. Tlingits also treated salmon respectfully, and processing them properly meant returning inedible parts to streams or burning to ensure reincarnation.

In addition to individuals following taboos to maintain harmony with spirits, Tlingit shamans used specialized knowledge in efforts to manipulate spirits in a variety of ways. Tlingits revered shamans for the power they could marshal. A shaman could, for example, heal the sick, affect the weather, make a hunting party or war party successful, send his spirit far away to communicate with other shamans and to gather news from them, predict the future, and expose witches (known to Tlingits as "masters of sickness"), among other things. Shamans, who were mostly men but sometimes women, managed all this through their relationships with spirits, who entered shamans' bodies and spoke to them or inspired them in other ways. Some, maybe all, of these spirits were souls of dead people. To maintain their powers, which can be thought of as maintaining their fitness to receive spirits, shamans lived by a special code. They fasted regularly and followed dietary restrictions and observed periods of sexual abstinence. Shamans could neither cut nor comb their hair.

Among shamans' many jobs, the most important might have been fighting witches, who might be thought of as shamans who sought to manipulate spirits for harm rather than for good or positive outcomes. A witch, for example, might use spiritual influence to inflict sickness on a person. Shamans used a spirit séance to discover witches, who were often an unsuccessful and jealous relative of the bewitched or a slave of the bewitched. A witch could be forced to release the bewitched by confessing and undoing the "spell." Getting a witch to do this involved dirty work, including torture. In some cases, witches were bound and left on the beach to be drowned by the rising tide, which, it was believed, would also wash away the witch's evil.

Shamans accrued power in Tlingit society because of their skills in manipulating the spirit world and this power also made them a focal point for outsiders. In the late 1800s, the period of early contact with the United States, US Navy officials seized shamans accused of torturing witches and destroyed the shamans' power by shaving their heads. From one perspective this might be seen as a humane policy designed to promote civility and the scientific thought of western civilization; from another perspective, it might be seen as a bald-faced attack on Tlingit religion. Much of the history of contact between American Indian and people of European origins related in this book involves attempts to destroy indigenous religions and to replace them with some form of Christianity.

Plains

The Lakotas, also known as Teton Sioux or Western Sioux, migrated to the northern Great Plains, probably in the seventeenth and eighteenth centuries, seeking horses first brought by Europeans but adapted by Plains Indians, shifting their way of life to buffalo hunting, and bringing with them religious beliefs developed in the Great Lakes region but that accommodated their new homes. The Lakotas consist of bands known as Oglala, Brulé, Minneconjou, Hunkpapa, Sans Arc, Blackfeet, and Two Kettles. They hold a fundamental belief system shared by many Plains tribes. Several themes run through Lakota belief and can be seen through to the present, indicating a willingness to maintain faith in longstanding beliefs and practices while adopting new ones such as the Ghost Dance and Christianity. As noted earlier, one hallmark of Lakota religion is belief in *wakan* as the foundation for their spiritual system; other hallmarks included the Sacred Pipe as a means of prayer and the development of the Sun Dance.

The dynamic nature of Lakota religious systems can be seen in the role of the Black Hills. By the mid-nineteenth century, after coming to the Great Plains from the Great Lakes region, the Lakotas claimed as their homeland a large area that included all or parts of present South Dakota, North Dakota, Nebraska, Kansas, Wyoming, Colorado, Montana, and parts of Canada. The Lakotas considered the Black Hills the center of their world, which it was geographically, even though the Black Hills had only recently become their center. But their consideration held deeper meaning. They saw the Black Hills as a sacred place and the home to powerful spirits.

As with virtually all American Indian belief systems, Lakota spirituality formed an integral part of everyday life. Lakotas recognized no distinction between sacred and secular. *Everything* they did and *every part* of their environment held a place in a system permeated with what non-Indians would call the sacred, not unlike virtually every group discussed in this chapter. Put another way, Lakotas did not recognize a difference between natural and supernatural the way most European thought did. They did mark a difference between human and non-human and the commonplace or everyday and the extraordinary or incomprehensible. Humans did not exist apart from those things, but coexisted with them and they accepted the extraordinary or incomprehensible as a part of life. Lakotas tried, to the best of their limited ability to manipulate the mysterious nature of the universe – *wakan* – to their benefit.

Wakan could be good or bad and could be invisible or personified by non-human beings that had human characteristics. *Wakan* beings watched humans all the time and controlled all events. Lakotas did their best to please *wakan* beings, lest they harm or cause grief to humans. Lakotas believed every object had a spirit and was *wakan*. *Wicasa wakan*, or holy men, gained special insight into *wakan* through dreams or visions allowing them to act as a conduit to those powers and to influence the *wakan*.

Lakotas' relationship to bison illustrates how belief and ritual linked them to their world, how their spirituality functioned, and how American Indian religion took on regional character. Lakotas believe that long ago bison had behaved aggressively toward humans. The Buffalo People sent an emissary, White Buffalo Cow Woman, a *wakan* being, to humans to deliver the Calf Pipe and to teach people its rituals, which would establish a benevolent relationship between bison and humans in which people would venerate bison and bison would provide food and other necessities to people. This spiritual and ceremonial relationship provides just one example of how Lakotas could call on *wakan* beings to provide kindness and generosity characteristic of good family members.

The nineteenth-century decline in the bison population highlights differences between Lakota and US worldviews. US Indian agents and others told Lakotas that bison were on their way to extinction and that Lakotas should adopt an agricultural economy. This made no sense to Lakotas, who agreed bison were disappearing. Lakotas believed the relationship between humans and bison had fallen into imbalance, which had caused bison to withdraw. If the proper balance and reciprocity could be restored, Lakotas believed the bison would return.

In the Lakota world, humans could relate to the spiritual world through prayer, which to Lakotas means both to call on someone for aid and to address someone using a kinship term. Put another way, prayer invoked the interrelatedness of all things and asked spirit beings to provide the kindness and generosity one would expect from a good relative. The pipe played a central role in prayer by providing a direct connection between the praying human and the spirit beings. Preparing the pipe involves its own ritual and is an important prelude to many other ceremonies. Lakotas believe White Buffalo Cow Woman herself is present in the pipe's smoke, which carries human prayers to the spirit beings.

In addition to individual manifestations of religion, which could include prayer and vision quests, Lakotas practiced a number of public group ceremonies such as the Sun Dance, which by the nineteenth century ranked as the most important public religious ceremony. The summertime ceremony involved the gathering of multiple bands in a celebration of tribal unity. The Sun Dance focused on prayers for the health and well-being of the Lakotas and of the bison population, but it also provided a venue for a number of lesser ceremonies.

For a nomadic hunting people, the Sun Dance served not only as an important ritual, but also as an important social event. Bands would gather at a spot agreed upon earlier and leaders selected a sacred tree. Honored women felled the tree and decorated it with sacred colors and the figure of a bison deity at the top. Once raised, the tree trunk became the Sun Dance altar. This shows how a variety of tribe members participated in the ceremony.

The Sun Dance ceremony lasted four days and included fasting, singing, mock battles against evil forces, and feasting. The climax involved the consecration of young warrior candidates to the buffalo deity via self-torture. Shamans purified candidates, who had demonstrated the four virtues of bravery, generosity, fortitude, and integrity. The shamans cut strips of flesh from the candidates' backs and inserted skewers, which were attached to a long leather strip connected to a bison skull. The candidates danced, with their eyes fixed on the altar, until at the signal of the shamans each dancer jerked at the thongs to release the bison skull. This produced gaping wounds and extraordinary pain. The telltale scars instantly identified the bearer as a revered warrior.

As an example of a Great Plains Indian religious belief and practice, Lakota spirituality shows similarities to other groups considered here. The role of shamans and the permeable boundaries between the natural and the supernatural can be found among other groups. The role of the Black Hills and the significance of bison, though, provide examples of how Lakota religion is embedded in a particular place, the Lakota homeland.

Plateau

The Sanpoil, a Salishan people who lived in the basin of the Sanpoil River of what is now eastern Washington state and are one of the Confederated Tribes of the Colville Indian Reservation, had a comparatively minimal social, political, and religious organization, which makes them representative of tribes in the Plateau culture area. Religiously, the Sanpoil focused on the vision quest and lived in a particularly egalitarian religious complex. Every man went on a vision quest and virtually all claimed success in contacting the supernatural, which meant virtually all Sanpoil men could claim spiritual experience. As a result, the Sanpoil did not see a big difference between the shaman and the layman. Shamans might have more spirit helpers than laymen or have access to more powerful spirit helpers. Furthermore, any layman who undertook another successful vision quest might recruit the help of more spirit helpers and assume the status of a shaman. In other words, the line between shaman and layman was easily crossed. The Sanpoil had no priests, no religious organizations, nor any standardized rituals.

The Sanpoil understanding of diseases helps to explain some of their convictions about the spiritual world. The Sanpoil divided disease into two categories, natural and supernatural. Natural illnesses included headaches, the common cold, and injuries from inanimate objects. Plant remedies could cure many of these illnesses, and knowledge of healing plants was widespread among men and women. Supernatural illnesses fell into five subcategories: injuries from animate non-human beings; diffuse internal illnesses; mental ailments; spirit sickness; and magical poisoning. Space limitations preclude in-depth discussion of each, but a sampling shows how the spiritual world interacted with the physical.

The Sanpoil interpreted animal injuries, such as a snake bite, as a result of the animal's spirit. The injured human might not have followed the advice of his spirit helper, which could have led to the snake bite. Jealousy between the victim's spirit helper and the animal spirit might also cause a bite. This reflects the importance placed on maintaining proper relationships with the spirit world on an individual level.

In other cases, shamans might be involved in bringing afflictions to people, in helping to cure afflictions, or both. A shaman might steal another person's spirit. In that event, the victim could recover the spirit by enlisting the aid of a shaman more powerful than the thief. A shaman might inflict an injury or an illness on a person by means we would consider magic. In those cases, the victim could enlist the help of a shaman to reverse the magic. If the healing shaman diagnosed an illness caused by a harmful spirit, he could use his expertise to remove

the spirit from the victim and neutralize it. This shows the insepa-
rable connection between spirituality and health and how the Sanpoil
saw the natural and the supernatural as manifestations of the same,
seamless world.

Great Basin

The people known today as Northern Paiutes were, at the time of
contact, a group of politically independent bands who shared a
common language. They practiced a semi-nomadic lifestyle and
depended on hunting, fishing, and gathering in what is now Nevada,
California, Oregon, and Idaho. Northern Paiutes believed power could
dwell in any object or phenomenon such as wind or thunder. Anybody
could seek power for assistance in life, but only shamans could gather
enough power to harness it to do good or to harm others.

Shamans could be male or female. Shamans might not seek power,
but could receive it unsolicited in dreams. The dreams often started in
childhood and could be repeated through the teen years and into
adulthood. The dreams usually included spiritual instruction by the
power source, which might be an animal or a spirit. The power source
would often tell the dreamer what items, which would be kept in a
special bag, would be needed for "doctoring" or to invoke spiritual
powers. The power also taught the dreamer a song or songs to use
when calling for spiritual assistance. Anyone who ignored the dreams
and refused to accept the power faced illness, maybe even death.
Power could also be inherited, along with the medicine bag and songs,
from a relative. Finally, a person could seek power by visiting certain
sacred sites throughout Northern Paiute territory.

Each person constructed a personal approach to the supernatural
within these bounds, which made religion largely an individual
matter, but Northern Paiutes also practiced some group rituals. For
example, people would pray and dance before group hunting or gathering activities such as an antelope or rabbit drive. People who lived
near Pyramid Lake or Walker River prayed and danced for seasonal
fish runs. Specialists directed such activities, but they might call on
others who had achieved a high degree of respect to lead prayers. All
times of group prayer and dancing doubled as festivals and might
include gambling games, races, and other forms of entertainment.

Northern Paiute shamanism resembled that of other tribes, but their relationship with elements of their environment such as salmon and antelope demonstrates the tight links between their beliefs and the place they called home. The importance they placed on dreams has parallels, too, in other groups, but is worth emphasizing here in a moment of foreshadowing because in the late 1800s a Northern Paiute named Wovoka had one of the most influential dreams in the history of the West. Wovoka's dream provided the foundation for the Ghost Dance movement that led to a tragic confrontation at Wounded Knee in 1890.

California

The Maidu, whose creation story we considered at the beginning of this chapter, live in the mountain valleys of what is now northeast California. Before the mid-1800s, an astonishing array of tribes lived in California and this chapter uses the Maidu as a vantage point by which to view California Indian religions generally. The Maidu settled in village communities, or clusters of small villages. A village community might contain three to five villages and each village had about seven dwellings. Each community centered on the village with the largest ceremonial earth lodge, which also served as the home of the village community's leader. The Maidu followed a seasonal subsistence economy. They lived in their villages during the winter, but in other seasons moved throughout their territory hunting and gathering.

Many mysterious powers and spirits inhabited the Maidu world. Coyote, for one, plays an important role as a foil to the Creator. The Maidu view the Creator as a wise and benevolent being, but they see Coyote as an opposing force. As a trickster, Coyote modified many beings from their ideal state at creation to the less-than-ideal form known by humans. He also introduced death. Other powers and spirits dwelled in Maidu country, residing in places such as cliffs, waterfalls, lakes, and the sky. Like many other tribes, the Maidu had shamans, each of whom received power and protection from one or many of these spirits.

Shamans exercised considerable power in Maidu society. The shaman, based on his access to spiritual guidance, selected the leader of each village community. And, should he learn the spirits no longer approved of a leader, the shaman gave word and the leader was deposed. Shamans led ceremonies and used their spiritual power to heal sickness. Shamans might be male or female, although female shamans generally were believed to act malevolently and to cause many problems. Shamans inherited their positions, but they underwent extensive education at the hands of experienced, usually older, shamans, especially in the healing arts.

Maidu shamanism had similarities with that of other tribes. Their creation story involving Earth Initiate and Turtle, demonstrates the close ties linking humans with the supernatural. It also shows the importance of place, as does the critical importance of shamans being able to commune with the local spirits.

Southwest

The Pueblos provide a sample of religion found in the Southwest, the area now defined mostly by Arizona and New Mexico. The Pueblos live mostly in what is now New Mexico and they are identified by their dwelling type – the pueblo – rather than by tribe. The people speak different languages and dialects, but share similar social, economic, and religious characteristics. At contact they lived probably the most urbanized lives of any Indians north of Mexico and had developed a highly sophisticated religious system centered on a religious structure in each village.

The Pueblos practiced agriculture in a precarious desert environment. They relied most heavily on corn, but also grew beans, squash, and other crops. Atypically for American Indian groups, men did much of the farming, although women helped with planting and harvest. Women and children gathered fruits, nuts, and plants to supplement agricultural production. Some Pueblo peoples irrigated their crops, but others practiced dry (non-irrigated) farming. Regardless, water and corn dominated their thoughts and played critical roles in their religious practices.

The Pueblo people lived in communities we might consider urban. They often built their towns on the top of mesas, which made them highly defensible. Hundreds or even thousands of people lived in multistoreyed rock or adobe dwellings that resembled modern

Figure 1.2 Spruce tree house kiva, Mesa Verde National Park, 1908.
Source: Photo by Nusbaum, Courtesy National Park Service, Mesa Verde
National Park (MEVE 9525).

apartment buildings. Secret chambers called kivas occupied central
locations in the pueblos (Figure 1.2). Only men could enter kivas,
which served not only as the location for certain ceremonies, but also
as a gathering place in the order of a clubhouse. Given the centrality
of religion to pueblo life and the degree of control exerted by religious
groups, one could consider pueblo society a male-dominated theocracy with order emanating from the kivas.

A class structure based on a person's degree of religious knowledge
provides another indicator of spirituality's importance to Pueblos.
The following example comes from the Tewa, a Pueblo group from
what is now northern New Mexico. The Tewas label common young
people and those uninitiated into religious practices "Dry Hardened
People," which refers to mythical ancestors who emerged from a
sacred primordial lake, hardened on dry land, and had not achieved
spiritual advancement. A higher class, "Persons," had attained some
spiritual experience and knowledge, and made up what could be
called the executive officers of the pueblo. At the top stood the "Made

People," the leaders who achieved high office through study and practice of spiritual knowledge and ritual practice. The Tewas also recognized a parallel group of spirit beings, the souls of deceased humans, divided into three classes that correspond to the three human classes.

Perhaps because of high population density, Pueblo communities emphasized solidarity and community and placed the group ahead of the individual. The religious societies that met in the kivas directed all activity and strived to maintain social order. Each society had its own priesthood, which contributed members to the town council, and the societies did everything from appointing civil officials to run the town to directing cures, organizing hunts, planning the town's military defense, and, of course, planning and directing ceremonial events. Religion pervaded and organized daily life, and through an elaborate year-round cycle of ceremonies attempted to guide the people in ways that would benefit the entire community. In fact, the "Made People" of the Tewas had a duty to perpetuate the world by conducting proper spiritual practice, which would preserve cooperation between humans and spirits. This harmonious relationship ensured rain would come, that plants would grow, and that game animals would present themselves to hunters.

Religious observations demanded a considerable amount of the people's time. By some estimates, religious obligations required half of a Pueblo man's time. Some ceremonies lasted for nine days and during some times of the year one ceremony followed immediately on the heels of another. Ceremonies aimed to accomplish any number of things, but commonly sought to ameliorate the gods so they would cooperate in bringing rain, a cure, or some other action that would help the people. Ceremonies frequently originated in the kivas.

Kivas acted as spiritual space in several ways. Sacred objects such as prayer sticks and the elaborate masks and costumes used in dances resided in the kivas. A stone-lined pit occupied the center of the kiva. Pueblos considered the pit a passageway from the "lower world" to earth and it symbolized Sipapu, a mysterious place in the north where humans first entered the world from underground. Boys first entered a kiva sometime between age five and nine to receive initiation into the religious societies. On reaching adolescence, usually between 11 and 14, boys returned for a second phase of their initiation, which included a long period of training. On marriage, adult men could become full members of the societies.

Common Themes

Having demonstrated that indigenous religions varied—and vary—significantly, just as Islam, Christianity, and Hinduism differ, it is nonetheless helpful to note some generic characteristics they shared and how these differed from the religions that non-Indians brought to the Americas after 1492. For one thing, indigenous religions depend on place; in fact, they are embedded in place. For practitioners of American Indian religions, no two places are alike. Home has unique characteristics that inform an individual's identity and a tribal identity. Each place, including the land and the plant, animal, and spiritual beings who dwell there, has a unique identity that informs belief and ritual. For American Indians, place meant everything and the "West" enshrined in American culture meant nothing. For many of them, the place they lived was the center and it was the most important place in the world. The west might be associated with the setting sun and special spiritual powers, but every cardinal direction, east, north, south, and west, even up and down, had spiritual significance of some kind.

Furthermore, most practitioners of indigenous religions view themselves as part of a seamless web of life that embraces place, plants, and animals. One writer called this a "nonchalance" regarding the division of animals and humans. American Indians often refer to birds and animals as "peoples" and, in certain circumstances, they can exchange forms. Everything and every act is religious in its own way. Hunting, for example, consists of a series of meditative acts. A hunter would pray and purify himself before setting out and, should he kill prey, would kill and butcher the animal in a sacramental way.

In indigenous religions supernatural spirits share many characteristics with humans. They have emotions, intelligence, and free will. They intervene in human affairs according to a code of ethics or, sometimes, just on a whim. This uncertainty contributes to a sense of mystery that virtually all tribes hold in regarding a universe that cannot be understood entirely. The spirits experience the range of human emotions and may act according to their emotional state at a given moment, which adds to their unpredictability. Furthermore, some spirits are good, some are evil, and still others are indifferent. Whatever their disposition and emotional state, most can be influenced by human actions. They typically listen to prayers, consider sacrifices, and might even respond to flattery or other emotional appeals.

Practitioners of many indigenous religions also share a common sense of a complex spirit world. This world includes a wide array of spirits – everything has a spirit. It also often includes an unknowable, mysterious, overarching spirit force. Carl Gorman, a Navajo, explained it this way:

> Some researchers into Navajo religion say that we have no supreme God because he is not named. This is not so. The Supreme Being is not named because he is unknowable. He is simply the Unknown Power. We worship him through his creation for he is everything in his creation. The various forms of creation have some of his spirit within them.[1]

The Lakotas call this force *wakan*, which translates roughly to holy, sacred, and mysterious wrapped into one, although it does not represent a Supreme Being, such as the Christian God.

Indians had a concept of an afterlife and they had ways of coping with the omnipotent force that drove the universe and the good and bad spirits present everywhere in their environment. Everything – rocks, plants, animals – had a spirit, and unseen spirits moved through the world. To succeed in any task, a hunt or a raid against another tribe, to name two examples, a person had to placate the spirits. Put another way, Indians sought to maintain harmony with nature and the spirit world. Religion explained how that world operated and proscribed methods for maintaining harmony. *Dis*harmony caused illness, pain, death, and other misfortunes and was to be avoided at all costs.

Another example of how religion ordered life in many tribes comes from the concept of clan membership. A clan is a group of blood-related families. Each clan had an origin story and claimed a common ancestor, a "totem," which acted much like a patron saint for the group and also provided the clan name such as deer, eagle, or buffalo. A person's clan association provided a link to the supernatural, which linked the person to all living things. The person's clan totem served as an intermediary to the world of spirits.

---

[1] Quoted in Huston Smith, *The World's Religions: Our Great Wisdom Traditions* (New York: HarperCollins, 1991), 378.

In terms of religious practice and ceremony, indigenous religions typically had both individual and group activities, and certain types of tribes might tend to have more of one than the other. Among hunting and gathering tribes, for example, the individual typically played a more important role than the group. A vision quest often ranked among an individual's most important spiritual events and marked the transition from youth to adult. The seeker would frequently leave the group to meditate and pray. If successful, the person would experience a supernatural vision which would indicate the spirit helper that would assist the individual in love, war, hunting, and other matters. Black Elk, an Oglala Lakota, had what is probably the best-known vision in American Indian spiritual history because it plays a prominent role in the widely read book *Black Elk Speaks*.[2] During his vision, Black Elk received a visit from the powerful Thunder Beings that directed much of his subsequent life. By contrast, tribal groups that practiced agriculture, such as Pueblo communities in what is now the American Southwest, generally practiced communal forms of spirituality. The Pueblo built religious structures – kivas – and they organized spiritual societies for men.

Conclusion

This lightning-quick tour of American Indian tribal groups and their spiritual practices barely scratches the surface of the West's indigenous religions. Spirits were everywhere and in everything. People had developed elaborate rituals, ceremonies, and taboos that were designed to shape their interactions with the spirit-rich world. Indigenous religious systems held some common elements, one of them being an intimate connection to the land and the things that lived on it. There was no West as we know it, but a land of many centers – one for each people. The people made no hard distinction between spiritual and non-spiritual matters. Religion and spirituality factored into everything they did. All told, the first human residents of North America west of the Mississippi River held a stunning diversity of highly developed religious systems. The Americas

[2] John G. Neihardt, *Black Elk Speaks* (New York: Morrow, 1932), 20–47.

held what was almost certainly their most diverse array of religions in the world before Europeans arrived. Together with other native peoples in the Americas they developed religious beliefs and rituals long before pharaohs sat on thrones in Egypt, before Moses led his people out of Egypt, before Rome rose as an empire, and before Christianity or Islam existed as religions.

Before Columbus arrived, religion in North America varied from group to group and most religions had intimate ties to the locales in which they existed. The "invaders" who showed up after 1492 decimated American Indian populations through warfare and the spread of devastating diseases. Many of those people brought with them a strict and aggressive Christianity that considered non-conforming religions as pagan and non-Christians as heathens. Many of those Christians spent much of the next 500 years attempting to eradicate Indian religions they considered inferior and trying to convert Indians to Christianity. That story plays an important role in most chapters in this book. Religiously speaking, the invasion of the Americas reduced the religious diversity evident in indigenous religions and attempted to replace it with a religious monoculture based on Christianity. Indian groups would resist this onslaught creatively, sometimes incorporating elements of Christianity into new spiritual movements. That story also plays an important role in this book into the twentieth century, when both Indian communities and their religious practices would experience renewal and growth.

Suggested Reading

Brown, Joseph Epes with Emily Cousins. 2001. *Teaching Spirits: Understanding Native American Religious Traditions*. New York: Oxford University Press.
DeMallie, Raymond J. and Douglas R. Parks, eds. 1987. *Sioux Indian Religion: Tradition and Innovation*. Norman, OK: University of Oklahoma Press.
Driver, Harold E. 1969. *Indians of North America*, 2nd edn, revised. Chicago, IL: University of Chicago Press.
Erdoes, Richard and Alfonso Ortiz, eds. 1984. *American Indian Myths and Legends*. New York: Pantheon.
Gibson, Arrell Morgan. 1980. *The American Indian: Prehistory to the Present*. Lexington, MA.: Heath.
Gifford, Edward W. and Gwendoline Harris Block, eds. 1930. *California Indian Nights Entertainments*. Glendale, CA: Arthur H. Clark.

Gill, Sam D. 1982. *Native American Religions.* Belmont, CA: Wadsworth.

Hultkrantz, Ake. 1979. *The Religions of the American Indians.* Berkeley, CA: University of California Press.

Glowacki, Donna M. and Scott Van Keuren. 2011. *Religious Transformation in the Late Pre-Hispanic Pueblo World.* Tucson, AZ: University of Arizona Press.

Josephy, Jr, Alvin M. 1968. *The Indian Heritage of America.* New York: Knopf.

Martin, Joel M. 2001. *The Land Looks After Us: A History of Native American Religion.* New York: Oxford University Press.

Nelson, Richard K. 1983. *Make Prayers to the Raven: A Koyukon View of the Northern Forest.* Chicago, IL: University of Chicago Press.

Sturtevant, William C., ed. 1978–2008. *Handbook of American Indians.* 20 vols. Washington, DC: Government Printing Office.

Underhill, Ruth M. 1965. *Red Man's Religion.* Chicago, IL: University of Chicago Press.

2

Missions to New Worlds

By the dawn of the nineteenth century, Russian fur traders had been working the Aleutian Islands and the coast of Alaska for decades. They worked with, lived with, and sometimes married Alaska natives. They settled trading outposts. But they did not come alone. Missionaries from the Russian Orthodox Church accompanied them. The missionaries provided some familiar comforts of home in the remote, forbidding land. The missionaries not only served Russian settlers, but also worked hard at the difficult and dangerous task of teaching their beliefs to Alaska natives and trying to convert them. A number of missionaries met their deaths trying to serve their God, but conversions mounted.

By the early 1810s, leaders of Russia's North American fur venture began looking south to the California coast. There, in a climate more favorable to growing crops, a new colony might be able to supply food for the Alaska settlements that struggled with agriculture. A California settlement could also provide a base to hunt sea otters and other lucrative fur-bearing animals. One Russian party, which included a number of Aleuts (a native Alaskan group) working for the Russians,

Inspiration and Innovation: Religion in the American West,
First Edition. Todd M. Kerstetter.

found its way into San Francisco Bay, home of the northernmost Pacific Coast outpost of the Spanish empire. The Spaniards told the Russians to leave, which they did. But, when the Russians returned, a party of Spaniards captured and imprisoned them.

The Spaniards not only objected to Russians encroaching on their territory, but also had concerns about some of the Aleuts, who had converted to Orthodox Christianity. (The eastern and western branches of Christianity had split in 1054 over doctrinal issues and disagreements about the authority of the pope.) A Spanish official, maybe several, encouraged the Aleuts to renounce Orthodoxy and to become Roman Catholic. One Aleut, a man named Chungangnaq (and also known as Petr, likely an adopted Russian name), drew special attention for refusing this suggestion. According to one story, the Spanish tortured the unfortunate Aleut expecting that the process would lead him to change his mind. They cut off a toe. Chungangnaq still refused. Another toe followed and, one by one, each of his fingers. Still, Chungangnaq held loyal to Orthodoxy. Next came disembowelment. Chungangnaq went to his grave true to his adopted religion. His adopted religion recognized his devotion by preserving the story of Petr the Martyr and ultimately honoring him with canonization as St. Peter the Aleut.

Scant documentation of the kind valued by academic historians leads many scholars to harbor doubts about this version of Chungangnaq's story. Whether or not the details of Chungangnaq's torture are true, the broad outlines of Russian and Aleut activity on the California coast and their interaction with the Spanish settlement at San Francisco Bay hold up and they drive home the point that religion was an important part of empire and colonization. In some cases religion helped drive imperial expansion and colonization, as missionaries backed by soldiers coerced native peoples; but, even where it did not drive policy, religion came along for the ride and, as in the case of Chungangnaq, Indians sometimes embraced it. The new religion changed people's lives, not always for the better.

Spain, France, Russia, and England built empires in North America beginning with Spain's sponsorship of Christopher Columbus' expedition in 1492. Those nations wanted to make money from their colonies, but they wanted other things, too. They competed with each other for prestige and resources, and sometimes they competed to spread Christianity. This was especially true for Catholic Spain and

France. English Protestants made some efforts in the colonial period, but they pale in comparison to Catholic missions. Because English Protestants had a negligible presence west of the Mississippi River, this chapter says little about them. It should be noted, though, that Protestantism had a profound influence on the United States and played an important role in US westward expansion, which will be discussed later. As Spain, France, and Russia reached into North America, their expansion included important religious components. European monarchs who ruled by divine right – the belief that the right to govern derives directly from God rather than the people – felt an obligation to serve their religion by expanding its presence. They also felt compelled to provide religious comfort, service, and guidance to the soldiers and subjects who toiled in North America. The monarchs and the clergy who served them also felt a zealous obligation to convert American Indians to Christianity. As the Europeans saw it, these conversions would benefit the Indians and bring glory to the missionaries who converted them. All told, Europeans saw Christianization as a vital part of subduing and civilizing the Americas, which they considered wild and barbaric. Christianity both inspired and provided justification for European expansion. This chapter focuses on religion in European imperialism and colonization in the trans-Mississippi region of what would become the United States. Spain's dealings on the Gulf Coast and in Florida take that narrative east of the Mississippi River, but, this chapter emphasizes Spain's activities in Texas, New Mexico, and California. The story of French efforts deals mostly with the St. Lawrence and Mississippi river valleys. French activity in the St. Lawrence River Valley, while obviously not in the trans-Mississippi West, acted as an important route to the West, allows for a comparative examination of French and Spanish Catholicism in North America, and offers context for later interactions west of the Mississippi. The story of Russia's activities covers from the Alaska coast to San Francisco Bay.

Spain

Spain expanded into the Americas with a uniquely aggressive Catholic agenda. What we know as the nation of Spain did not exist in the 1400s. A variety of Spanish kingdoms had combined into two: Aragon and Castile. The marriage of King Ferdinand of Aragon to Queen Isabella of Castile united the kingdoms in 1469 in a new monarch, but the union was largely a personal one. The kingdoms shared no political, judicial, or administrative institutions, nor did they share a "Spanish" identity. What the kingdoms did share was a sense of belonging to the Spanish Catholic church. Aragon and Castile had emerged from centuries of crusades in which Catholics cooperated to drive Muslims from the Iberian Peninsula, the land mass currently occupied by Spain and Portugal. By the 1400s memories of the Catholic crusades united residents of Aragon and Castile, and the Spanish Catholic church was the one institution that functioned across both kingdoms. Ferdinand and Isabella worked to unify their kingdoms around the church. This created an atmosphere of hyper-Catholicity. In 1492 Ferdinand and Isabella drove the last Moors, who were Muslims, from the Iberian Peninsula and expelled Jews. Nationalism and Catholicism became one and the only way to be a good Spaniard was to be a good Catholic. Spain remained on a great crusade, expanding Catholicism to the Americas and defending it against threats worldwide.

A major threat to Catholicism emerged in the early 1500s. Reformers objected to certain practices of the Roman Catholic Church and set out to change it. Conflicts between reformers and the Catholic Church produced Protestantism, which grew into a major branch of Christianity. Among other things, Protestants rejected the authority of the Pope, the leader of the Roman Catholic Church. They also believe the Bible, rather than church tradition, is the supreme source of authority for all Christians. It might help to think of Protestants as religious revolutionaries who believed Roman Catholic practices were misguided and abusive and that the church was wrong in principle. For more than a century these revolutionaries hoped "popery" would fail everywhere. During that same period, defenders of Roman Catholicism tried to destroy or reconvert the revolutionary "heretics." This grossly simplified explanation might not seem like a big deal, but it led to decades of competition – even bloodshed – between Catholics and Protestants that spilled into the Americas and significantly influenced colonization efforts by European powers.

For example, in 1565 Spanish troops challenged a French settlement, Fort Caroline, established the year before, in what is now Florida. The settlers were Huguenots, French Protestants. At dawn on a September morning Pedro Menéndez de Avilés led an attack on the French and caught them by surprise. The Spaniards killed more than 130 French settlers, but spared women and children. Menéndez referred to the victims as members of "the evil Lutheran sect." His chaplain believed the "Holy Spirit" had intervened in the Spanish routing of the French Huguenots.

Not long after, Menéndez met more French settlers who had left the fort, but who had been stranded when their ships were wrecked in a storm. The French offered to surrender if Menéndez would spare their lives. Menéndez responded that if the French would disarm and put themselves at his mercy, he would "deal with them as Our Lord command me." The French accepted. In this second episode, Menéndez spared Catholics. As the Protestant Frenchmen came into the Spanish camp in small groups, Menéndez had them led out of sight, had his men tie the Frenchmen's hands behind their backs, and had most of them, the Protestants, killed.

The contest for empire among European nations bred considerable violence, but these incidents stand out because they say something about the nature of those conflicts. The bulk of the Frenchmen Menéndez and his soldiers killed belonged to the Huguenots, French followers of the influential Protestant leader John Calvin. Thus, Menéndez believed he was fighting heresy. He also believed the Protestants – and the local Indians – "held similar beliefs, probably Satanic in origin." Killing both the French and the Indian heretics did a service to God and to Menéndez' earthly ruler, Felipe II, Spain's Catholic king. Simply put, Spain wished to achieve profit and the spread of Roman Catholicism in the Americas. It is difficult to say which goal figured more prominently in the Spanish empire as a whole, but religion sustained Spanish activity in what would become the American West for more than a century.

In the 1600s, Spanish explorers failed to find the instant economic wealth they expected. Settlements in Florida and New Mexico sat at the remotest northern parts of the Spanish system. They proved so expensive to maintain that the Crown considered abandoning them. Instead, they sent in missionaries to help settle the colonies. Though this chapter will focus on New Mexico, Spanish missionaries followed virtually identical strategies around the West. Those missionaries, Franciscans, named because they followed the teachings of St. Francis of Assisi, convinced the Crown to continue subsidizing money-losing settlements as missions, which were more cost-effective than military outposts. More importantly, souls were at stake.

Franciscans also had the support of the Spanish Crown, which subsidized mission work partly out of obligation to the Catholic Church and partly for practical reasons. The Crown sent tools, building supplies, food, and clothing to support the missions. In doing so, the Crown met its obligation to the Catholic Church to convert natives. In the long run, the Crown hoped the missions might accomplish other goals. First, if the missionaries succeeded, they would add to the number of laborers and taxpayers in the Spanish empire. Second, missions had the potential to pacify large areas of the empire more inexpensively than military campaigns. In some cases, mission settlements served the dual purposes of pacifying an area and acting as a defensive claim to territory in regions such as Texas, New Mexico, and California, which were remote from power centers of New Spain. So, the Crown hoped both to make money and save money from its investment in missions.

Franciscans came to the Americas in 1493 with an aggressive spiritual agenda. They accompanied Spanish expeditions so that Spanish conquest might be considered an act of Christianity rather than butchery. In some cases, missionaries provided legalistic justifications for butchery as a defense of Catholicism or its expansion. They also wished to save souls by bringing Christianity to non-Christian natives and to reform native cultures. They aimed to create utopian Christian communities of converted Indians serving God in an earthly paradise. Of course, Catholic priests and missionaries also went to the Americas to serve the spiritual needs of the conquistadors and the settlements that resulted from their work. When King Felipe II issued the Orders for New Discoveries in 1573, the rules for Spaniards developing the Americas changed, with important implications for religion's role in the process. Atrocities committed during the first decades of Spanish conquest upset King Felipe II, who wished to improve the process. The new rules forbade calling the process "conquest" and instead used "pacification." Parties wishing to attempt pacification had to get a license from the Crown, and the rules made missionaries the main agents for exploration and pacification. Thanks to the Orders for New Discoveries, Franciscans would spearhead Spanish "pacification."

In 1581, the Crown approved the request of Agustín Rodríguez, a Franciscan, to enter what is now New Mexico to conquer and pacify new people. Rodríguez wasted no time and set out that same year with two more Franciscans and an escort of seven soldiers. The party crossed the Rio Grande and continued hundreds of miles to the land of the Pueblos. The Spaniards imposed a new name on the region: San Felipe del Nuevo México. Most of the expedition returned to New Spain and their report of what is now central and southern New Mexico stirred new interest in developing the region. Rodríguez and another Franciscan remained to pursue their work at a pueblo they knew as Puaray. For reasons we can only guess, residents of Puaray killed both Franciscans, who sacrificed their lives to spread their Christian beliefs and vision of Spanish civilization into a frontier area they saw as the north. Their deaths did nothing to lessen the Spanish desire to convert the Indians.

In 1598, Franciscans accompanied an expedition led by Juan de Oñate that brought permanent European settlement to New Mexico in 1598. Whatever good intentions motivated the Orders for New Discovery, the presence of soldiers complicated matters. Oñate wanted to develop New Mexico for his own political and economic gain, but to garner royal approval he carefully emphasized missionary work as his primary motivation. Thus the force he took north into New Mexico included about 130 soldiers, families, servants, and slaves of the soldiers, and 10 Franciscans. In an act of speculation, Oñate financed most of the expedition himself; the crown paid for the Franciscans, the typical arrangement for subsidizing mission work. The partnership put the burden of colonization on those who would benefit the most financially and ensured the Crown policy of extending Catholicism.

Oñate planted a Spanish settlement among the Pueblos and almost immediately the two groups clashed. The poorly supplied and even more poorly behaved Spaniards demanded food and clothing from the Pueblos and committed torture, rape, and murder. Residents of Acoma fought back, killing 11 soldiers, including Oñate's nephew. Before responding, Oñate asked his Franciscan missionaries if the circumstances allowed him to retaliate with a "just war" against Acoma; and, if so, to delineate how far he might go in waging such a war. The Franciscans ruled the Pueblos had violated their oath to the king and stood in the way of peace, which provided two causes for a just war. The missionaries told Oñate that those Pueblos who had killed Spaniards were at his mercy. As for those Pueblos who stood in the way of peace, the missionaries told Oñate he could exterminate and destroy them. Of course the missionaries urged Oñate to protect the innocent and to avoid bloodshed and death as much as possible as God finds those distasteful. The Spaniards attacked Acoma and, over three days of fighting, killed about 500 men and 300 women and children. They took prisoner about 80 men and roughly 500 women and children. Oñate put the captives on trial, providing them with a defense attorney, found them guilty, and meted out a harsh sentence designed to serve as an object lesson to other Indians who might consider resisting the Spanish. Those older than 25 had a foot cut off. The Spaniards sentenced those between 12 and 25 to 20 years of servitude. As for children younger than 12, Oñate exonerated them but turned them over to the Franciscans for spiritual training.

This episode shows how closely Spanish colonizers linked religion and imperial conquest. In many ways church and state were one, and the Spanish saw extending Catholicism as an important part of their imperial endeavor. Furthermore, the Spanish met in the Pueblos a people for whom religion and spirituality ran through all aspects of life (see Chapter 1). To the Spanish, converting American Indians to Catholicism amounted to doing them a favor and helping them make a vital step toward civilization. As far as they were concerned, the Spanish extended their national power and Catholicism with divine guidance and sanction.

As the 1600s began, Spain faced a dilemma with its North American colonies. As costs mounted, the empire considered withdrawing but the Franciscans persuaded the Crown to continue supporting missionary work even as it lost money. They wanted souls above profit and the Crown eventually agreed. Franciscans dominated missions where Spain pushed into new territories and they played an important part in Spain's empire until it collapsed in 1821. Franciscans ministered to Spanish settlers and planned to spread Christianity to American Indians, while at the same time destroying indigenous religions. How did the Franciscans pull this off? Some Franciscans credited divine intervention. Fray Alonso de Benavides described several magical events or miracles that he claimed helped Franciscan efforts in New Mexico.[1] In one, an infant believed to have died was brought back to life

---

[1] David J. Weber, *The Spanish Frontier in North America* (New Haven, CT: Yale University Press, 1992), 99.

through baptism. In another, a Hopi boy regained his eyesight thanks to a Christian cross. A group of Indians from Picurís Pueblo went to murder a Catholic priest, only to have the priest vanish from sight, which saved his life. In a different kind of message, a thunderbolt killed a "sorceress" at Taos Pueblo. These events suggested to Fray Alonso that his God was at work in New Mexico. This kind of thinking was common at the time among both Christians and many non-Christians such as the American Indians the Spanish sought to convert.

On the other hand, a number of Franciscans found martyrdom, like Agustín Rodríguez. Some even welcomed it. They believed it would help them in the afterlife, for one thing. For another, what could be better than giving one's life for Jesus? Whatever the rationale, it reflects a zeal that sustained the Franciscan mission and demonstrates how religion drove people and ideas into new territories.

When miracles and zeal failed, stagecraft and gifts could help. Franciscans sought to inspire awe through music, paintings, statues, ceremonies, and church buildings. Missionaries gave exotic gifts such as beads, cloth, hatchets and other very useful metal tools. They might also give gifts of food. Whatever the gift, it aimed to demonstrate the power of the Franciscans' Christian and Spanish ways, to inspire confidence, and to build bonds of reciprocity. The gifts not only represented exotic and useful items to Indians, but also demonstrated Spanish willingness to follow social customs familiar to Indians. Many Indians also found elements of Christianity appealing. As discussed in Chapter 1, many Indians practiced an open-minded spirituality and would have seen nothing wrong with adopting bits of Christianity to use in conjunction with their own spiritual traditions. As we will see, most Christians did not share that attitude and sought to make Indians exclusively Christian.

With a sense of confidence and reciprocity established, missionaries turned their attention to spiritual matters with special emphasis on two influential audiences. Franciscans targeted existing leaders with the expectation that influence would trickle down to the rest of a community. Missionaries also targeted children. Children not only had the perceived benefit of being more teachable than adults, but also represented the next generation of leaders. Using this generational strategy, the Franciscans sought to Christianize and, as they saw it, civilize native peoples they viewed as savage and heathen.

This model had a dark side. Although the Spaniards relied on education and freewill to convince Indians to convert, those who adopted Christianity faced a heavy-handed system. Franciscans called on soldiers to keep baptized Indians – neophytes – in the mission communities, for example. Franciscans feared new converts might backslide in the company of Indians who had not forsaken their old ways. Franciscans could also call on soldiers to punish baptized Indians who failed to adhere to Catholicism or who practiced their original religion alongside Catholicism, often called syncretism. In this way, the Spanish practiced a form of coercive Christianity, interweaving enforced religious practices with efforts to encourage individual faith. Priests tried to destroy or eliminate sacred objects used in native ceremonies and did their best to prohibit ceremonies. They also pressured native religious leaders to abandon their practices. The Franciscans sought to erase native religion and its influences as they "civilized" Indians and they would use violence to achieve their goals.

Why cooperate at all with these invaders? Sometimes native peoples did not cooperate. But when they did, they felt they had too much to lose by not cooperating or they believed they had something to gain by cooperating with the Franciscans. On a very basic level, Franciscans offered natives access to certain trade goods and technology like metal goods and cloth that could be obtained only from the Spanish. In some cases, a group might identify the Franciscans and Spaniards as an ally against unsavory Spaniards or against a threatening tribe, often a familiar enemy who seemed a more immediate danger. Thus, conversion created an alliance with the Franciscans. Spiritually, virtually all natives had first-hand experience with priest-like holy figures and some no doubt saw the Franciscans as offering access to a new and different type of spiritual power. Those interested in Christianity often adopted the parts that appealed to them. For example, they typically *added* elements of Christianity to their existing belief system rather than abandoning it. They might add Jesus and Mary, for instance, to their existing cast of religious figures and they might view Franciscans as additional shamans. A Franciscan who declared New Mexico free of "idolatry" in 1638 got it wrong or deliberately overstated the case. Another wrote in 1696 that New Mexico's Pueblos still had more interest in their own beliefs than in Christianity. So, Indians cooperated with the Spanish for a variety of reasons and together they created a complex new religious environment.

This messy environment, in which Spaniards expected and demanded complete conversion, while Indians retained religious ideas and practices while selectively adopting parts of Christianity, created conflict. Pueblos, for example, continued to practice their ceremonies, secretly where necessary. At Taos Pueblo, Indians protested by serving their priest tortillas made with urine and rodent meat. As mentioned earlier, Indians such as those at Puaray murdered missionaries. Whether adopting Christianity or fighting it, Indians made choices and, by the late 1600s, violent resistance became more common.

Indeed, revolts spanning the 1600s in New Mexico leave no doubt that the native population chafed under Spanish rule. Spanish officials reported uprisings in 1632, 1639, 1644, 1647, 1650, and 1667. Because Pueblo people lived in relatively small communities and did not share a language, Spaniards had little trouble stopping the rebellions, often by hanging leaders and selling suspects into slavery. In rare cases, two or more communities united in rebellion. The Spaniards succeeded in halting those, too, for a time.

About 1660 the Pueblos entered a particularly difficult period. Drought settled over New Mexico along with higher than normal temperatures. Plants and animals both struggled to survive and people died of hunger. At the same time, Apaches, Navajos, and other neighboring tribes raided Pueblos. The Spaniards and their Christianity proved unable to provide for the Pueblos or to protect them. In these difficult times, many Pueblos turned to their own religious leaders and traditional Pueblo religion experienced a revival. This reminds us that even though the Pueblos had a degree of open-mindedness when it came to religion, religious beliefs were central to their lives.

Spaniards viewed the revival as a threat to civilization and Christianity and responded violently. Spaniards tried to stamp out native religious ceremonies and they punished Pueblo religious leaders with beatings, imprisonment, and execution. In 1675 Spanish officials meted out some of the harshest punishments. They hanged three Pueblo shamans and whipped 43 others. Yet another killed himself while imprisoned. This crackdown helped convince many Pueblos the Spanish had gone too far. In 1680 the combined effects of drought, raids, and the Spanish crackdown pushed the Pueblos to the breaking point. Pueblos across New Mexico united in a revolt against Spanish rule and forced all Hispanics – and a number of Christian Indians who did not wish to rebel – in New Mexico south to El Paso. Religion played a central role in what has become known as *the* Pueblo Revolt.

One of the Pueblos punished in 1675, a religious leader from San Juan Pueblo named Popé, channeled his anger and opposition into organizing a widespread offensive. The Spaniards saw it as a rebellion, but to the Pueblos it must have seemed like a fight for freedom. Popé's movement came to include about 17 000 people from more than 24 independent towns spanning several hundred miles. Popé's followers spoke six or more different languages and even more dialects. The movement reflected the complexity and diversity of Pueblo society and politics, but it doesn't tell the whole story. Not all Pueblos joined the movement. Popé and his lieutenants did not trust every town, so some did not receive an invitation to join the rebellion. Some towns invited to join the movement refused. Even within towns dedicated to the movement, some individuals remained loyal to the Spanish.

From a base at Taos Pueblo, Popé's followers planned to attack Spanish strongholds on August 11, 1680. Word of the impending attack reached Spaniards on August 9, which led Popé's followers to advance their plans by a day to maintain some semblance of surprise. Even with a warning, the Spaniards were unprepared for the scope and magnitude of the attacks that came that day and in the days that followed. The natives killed more than 400 of the 2500 foreigners living in New Mexico and, by the end of September, had forced surviving Hispanics south to El Paso. Amid the tumult, Popé and other leaders discussed purging Pueblo society of all hints of Spanish influence, essentially advocating a type of ethnic cleansing. In the end, Pueblos continued growing crops and livestock brought by the Spanish and retained items deemed beneficial.

Religion played an important role in the movement. The Pueblos killed 21 of the 33 missionaries in New Mexico. In some cases they tortured the Franciscans before killing them. They defiled or outright destroyed churches. According to one eyewitness, Popé himself traveled among the participating towns directing followers to destroy symbols of Christianity in the churches. He also told those who had been baptized to immerse themselves in rivers to undo the effects of that ceremony and to restore them to their pre-Christian state. Christian Indians who had not fled to El Paso and who resisted Popé's revival message were killed. Popé also urged Pueblos to rebuild kivas and to resume traditional ceremonies and dances, especially those that would bring rain.

In hindsight, it seems clear the Pueblos acted to express disapproval of Christianity. At the very least, they seem to have focused on religion as an important symbol of Spanish oppression. To many Spaniards of the day, Crown policy and actions of soldiers and Franciscans had nothing to do with the rebellion. They considered the violent uprising an expression of God's wrath exacting punishment for Spanish sins or simply as the work of the devil. In other words, they saw the supernatural at work, but not a repudiation of their efforts to spread a superior religion to a benighted people.

Pueblos held their independence for about 12 years until Diego de Vargas initiated Spain's reconquest of New Mexico in 1692. The reconquest involved diplomacy and force, but it also had religious overtones. Even with Christianity banished and traditions restored, the Pueblos continued to suffer from drought and raids from enemy tribes through the 1680s. This likely contributed to factionalism among the Pueblos and to conditions that allowed Spain to return to New Mexico in the 1690s. When Spaniards stormed Santa Fe in 1693, they invoked the name of Santiago, or St. James (the apostle and patron saint of Spain). They also called on a three-foot-high statue for help. Called *Nuestra Señora de la Conquistadora*, or more commonly *La Conquistadora*, the image of the Virgin Mary had been taken from Santa Fe in 1680 during the Spanish evacuation. The statue first came to Santa Fe in 1626 with Fray Alonso de Benavides. Now the Spanish force brought it back and asked the icon for help in reclaiming New Mexico. The Spaniards and their Indian allies (Pueblos who had not supported Popé or who had since abandoned the cause) reclaimed New Mexico. *La Conquistadora* still resides in Santa Fe and enjoys the distinction of being the oldest continuously venerated image of the Virgin Mary in the United States.

As before, missions staffed by Franciscans played a central role in Spain's New Mexico. Franciscans re-establishing missions in the 1690s found many Pueblos still held hard feelings about the Christian endeavor. Many Franciscans who had ventured into the countryside felt it prudent to retreat to the safety of Santa Fe. One priest admitted to Vargas that while he and his colleagues welcomed the opportunity to shed their blood for the gospel, they would prefer not to do so unless some gain would come of it. The Pueblo Revolt frustrated Spanish colonizers, but priests remained doggedly determined to spread Catholicism and they would sacrifice their lives to do it.

In June 1696 dissatisfied Pueblos again attacked missions in New Mexico. They killed five Franciscans and burned churches. Vargas responded with a war of attrition. Spain regained control of most pueblos after six months and after this rebellion the Spaniards finally changed their approach. The Franciscans relaxed their efforts to eradicate Pueblo religion and the Spanish colonial system demanded less of its Pueblo workforce. Pueblos suffered a population decline from about 17 000 in 1680 to about 14 000 in 1700, and they had endured social disruptions from the decades of turmoil. But, they prompted the Spanish colonial system to moderate its demands. Those adjustments, combined with facing a growing threat from Utes, Apaches, and Navajos, led Pueblos and Hispanics into a period of peaceful coexistence. In the end, though, religion played an important role in the Pueblo Uprising.

The Spanish policy of expanding and defending its empire in North America continued to rely on the institution of the mission in Texas. In this region, Spain responded to French expansion by establishing missions in 1690 in what is now east Texas. Two missions among the Hasinai Indians established a Spanish presence. The Hasinais tolerated the missions for a few years, but a smallpox epidemic turned sentiment against the Franciscans. The missions' remote location and trouble in New Mexico made it extremely difficult to sustain the far-flung east Texas missions in anything but a completely cooperative atmosphere. When the natives gave the missionaries two choices, leave or die, the Franciscans abandoned the missions in 1693. Spain let the Texas mission field lie fallow for 20 years.

A French move into east Texas in 1713 prompted Spain to make another effort at establishing missions in the region. In 1716, Spaniards built five missions in east Texas and what would become Louisiana. One, San Miguel de los Adaes, would become the capital of Spanish Texas. These missions still sat far from any significant Spanish settlement. To ease the task of supplying the east Texas missions, Spain sought additional settlements between the Rio Grande and east Texas. A Franciscan, Antonio de San Buenaventura de Olivares, had found an excellent riverside site for the purpose. In 1718, Spain built presidio San Antonio de Béjar on the site that would become the city of San Antonio. It also built a mission, San Antonio de Valero, whose chapel, later known as the Alamo, would play a critical role in Texas history and mythology.

Missions in east Texas struggled. With the nearby French offering trade, including weapons, Indians in the region had choices and

Figure 2.1   Mission Nuestra Senora de La Purisima Concepcion. Source: Courtesy of the Library of Congress Prints & Photographs Division, HABS (HABS TEX, 15-SANT.V,1--2).

resources to resist Franciscan appeals. Frustrated friars requested troops to force Indians into the missions, to help keep them there, and to destroy Indian sacred sites. The troops never came and three of the east Texas missions had been abandoned by 1731. The others survived into the 1770s, but produced few converts. Without the military and trade behind them, the Franciscans did not fare well in Texas.

Where missions survived, hard times seemed to be the key to success. Namely, they seemed to serve a population that faced poor choices. Away from the missions, the Indians faced Spanish expansion encroaching from the south and Apaches from the north. At the missions, they found some measure of safety and a reliable food supply. The five San Antonio missions, the most successful in Texas, met these needs and by the mid-1700s counted a stable population of about 1000 (Figure 2.1).

While these missions found some success, they also played a role in discouraging colonization. The missions enjoyed government subsidization and had an inexpensive communal labor force with which to build irrigation projects. Tejanos, or settlers from Spain, could not compete with crops and livestock produced under those conditions. The missions provided defensive outposts to hold the edges of empire, but at the same time stunted development.

Spain turned its imperial vision to the Pacific coast of North America in the second half of the 1700s, which brought the founding of New California in 1769. Franciscan missions would, as they had in New Mexico and Texas, play a central role in the Spanish enterprise. José de Gálvez, appointed Secretary of the Indies in 1776, had pushed Spain into this arena to stave off competition from Russia, England, and Holland. Gálvez ordered what he sometimes called the "Sacred Expedition" to establish a Spanish presence at Monterey. Under Capt. Gaspar de Portolá, the expedition built a presidio at San Diego in 1769. Father Junípero Serra, the expedition's spiritual leader, added the mission of San Diego de Alcalá. The following year, the duo of Portolá and Serra established a presidio at Monterey with the mission of San Carlos to handle spiritual matters and Gálvez had the capital of Alta or New California in place to thwart imperial rivals and to spread the gospel to the Indians of California.

Again, the odd pairing of soldiers and clergy produced shameful results and brought changes to Franciscan policy. Spaniards turned local Indians against them by stealing food and livestock. Though Father Serra encouraged soldiers to marry Indian women, and some did, others resorted to rape. This violence led Franciscans to try to keep non-Indians out of mission communities. The Spaniards, with few gifts to offer California Indians, relied on intimidation (whippings, executions) in an attempt to maintain control. As had happened in New Mexico, Indians retaliated. In 1775, Ipai Indians burned the mission at San Diego and killed the priest. Other Indian attacks against California missions followed.

Things changed in the 1780s as the number and size of missions grew even as the mission lifestyle proved harmful to Indian neophytes. Reformers wished to change policy at California's missions to include Hispanic residents. Elsewhere, the model of creating separate communities for Indians and Hispanics had failed. Reformers hoped that adding Hispanic role models to the mission communities would help acculturate Indians. The Franciscans running California's missions resisted. Many of these priests came from Spain and were prejudiced against Mexican-born settlers. The priests also deplored the soldiers' immoral behavior. Rather than mix the populations, they preferred to keep the Indians separate until they were, in the eyes of the Franciscans, ready to participate in the Hispanic world. The Franciscans prevailed.

Also during the 1780s, the missions began producing agricultural surpluses. This meant the missions generated money, which could be used to pay for imported goods. It also meant that shipboard cargo space previously dedicated to foodstuffs to sustain the missions could be allocated to other goods. As the missions improved their inventories of goods, they found it easier to attract converts. More converts meant more workers and, often, larger surpluses. The system boomed. In 1784, about 4650 Indians lived at California's missions. By 1800, the number reached 13 500. When Spain's rule ended in 1821, Franciscans counted more than 21 000 mission Indians.

Even as the population of mission Indians increased, the population of Indians in what is now California decreased. Disease took a high toll and birth rates declined. Indeed, some missionaries lamented that Indians died as fast as they could baptize them. Estimates place California's Indian population at about 300 000 in 1769. By 1821, it had fallen to about 200 000. As had happened in Texas, the mission system likely discouraged colonization in California. The missions held large tracts of the best arable land. They dominated the Indian labor supply. The Franciscans fought the establishment of civil towns and private landholdings. So while trying to increase converts, the Franciscans in California discouraged settlement, yet failed to protect the Indians from outside incursions.

By the 1780s, Spanish officials facing the difficulty of drawing settlers from Spain or Spain's American colonies began trying to attract colonists from the United States to live in Louisiana and the Floridas. In addition to offering large grants of free land, Spanish officials relaxed religious requirements for settlers. Previously, Spanish policy demanded Protestant immigrants convert to Catholicism. Under new policies, immigrants had to swear allegiance to Spain, but they were not required to convert to Catholicism. Spanish officials hoped priests could convert at least some of these adults and they expected religious instruction to make the next generation Catholic. Even as they offered a limited religious freedom, they assumed that Catholicism would triumph.

In Texas it became clear by the late 1700s that the missions were not achieving the goal of turning American Indians into tax-paying

Christians, as historian David Weber put it. The missions effectively isolated Indians in communities segregated from Hispanics. Missionaries continued to hold the paternalistic view that Indians would never be able to fully understand Catholicism and could never become fully functioning members of Hispanic society. At the urging of its Franciscan leader, San Antonio de Valero underwent secularization in 1793. This meant it became a parish staffed by parish-supported priests. It also led to mission lands being divided and distributed to remaining Indian residents of the mission. The other four San Antonio missions began secularizing in 1794, a process that continued into the 1820s. As for Spain itself, by 1821 diplomacy and the Mexican revolution removed it from areas that would become the United States.

While the missions served their purpose as outposts of empire and produced a mixed, if not dark, legacy with respect to bringing Catholic Christianity to American Indians and attempting to erase indigenous religion, they have largely been remembered as romantic, benevolent institutions they certainly were not. Why this happened is not entirely clear, although steps in the process can be traced. As the actual events receded into history, it became easier to forget or sanitize them. By the mid- to late 1800s people perceived the closing of the frontier and the rise of cities and industry. These developments proved unsettling and encouraged some to romanticize a golden age that never really existed. For example, in 1886 a well-known historian of California wrote of the Spanish period, "Never before or since was there a spot in America where life was a long happy holiday, where there was less labor, less care or trouble."[2] In the 1880s California gave birth to an architectural style called Mission Revival featuring red tile roofs, stucco walls, and bell towers. Thanks to exposure at Chicago's World Columbian Exposition in 1893, Mission Revival architecture spread to parts of the country far removed from the Spanish missions. Areas where actual missions had functioned capitalized on nostalgia and a sanitized history to create tourist attractions based on missions. California boosters, especially, played mission history effectively by refurbishing the state's 21 missions and promoting them as scenic destinations. Texas and New Mexico have also played on this religious past for tourist profit. In recent decades, discussions of the missions and their legacy have acknowledged their dark side. For example,

---

[2] Hubert Howe Bancroft quoted in Weber (1992), 341.

when Pope John Paul II beatified (the second of three steps required for sainthood) Father Junípero Serra in 1987, many Indians and scholars objected based on the harsh living conditions for Indians at missions and Serra's support of beatings for those who violated mission policy.

Spain's history in the Americas and in the American West cannot be separated from Catholicism. Religion motivated Spain's imperial expansion and provided justification for acquisition of new territories and the treatment of people living in them. Religion played a central role in American Indians' lives, too. Some of those people, namely the Pueblos, fought Spanish expansion in what was essentially a religious war. In the late 1700s and early 1800s, religion's influence on Spain's efforts receded, but it never disappeared. By the late 1800s, historical memory sanitized and romanticized the Spanish colonial period. But, as the story of Father Serra illustrates, what had been swept under the rug remains.

France

France lagged behind Spain in exploring, claiming, and trying to develop North America, but not by much. The fur trade, fishing, and trying to find a shortcut to Asia drove French interest in North America, but so did the desire to spread Catholicism. In 1534 and 1535, Jacques Cartier found the Gulf of St. Lawrence and the St. Lawrence River leading the French to hope they had also found the much desired shortcut to Asia. France settled a colony in the St. Lawrence in the 1540s, but high costs and poor relations with the Iroquois doomed it to a short life. Religious problems in France contributed to the difficulty of maintaining the colony and distracted the nation from developing North American colonies. The Reformation, which pitted Protestants against Catholics, took France to the brink of religious war for much of the late sixteenth century. France, a predominately Catholic nation, granted civil rights to Protestants in 1598. This calmed the conflict and allowed France to turn its attention elsewhere, including the development of North America. Even with renewed attention, the French effort paled in comparison to those of Spain and England. By the 1660s, about 3000 French colonists lived in what is now Canada. Nearby to the south at the same time, about

40000 English settlers lived in the New England colonies. Partly because of their small numbers and partly because the fur trade, the economic foundation of their North American enterprise, depended upon American Indian labor and commerce, France took a unique approach to colonization. France approached North America with a relatively light hand and that extended to its religious endeavors. France extended Roman Catholic influence in North America and the dramatic experiences of missionaries help us understand how it was done and the role religion played in New France. Although many of the stories related here occurred east of the Mississippi River, they can be seen as a template for French colonization of the Great Lakes region and into the Mississippi River Valley.

In the French system, missionaries eventually adopted a strategy of following the fur trade, establishing missions in Indian villages far from French farming settlements. Samuel de Champlain, considered the "Father of New France," provides an excellent example of how the French system worked. Champlain wanted to make money in the fur trade, but he also wanted to plant self-sufficient settlements in North America and to spread Christianity. Champlain established Québec in 1608 on the St. Lawrence River. Québec became an important base in developing New France. Over the course of a century, France would extend its influence from the mouth of the St. Lawrence River to the mouth of the Mississippi, an area that has been called the French Crescent. Champlain raised money to bring four Recollet friars to Québec in 1615 to convert Indians. The friars held the Indians in low esteem, which might help explain their poor record of conversions. The Recollets' strategy was to establish villages of Indians nearby French settlements, presuming that Indians would be attracted to them, and assuming that Christianizing them required "civilizing" them, inculcating them with French ways and the French language.

In 1625 a contingent of Jesuits joined the Recollets at Quebec. They gradually adopted a very different strategy from that of the Recollets. These missionaries, too, had been brought to Québec with private funds, this time by the viceroy of New France, Duc de Ventadour, a devout Catholic. Jesuits belonged to a Roman Catholic order called the Society of Jesus founded in 1534 by Ignatius Loyola. They quickly gained a reputation for education and for undertaking missionary work virtually anywhere in the world to evangelize people who had not heard the Gospel. Jesuits had two major goals for their missionary work in the New World. First, they wished to convert American Indians to Catholicism. Second, they wished to fight the spread of Protestantism. The presence of Protestant traders in the St. Lawrence River Valley and in English and Dutch colonies on the eastern coast of North America inspired Jesuits, who came to dominate French missionary efforts in North America.

The Jesuits arrived at about the same time the French government adopted policies favorable to Catholics. In 1627, the French government withdrew the trade monopoly it had granted to a group of merchants that included both Catholics and Protestants. The government granted a new trade monopoly to the Company of One Hundred Associates, sometimes known as the Company of New France, a strictly Catholic organization. By 1632, the government had granted a mission monopoly on the St. Lawrence River to the Jesuits. Jesuits had the territory to themselves until 1657.

Father Paul Le Jeune led the Québec mission from 1632 until 1639. Le Jeune's experiences show us how the Jesuits functioned within the French system and how they worked to convert Indians to Catholicism. The French came to North America in small numbers and so did Jesuit missionaries. The Indians who lived in New France were never conquered and the French never had the ability to force their will on these Indians. These Indians remained highly independent, which forced Jesuits to approach them in a relatively accommodating way. Missionaries lived in the Indian communities they targeted for conversion. This practice helped them learn the Indians' language and customs, which the Jesuits expected would ease religious instruction. In other words, rather than trying to get Indian communities to adapt to them, they began by adapting to the Indians. Le Jeune spent the winter of 1633–1634, his second in Canada, with the Montagnais. He learned much about them and the Montagnais learned much about Le Jeune.

Le Jeune paid special attention to Montagnais ceremonies and spiritual matters. He noted the special care given to disposing of animal remains. This was part of hunting's ritual nature and an example of how spirituality permeated every aspect of life for virtually all American Indians. To the Montagnais, more than skill went into hunting. To them, the human hunter and the prey enjoyed a mutual relationship, one of the many relationships between humans and animals. Among other things, hunters had to show respect to the animals they killed by disposing of remains properly. If hunters failed to show proper respect, animals might withdraw and leave hunters and their families hungry. Le Jeune seemed not to appreciate the significance of these rituals. To him, they proved the Montagnais' simple nature and reinforced the idea that they would benefit from adopting Catholicism and other French ways.

That winter Le Jeune spent much time observing a Montagnais shaman, essentially Le Jeune's counterpart, named Carigonan. According to Le Jeune's records, he saw Carigonan lead a ceremony to forecast results of a hunt and health of members of his group. Le Jeune also noted that Carigonan used his spiritual powers against a rival shaman and claimed to have caused his death. In contrast to his own Christianity, Le Jeune noted that in Montagnais belief shamans played an active and necessary role in manipulating spiritual power, and that a Montagnais shaman might use spiritual power for both altruistic and hostile ends. As far as Le Jeune was concerned, Montagnais belief amounted to little more than superstition. Le Jeune did his best to discredit Carigonan among his Montagnais followers, which must have complicated Le Jeune's task of converting them to Catholicism.

As Le Jeune tried to convince his companions of the benefits of Christian doctrine, such as the first commandment, the Montagnais tried to teach *him* how to behave properly in their world. They thought Le Jeune behaved strangely. They thought his beard was ugly. They tried to get him to act appropriately by poking fun at his strange behaviors. After spending a winter with the Montagnais, Le Jeune concluded their seasonal economy based on fishing, hunting, and gathering posed an obstacle to their progress. They needed to adopt a more sedentary, settled lifestyle, Le Jeune decided, if they were to enjoy a more stable and higher standard of living. In other words, they need to be French, economically, politically and religiously. It would also make Le Jeune's task of teaching Christianity much easier. The French eventually built a village for the Montagnais, but it failed to live up to Le Jeune's expectations and it was abandoned.

Le Jeune and his Jesuit colleagues held higher hopes for the Hurons, who lived a more sedentary lifestyle based on growing corn. Hurons supplemented their corn crop with hunting and gathering, but their village-based society provided an attractive target for Jesuit missionaries. On learning more about the Hurons, the Jesuits realized converting them to Christianity would be more difficult than they first thought. At first glimpse, the Jesuits saw no institutionalized religion among the Hurons. More accurately, the Jesuits saw nothing *they recognized* as religious among the Hurons. Converting them would be easy, the Jesuits hoped.

The Jesuits quickly learned the spiritual setting was much more complicated. Religion and spirituality ran through virtually everything the Hurons did, it turned out. Cures for diseases, games, fishing, hunting, growing crops, trade – everything – had some "diabolical" ceremony associated with it, or so one Jesuit observer put it. "Superstition" as that Jesuit viewed things, "has contaminated nearly all the actions of their lives."[3] As for the most important religious ceremonies, they literally made the world go around. Hurons called these ceremonies, dances, and feasts *onderha*, which translates to the "prop" or "foundation" of the country. When some Hurons converted to Christianity and refused to participate in these critical ceremonies, non-Christian Hurons said the converts were trying to destroy the community. The same went for the Jesuits, whose teachings threatened the Huron cycle of life. The Jesuits wished to replace the spirituality that ordered the Huron world with a moral, social, and political order based in Christianity. Religion ran to the core of both the Hurons and the French, at least the Jesuit, world. And unlike most missionaries, the Jesuits worked to learn about the people they sought to convert and were more willing to adapt aspects of Christianity in order to encourage conversion.

Despite the challenges, Jesuit missionaries made the Hurons the focus of their missionary work in New France in the mid-1600s. Champlain encouraged French fur traders to assist the Jesuits. Some Hurons accused the Jesuits of practicing what we would consider witchcraft or sorcery, and argued the missionaries should be killed. Others, many others, resisted this and protected the priests. These Hurons, whatever they thought about the missionaries, wanted to stay on good terms with the French so they could enjoy the benefits of the fur trade. In 1639, Jesuit missionaries established Sainte-Marie, a fortified settlement in the heart of Huron country. Sainte-Marie lasted a decade. Conflict between the Hurons and neighboring Iroquois led the Hurons to abandon their villages in the late 1640s. Some Hurons

[3] Quoted in Carole Blackburn, *Harvest of Souls: The Jesuit Missions and Colonialism in North America, 1632–1650* (Montreal: McGill-Queen's University Press, 2000), 38.

joined friendly neighboring groups. Most of the Christian Hurons followed the Jesuits, who, after burning Sainte-Marie in the spring of 1649, fled to the safety of Québec.

The way Jesuits described North America and its human inhabitants tells us how religion influenced their perceptions and gives us some clues about how the French viewed their work on the continent. Jesuits described the landscape they encountered as wilderness. As they saw it, the land had not been improved according to uses they recognized and approved, such as agriculture. Their theological background led them to consider wilderness as a place forsaken by God and hostile. Similarly, Jesuits described American Indians as savages, rude people who lived apart from the benefits of Christian civilization. This view contrasted mightily with the worldviews of Hurons, Montagnais, and other longtime residents. They felt completely at home in and spiritually connected to what the Jesuits saw as foreign and hostile. Although the Jesuits used a lighter, more accommodating approach to converting American Indians than did the Franciscans, the Jesuits and Franciscans both saw themselves as important agents of domestication and civilization to be achieved in large measure through Christianization.

The complicated intersection of Jesuit and American Indian beliefs can also be seen in the way each group viewed disease. Shortly after the Jesuits arrived among the Hurons, a series of epidemics swept the population. Disease killed nearly half the Hurons. The Jesuits and other French became ill, but typically recovered. How could this be and what did it mean? Jesuits interpreted the disease as a heavenly scourge. Father Le Jeune wrote that an affliction such as an epidemic "opens the eyes of the understanding."[4] Suffering and death undermined the pride that prevented Indians from truly converting to Christianity. Hurons saw things differently. Many considered the Jesuits sorcerers, but the Hurons disagreed on Jesuit motives. Initially, they thought the priests had the power to protect themselves and to cure others and Hurons sought that help, sometimes through conversion. As disease continued to kill unabated, their interpretation changed. They came to see the priests as sorcerers who could protect themselves from the disease. How else could they spend so much time among the sick and not pay with their lives? In fact, some

[4] Quoted in Blackburn (2000), 105.

Hurons concluded the Jesuits had conjured the disease. Whatever the epidemics' origins, the Hurons considered it bad form to have the ability to cure disease and not use it to help the sick. For some, this strengthened their resistance to the Jesuit mission. Others saw the hideous damage inflicted by the epidemics as evidence that Huron traditional healers were ineffective against the sickness. Some warmed to the possibility of accepting Christianity, seeing it as a possible ally against the disease and an alternative or adjunct to their old beliefs. The Jesuits found themselves busy with conversions in the aftermath of the epidemics.

Jesuits found a receptive audience among Huron women, too. Huron women, like those in many tribes of northeastern North America, had considerable power over their lives. For example, they chose lovers and husbands. They could, and did, choose their spiritual path. Huron women found appeal in the cult of the Virgin Mary, Jesus's mother, and their veneration of women saints. The Jesuits also took seriously the abuse of Huron women and worked to stop it. Huron women who accepted Christianity helped Jesuits make inroads to greater Huron society. By the 1640s, Jesuits had converted about 40 percent of Hurons.[5] Tactical accommodation to Huron ways, in the interest of conversions, succeeded to a notable degree.

In the 1650s and 1660s, French and Jesuit ties to the Iroquois deepened and brought significant political, social, and cultural changes, many with strong religious components. After years of strong ties to the Dutch, the Iroquois shifted their allegiance to the French in the mid-1660s. The Iroquois–Dutch relationship revolved around trade almost exclusively. Dutch goods transformed Iroquois life, but the Iroquois kept the Dutch at arm's length. Shifting to French trade brought the unintended consequence of French missionaries bent on converting the Iroquois. That, in turn, meant close contact as missionaries came to live with the Iroquois.

Allying with the French exacerbated political divisions among the Iroquois. One group of Iroquois leaders had for some time sought a closer relationship with the French. Generally, this group recognized that trading with the French and allying with them in war also meant converting to Christianity and they did not object. Other Iroquois

[5] Robert V. Hine and John Mack Faragher, *The American West: A New Interpretive History* (New Haven, CT: Yale University Press, 2000), 51.

leaders wished not to ally with the French and saw religious conversion and compliance with other French policies as a form of capitulation. By the late 1660s and early 1670s, those leaders who favored the French had charge of almost every Iroquois town.

The ethnic diversity of Iroquois communities helped motivate closer ties with the French. Hundreds, maybe more than a thousand, Hurons and Algonquians lived among the Iroquois. They had been captured and adopted by the Iroquois. Before that, many had converted to Christianity. They maintained their faith while living among the Iroquois and regularly asked for access to priests. Iroquois diplomats arranged for French priests to establish a mission in the mid-1650s. Iroquois hostile to the French forced the mission to close by 1658. The short-lived mission showed the religious diversity of Iroquois society and the role religion played in Iroquois politics.

Iroquois–French relations depended on priests as a type of guest-hostage. When Indian enemies reached a peace agreement with each other, they usually sent members to live in their former enemy's village. These guests acted as a type of insurance. Presumably, warriors would not attack a village where relatives lived. To Europeans, these guests might seem like hostages. During the seventeenth century, nearly every Iroquois request for French missionaries came during peace negotiations. The Iroquois probably saw the missionaries as more than "peace hostages," but the priests interested them for reasons other than their knowledge of Christianity.

In the 1660s and 1670s, social divisions between Christian and non-Christian Iroquois brought disruptions to Iroquois society and led Jesuits to change their recruiting tactics. Iroquois society expected members of a minority faction to subordinate their desires to the will of the majority in order to achieve consensus. For example, a Christianized Iroquois might continue to participate in Iroquois ceremonies while practicing Christianity. The Jesuits disapproved of this and pressured converts, especially those with leadership roles, to abandon Iroquois beliefs and ceremonies that conflicted with Christianity. Those who did earned the scorn of their non-Christian tribesmen. To non-Christians, Iroquois who followed this path had become French and were no longer Iroquois. The Christian Iroquois suffered verbal and physical abuse and, if they had a leadership position, they likely lost it. This suggests that it wasn't just Catholic Franciscans and Jesuits who linked religion and identity. Iroquois who completely abandoned traditional beliefs and practices effectively abandoned their Iroquois-ness and found themselves outcasts.

Following Iroquois custom, these outcasts left to settle a new community. Christian Iroquois left to settle closer to the French. A trickle of Christian refugees turned into a flood after the Jesuits adopted a new policy in 1673. Rather than continue to live and pros- elytize among the Iroquois, the Jesuits began gathering converts to villages established for Christian Indians. By 1682 one of the largest villages, Kahnawake (also known as the Saint François Xavier du Sault mission), had as many as 600 residents and at least three other villages received Christian Iroquois who had fled conflict. This reflects the complicated results of religious change and how the Iroquois still held significant power in the 1680s and could shape European coloniza- tion and forestall the spread of Christianity.

The missions also served as havens for people who lacked family and friends. Kateri Tekakwitha, a Mohawk, lost both her parents to smallpox when she was about four. An uncle, a vocal opponent of Christianity, raised her. Twice she refused marriage matches arranged by her aunts. Her reasons remain obscure, but seem to include a dis- like of men, aversion to marriage, and a dedication to maintain her purity by avoiding sex. Tekakwitha's mother had been a Christian Algonquin and her aunts interpreted her refusal to marry as evidence she had turned her back on the Iroquois nation. They rejected her. Tekakwitha followed her mother's footsteps by adopting Christianity with a baptism on Easter 1676. She then began a life of what one historian called "almost pathological piety."[6] Her new habits and her refusal to work on Catholic holy days brought more hostility, including attacks and death threats. In the fall of 1677 she fled to Kahnawake. Her continued aversion to marriage and her devotion to Catholicism led one priest to comment that she wished to have none other than Jesus as her spouse. At the mission, Tekakwitha continued her extreme fasting and physical penance. Priests urged her to moderate her behavior, but it likely contributed to her death at age 24. The Roman

---

[6] Daniel K. Richter, *The Ordeal of the Longhouse: The Peoples of the Iroquois League in the Era of European Colonization* (Chapel Hill, NC: University of North Carolina Press, 1992), 126–128.

Catholic Church began the process for her canonization in 1884 and in October 2012 she became the first indigenous woman from the Americas to attain sainthood.

Jesuits continued mission work elsewhere in the St. Lawrence region and also accompanied French activity farther west in the Great Lakes and along the Mississippi River. Father Isaac Jogues established a mission to the Ojibwes in 1641 on the peninsula between Lake Michigan and Lake Superior. The community at Sault Sainte Marie grew into a major settlement. A Jesuit named Jacques Marquette undertook missionary work in what is now Wisconsin in 1669. While working there, Marquette explored the upper Mississippi River. With explorer Louis Jolliet, Marquette headed an expedition down the Mississippi River in 1673 that provided France with the justification to claim territory (and the Jesuits to extend their potential mission field) from the mouth of the St. Lawrence to the mouth of the Mississippi. In the following decades, Jesuits would play important roles in establishing a Catholic presence in French settlements at Biloxi, Mobile, and New Orleans.

By 1763, though, the extensive Jesuit missionary effort would be considerably reduced and the French would lose their dominance in interior North America. By the mid-1700s, the Jesuits had become so wealthy and powerful that the French Crown – even the Roman Catholic Church – worried about the organization's influence. In 1763, the French Crown essentially recalled Jesuit missionaries. News of the suppression arrived in New Orleans on the same ship that brought news of the Peace of Paris. The Peace ended the Seven Years' War between France and England. In it, France ceded to England all its North American territory east of the Mississippi River and all its territory west of the Mississippi to Spain. French cultural influence remained, but the French religious presence was a shadow of what it once was. Still, a powerful Roman Catholic presence endures in the French Crescent from Mobile to New Orleans to St. Louis to the St. Lawrence River Valley.

As it did in New Spain, religion played an important role in New France. French Catholic religious figures came to North America to minister to the needs of French settlers. French Catholic missionaries also sought to extend Catholicism's reach among American Indians. National, political, economic, *and* religious interests motivated and shaped French expansion into North America. Efforts to convert

American Indians to Catholicism vividly demonstrate French cultural superiority and help explain French attitudes about colonialism. The degree to which American Indians were willing to consider or even adopt Catholicism reveals American Indian culture's dynamism and shows how the balance of power between Indians and the French shifted. Even though the French were expelled from interior North America as an imperial force by 1763, French influence remained – and remains – in the form of French Catholic landmarks and practice in the French crescent, which reaches from the St. Lawrence Valley to the Mississippi Valley, including the important gateway cities of New Orleans and St. Louis.

Russia

On the other side of the continent, Russia's imperial ventures in North America focused on Alaska, beginning in 1741, and from the outset involved attempts to Christianize native peoples. The Russian American Company (RAC) drove Russian involvement in North America and capitalism drove the RAC. The RAC functioned as an arm of Russia's imperial government and its job was to take control of Russia's claims along the northwest coast of North America. Profit drove the RAC, but so did its charter obligations, which included spreading Russian Orthodox Christianity. In this sense, Russia followed the pattern of other European states, but with its own state religion. Spreading religion meant building and maintaining churches for Russian settlers and indigenous converts and supporting missionaries. The church and its missionaries played an important role in Alaska throughout the Russian period, which ended in 1867 when Russia sold the colony to the United States, and continued in the era of American control. During the Russian period, the church acted as the custodian of the colony's morals and made continuous efforts to convert and educate native Alaskans.

Russian explorers likely baptized Alaska natives as early as the 1740s. In 1759, the explorer Ivan Glotov baptized the young son of a clan chief of the Fox Island Aleuts. Glotov took the boy to Kamchatka, where the boy learned to speak, read, and write Russian. On his return to Alaska, the boy became a leader and contributed to the spread of Christianity among Alaska natives.

The nature of the Russian fur trade in Alaska also inspired missionary work. According to Ioann Veniaminov, perhaps the most accomplished Orthodox missionary of Russian America, the desire for laborers to serve the RAC led to a search for converts. As Veniaminov tells it, Aleuts who converted revered their godfathers as much as their biological fathers. They would work willingly for their godfather and only for their godfather. So, the Russian fur trader would by baptism not only expand his workforce, but also create a labor pool that would not work for a competitor. Religion boosted profits. More than that, it created social relationships between Aleuts and Russians, reflecting beliefs common among indigenous peoples in the Americas that trade was not separate from general social relationships and mutual obligations.

Empress Catherine approved an Orthodox mission for Alaska in 1793 and from the arrival of the first missionaries at Kodiak Island in 1794 the church worked hand-in-glove with the RAC and Russia's civil government. As the government saw it, the church's mission was to minister to Russians in America and to Russianize – to "civilize" as the Russians saw it – natives in areas occupied by Russians with financing and logistical support provided by the RAC.

Russia applied the same tools of cultural imperialism in Alaska as it used in other occupied countries. Baptism conferred not only membership in Orthodoxy, but also Russian citizenship, social rank, and entitlement to elementary education. Education served important practical purposes. Gifted students could go to Russia for training in seamanship and other trades that would serve both the student and the RAC. As for the church, it sought to develop Russian-speaking congregations for its own ostensibly higher purposes. The curriculum focused on religion, but also included writing, reading Russian, basic math, and singing.

On arrival at Kodiak, missionaries began aggressively working with native Alaskans there and throughout southern Alaska. Missionaries claimed hundreds of baptisms and found their efforts to remake a people's spiritual world challenging, dangerous, fatal. The work of Hieromonk Iuvenalii (a hieromonk is a monk who is also a priest) illustrates the complexities and dangers of missionary work. Hieromonk Iuvenalii began a "tour of baptism," traveling among the natives and conducting baptisms, on Kodiak Island in 1795. He crossed onto the Alaska mainland and continued baptizing hundreds of natives until his death in 1796. Accounts of his death vary widely. A complimentary version says "wild natives" killed Iuvenalii probably because he prohibited polygamy among those he baptized and because tribal leaders gave their children to Iuvenalii for schooling at Kodiak. In this version, the natives changed their mind about letting their children leave home with the missionary and attacked him. Rather than flee or fight, Iuvenalii allowed himself to be killed. Another version of Iuvenalii's story sounds more credible. According to a report submitted to directors of the Russian-American Company, Iuvenalii baptized the natives by force, married them, and took away girls from some and reassigned them to others, apparently in an effort to end polygamy. The natives endured Iuvenalii's boorish and violent behavior for some time before deciding they could rid themselves of this "monster" by killing him.[7]

Whatever happened, spiritual and ethnic cultures clashed. The natives, for some time, told that Iuvenalii rose from the dead and pursued his murderers. The natives attacked the spirit and beat him, only to see the spirit rise again to continue the pursuit. When repeated beatings failed to subdue the spirit, the natives chopped him to pieces, which finally stopped the spirit. But then, they reported, a pillar of smoke rose from the pile of remains and reached toward heaven.

For 20 years after Iuvenalii's death mission work slowed dramatically for several reasons. The church lacked clergy. From 1796 through 1816 a single priest served more than 7000 followers. Enormous distances, as much as 600–1500 km, separated churches. That, too, made missionary work difficult. And, in some ways, Russian Orthodox success among the Aleuts hindered their ability to convert members of other tribes, namely the Tlingits. The Tlingits, not surprisingly, had great attachment to their own religion. Furthermore, as they saw it, the Aluets who had accepted Christianity through baptism at the same time enslaved themselves to the Russians. The Tlingits had no interest in following the same path.

Things changed in the mid-1830s. Ioann Veniaminov, almost certainly the most important Orthodox figure in Russian America, left an account of the change that shows how religion permeated his

---

[7] Robert Nichols and Robert Croskey, translators and editors, "The Condition of the Orthodox Church in Russian America: Innnokentii Veniaminov's History of the Russian Church in Alaska," *Pacific Northwest Quarterly* 63 (Apr. 1972): 43.

outlook and, in all likelihood, that of the Tlingits. Ordained a priest in 1821, Veniaminov answered a call by the Alaskan Russian–American Company for a priest in 1824 and went to Unalaska, Aleutian Islands, where he raised a church and a parish house. He studied the Aleutian-Fox dialect and wrote a dictionary, grammar, and primer in the dialect.

Veniaminov moved to Sitka after 10 years and continued his work on a larger scale. Veniaminov claims that the Tlingits would have maintained impenetrable opposition to Christianity "if Providence had not sent them a disease which they had apparently never before encountered."[8] The disease, most likely smallpox, ravaged the Tlingit population in early 1836. By Veniaminov's estimate, nearly half the Tlingit population died. Old Tlingits, those who disliked the Russians most and who held the strongest influence in making policy, suffered the most. With many of them gone, a new generation of policymakers took over. The fact that Russians suffered much less than the Tlingits in the epidemic convinced many Tlingits, according to Veniaminov, of the superiority of Russian science and overall knowledge. Russians had tried to vaccinate the Tlingits, who refused. Finally, the inability of Tlingit shamans to forestall the epidemic in others and in themselves seems to have rattled their followers' faith. In the epidemic's aftermath, Veniaminov reported about 1500 Tlingits attended and intently observed one of his services. As of 1840, he wrote that while the Tlingits might not be Christianized, they were ready at least to consider converting and that they had experienced a striking and quick change of heart.[9]

Despite the fact that Russians reported that Aleuts accepted Christianity, at least baptism, much more readily than Tlingits, Aleuts kept Christianity at arm's length through the mid-1800s. They rarely attended church, and they continued to value their shamans. When a pox epidemic ravaged Kodiak Island, Aleuts living there refused medical help from the Russians. Nearly one-third of the Aleuts living on the island died.

By contrast, Aleuts living at Unalaska reportedly accepted baptism readily and made a quick and thorough conversion to Christianity. According to Veniaminov, they abandoned shamanism and destroyed

[8] Nichols and Croskey (1972), 47.
[9] Nichols and Croskey (1972), 48.

masks and clothing used in their traditional ceremonies. Veniaminov also wrote that native Unalaskans forsook many of their ceremonial songs. What this really meant is anyone's guess. Aleuts at Unalaska might well have converted as thoroughly as Veniaminov reported. They might have been more successful in observing their original religion in complete secrecy. Or the truth might rest somewhere between the two extremes. When the pox epidemic that devastated Kodiak's population hit Unalaska, the Unalaska Aleuts accepted medical help from the Russians. They lost 80 people out of a population of about 1200, a much better survival rate than Kodiak experienced.

Orthodoxy's reach extended with the RAC as far south as present California. During the first decades of the nineteenth century, the RAC probed south. In 1812, the RAC established Fort Ross (an Americanization of Rossiya, an archaic name for Russia) about 90 miles north of San Francisco. Fort Ross not only to expanded the RAC's reach for resources, but also served Russia's rivalry with Spain for colonial expansion. The RAC intended Fort Ross as a base to grow food for settlers at Kodiak and Sitka and as a trapping and trading outpost. The settlement grew to more than 400 Aleuts, Russians, and local Indians. Though small and remote, Fort Ross maintained an Orthodox church for nearly 30 years. According to one account, the church had more than 40 native (most likely local Pomo Indians) members during that span. As of 1838, the church had 255 members, mostly Russians but also Creoles, Aleuts, and local Indians. The Russians sold the remote and difficult to maintain settlement in late 1841 and departed on January 1, 1842.

Russia's forays into California also produced the important, if apocryphal, story that opens this chapter. An Aleut named Chungangnaq tells us about religion's role in imperial rivalry as well as Orthodoxy's enduring legacy in the West. In addition to establishing Fort Ross during the 1810s, the RAC sent several ships south to trade for food at San Francisco and to poach along the coast south of Vancouver Island. One of these ships landed a party just inside San Francisco Bay. The Spanish ordered them away, but the Russian party lingered and later returned to shore. The Spanish captured the party's Russian leader and 24 Aleuts, who were held at various missions where they served as laborers. Years later, a Russian rescued one of the Aleuts, who told a horrific tale. According to the story, Spanish missionaries demanded Chungangnaq, also known as Petr, renounce his adopted

Orthodoxy and convert to Catholicism. Petr refused, which resulted in his being tortured to death. The church canonized Chungangnaq as St. Peter the Aleut. Despite the canonization and the fact that the tsar believed the story, sources do not corroborate the report and such acts would have violated the policy of Franciscans operating in California at the time. Whether or not the story is true, St. Peter the Martyr enjoys a living legacy in the form of churches dedicated to him in Calgary, Minot, North Dakota, Lake Havasu City, Arizona, and Abita Springs, Louisiana.

Orthodoxy had a steadier presence in Alaska. Veniaminov left Alaska in 1838, but returned in 1841 as Innokentii (Innocent), bishop of Kamchatka, the Kuriles, and the Aleutian Islands, a newly established diocese. That position took him to scattered, remote Russian posts in Alaska where he helped establish more schools and missions. In 1846 he consecrated St. Michael's Cathedral in Sitka, the first Orthodox cathedral in America and seat of the diocese (see Figure 2.2).

Innokentii made the cathedral's belfry clock and also made barrel organs, including one he delivered to a Franciscan mission in California. This showed both his diverse skills and that relations with the Spanish had apparently improved since Chungagnaq's day.

Figure 2.2 Saint Michael's Russian Orthodox Church, Sitka, Alaska, 1887.
Source: University of Washington Libraries, Special Collections, UW 26281.

St. Michael's served as seat of the Diocese of Alaska after the Russian era ended. The original structure burned in 1962, but a replica occupies the site and maintains the Russian legacy.

Russia's sale of Alaska to the United States in 1867 ended the Russian Orthodox Church's monopoly on mission work there, but its influence lingered. It's difficult to say how Alaska's sale affected Alaskans who had been trained that to serve the church also meant to serve the tsar. US control brought new Christian sects competing for influence among Alaska's native peoples. That situation brought new turbulence. During the Russian era, natives, sometimes entire villages, returned to shamanism. The arrival of additional, competing religious groups increased the frequency of that phenomenon. Orthodoxy's influence can still be seen in Alaska's religious life and in its architecture, and the religious legacy of imperial competition still echoes in the living congregations of St. Peter the Aleut churches in the American West.

Conclusion

European expansion into the Americas functioned as missions in more than one sense of the word. Spain, France, and Russia were on a secular mission to expand their national influence and to enrich their national treasuries. From the 1400s through the 1800s, though, it was difficult, if not impossible, to separate those missions from spiritual matters. In some ways, Europe's divine right monarchies and the people who lived in them weren't all that different from the American Indians they encountered. Both the Europeans and the indigenous peoples existed in a world imbued with religious significance, where political alliances, wars, and governmental expansion were outward expressions of their collective religious worldviews. The monarchs believed they governed by virtue of God's will and they staked claims on what were to them new lands based on providence. Spain and France had close relationships with the Roman Catholic Church and they sought to expand Rome's reach at the same time and as a part of their national agendas. Russia sought to expand the Russian Orthodox Church. To varying degrees each of these nations saw the expansion of its way of life, including religious systems and values, to new territories and new people as an important function of colonialism. Religion inspired expansion and the extraordinarily difficult work of creating new societies and it provided ideals to which the pioneering Europeans aspired. They brought religion to serve their colonial settlers' needs and as a kind of moral export commodity to bestow upon the American Indians they met. In a broad sense the Europeans could probably agree that bringing their religion to American Indians represented a noble, civilizing mission, but in the details – the type of religion – they disagreed, sometimes intensely. American Indians, were they Pueblo, Huron, or Aleut found new ideas in these religions and, in a sense, found themselves in a new world even without leaving home. Some adopted these new ideas, some rejected them, and some fell in between as they adopted concepts they found useful and rejected those they did not. Europeans used Christianity to inspire and justify imperial expansion. Christian missionaries and their indigenous counterparts changed the religious landscape of the Americas as they worked or innovated religious systems to navigate the reality of their shared new world.

The legacy of religious missions in service to empire remains imprinted on the people and landscape of the American West. Descendants of converts among native peoples still live and worship in the West. In some cases they observe only imported religion, but in others they observe both the import and their traditional religion. Physical reminders include landscapes altered by Catholic missions in the Southwest and buildings such as the San Antonio missions in Texas and others in California and the Southwest. Buildings left by Russian missionaries can still be seen in Alaska. The living legacy of the Russian Orthodox mission to Alaska can be seen even in the lower 48 states. In 1980, a congregation in Minot, ND, built the St. Peter the Aleut Church, which operated into the twenty-first century.

Suggested Reading

Black, Lydia. 2004. *Russians in Alaska, 1732–1867*. Fairbanks, AK: University of Alaska Press.

Eccles, W. J. 1983. *The Canadian Frontier, 1534–1760*. Albuquerque, NM: University of New Mexico Press.

Gaustad, Edwin and Leigh Schmidt. 2004. *The Religious History of America: The Heart of the American Story from Colonial Times to Today*, revised edition. New York: HarperSanFrancisco.

Greer, Alan. 2005. *Mohawk Saint: Catherine Tekakwitha and the Jesuits*. New York: Oxford.

Haycox, Stephen. 2002. *Alaska: An American Colony*. Seattle, WA: University of Washington Press.

Hudson, Winthrop S. and John Corrigan. 1999. *Religion in America: An Historical Account of the Development of American Religious Life*, 6th edn. Upper Saddle River, NJ: Prentice Hall.

Starr, S. Frederick, ed. 1987. *Russia's American Colony*. Durham, NC: Duke University Press.

Thwaites, Reuben Gold, ed. 1959. *The Jesuit Relations and Allied Documents; Travels and Explorations of the Jesuit Missionaries in New France, 1610–1791*. New York: Pageant.

Williams, Peter W. 2002. *America's Religions: From Their Origins to the Twenty-First Century*. Urbana and Chicago, IL: University of Illinois Press.

3

Migrations, Manifest Destiny, and Mormons, 1803–1860

Winter is not a good time to travel the prairies and plains. The weather might bring fairly comfortable temperatures, or it might bring bitter cold. Early February 1846 brought moderate temperatures to western Illinois, which made it possible for the refugees leaving Illinois' second largest city to cross the Mississippi River on flatboats. The city would be nearly empty by year's end. While the crossings might have been routine, they certainly were not easy. One refugee, maybe in mischief or maybe by accident, spit tobacco juice into the eye of an ox crossing the river on a loaded flatboat. The irritated beast plunged overboard, pulling another ox with it and damaging the boat. The oxen drowned and the boat sank taking with it food and other supplies the refugees needed desperately. A run of cold weather took overnight temperatures below zero, making the refugees' tent camping miserable and chilling the already cold river nearer and nearer the freezing point. By the end of February, the Mississippi had frozen. Some of the refugees, Mormons fleeing their holy city-state of Nauvoo, Illinois, considered the river's freezing a miracle as it allowed them and their livestock to walk across the Mississippi. Other miracles graced their evacuation.

Inspiration and Innovation: Religion in the American West,
First Edition. Todd M. Kerstetter.
© 2015 John Wiley & Sons, Inc. Published 2015 by John Wiley & Sons, Inc.

As for the ancient people of Israel in the desert, as told in the Bible, thousands of quail appeared and fed starving stragglers who fled Nauvoo in October 1846. The refugees saw that as a clear sign of God's favor. The people of the City of Zion had become the Camp of Israel as they began an exodus from years of persecution in the United States to what they hoped would be a promised land in the Rocky Mountains.

The region west of the Mississippi River underwent extraordinary changes during the nineteenth century, none more important than conquest by the United States. Through warfare, diplomacy, and purchase the United States became a transcontinental nation and constructed the boundaries we recognize today. Conquest by the United States opened a new chapter in the West's history, one in which religion and religious people played important roles. This chapter deals with the period in which the United States extended its influence over the region west of the Mississippi River. This involved incorporating the region into the nation economically, politically, and culturally. The process, permeated by religion, unfolded over the span of the 1800s but the United States took important first steps in events described here.

This chapter starts with the Louisiana Purchase in 1803 and extends through to 1860 when Abraham Lincoln's election triggered events that led to the US Civil War. Spain, France, Britain, and eventually Russia departed the scene, but left their marks socially, culturally, and religiously. The United States entered the scene and set out to make its marks. The United States created a series of administrative units called territories, most of which became states during the 1800s. Texas and California skipped this territorial stage and joined the nation as states in 1845 and 1850, respectively. For virtually the entire West, political, economic, and social institutions had to be established in areas populated for centuries by people with their own distinctive religions. Protestant citizens of the United States thought American Indians living in the region racially and religiously inferior and ripe for "enlightenment." The United States also took over regions where imperial nation states had transplanted Roman Catholicism and Russian Orthodox Christianity and transformed people and landscapes. Protestant Americans considered Catholic Mexicans, like American Indians, racially and religiously inferior.

Religious people and institutions joined the task of transforming the West. Mormons moved about the Midwest and crossed into the trans-Mississippi West where they established a homeland they hoped might become the kingdom of Zion. Mormon attempts to conquer the West led them into a complex relationship – sometimes partner but more often foe – with the United States. Christian missionaries took leading roles in what many saw as the civilizing or redeeming of the region. In a number of cases, they worked in close partnership with the US government in trying to establish what they hoped would be a "Protestant Empire" or "Christian America." They achieved a large measure of success in social and political influence, but the American West, thanks to the diversity of its people, developed a unique regional religious life marked by the absence of any predominant norm. By 1860 boundaries on maps would clearly indicate the trans-Mississippi West from the Rio Grande to the 49th parallel belonged to the United States, but the religious West remained a varied and hotly contested landscape.

Transplanting Religions in the US Imperial Period

Protestantism

The rapidly growing US empire struck early nineteenth-century Protestant leaders in different ways. Timothy Dwight, the Congregationalist president of Yale University, worried about the character of people moving into the new territories. Dwight saw *too much* independence and egalitarianism at work in new settlements. He saw many pioneers as anti-intellectual social misfits and held low expectations for what they would create as they moved west. Another influential Congregationalist minister, Lyman Beecher, feared the same problems, but he held high hopes for the region. Sure, the raw, booming West had its challenges, Beecher thought, but if morality and religion could be imposed upon it, the region had glorious prospects. Protestant missionaries set out to ensure that glorious future by spreading religious institutions to new American settlements and by aggressively converting and civilizing, which they saw as two sides of the same coin, American Indians.

Within a decade of the Louisiana Purchase, Protestants sent observers to the West to report on the region. What they found confirmed Dwight's concerns. They viewed Indians as pagans, of course.

They reported widespread ignorance of "divine things," even among Catholics. Their Protestantism likely shaded their interpretation. They also reported intemperance (drunkenness), widespread vice (sex outside of marriage), and little observation of the Sabbath. In fact, they suspected westerners of committing more sin on Sundays than on any other day of the week. What could guardians of respectable, moral society do to improve the amoral society they found on the frontier, far from the controls of established society? Might the sinful state of frontier society corrupt the nation's moral fabric? The solution to the problem: send missionaries. Missionaries could distribute Bibles, promote revivals, teach people to read and write, and otherwise instill morality and civilization in a depraved region. Protestants applied this strategy throughout the continental West and in Hawaii and Alaska.

The daunting challenge of bringing Protestantism to the vast, "heathen" West led Presbyterians and Congregationalists to agree to a Plan of Union in 1801. According to the plan, the two socially influential Protestant denominations combined their resources to spread the gospel in the West, which meant everywhere west of the Appalachian Mountains, beyond the coast of California and into the far reaches of the Pacific Ocean. A group of Connecticut missionaries and their wives established a mission in the village of Kailua on the island of Hawaii, then called the Sandwich Islands, in 1820. The missionaries made important converts among the Hawaiian royal family. The mission rose in influence, and between 1825 and 1853 two of its leaders acted as prime ministers to the Hawaiian monarchy. The missionaries accrued such power they have been described as de facto dictators during those years. By 1837, more than 80 missionaries served 17 churches in Hawaii. Gerrit Judd, the second of the two missionary prime ministers, oversaw in 1848 implementation of a land distribution act. The act replaced traditional Hawaiian land ownership with private ownership, which effectively destroyed traditional Hawaiian society, turned most native Hawaiians into landless peasants, and opened the way for foreign ownership of Hawaiian land. On the other hand, because Protestant missionaries in Hawaii believed that salvation depended on a personal understanding of the Bible, they worked hard to spread literacy among Hawaiians. The first Protestant missionaries brought a printing press with them and they produced religious tracts and other items as early as 1822. The missionaries also pushed for public education, which became mandatory through to age 14 by 1840. By 1848, Hawaii boasted a literacy rate of 80 percent, one of the highest rates in the world at the time. Missionary activity in Hawaii reminds us that US expansion across the North American continent occurred within the broader context of US and European expansion overseas. Missionaries not only worked to spread the gospel, but also spread the cultural and social values of their home nations. In the case of Hawaii, missionaries helped pave the way for conquest by the United States by the end of the nineteenth century.

Protestant missionaries risked life and limb to advance God and flag in dramatic events in the Oregon Country, too. By the 1820s, both the United Kingdom and the United States claimed Oregon Country, but neither could truly control it and the nations agreed the territory should remain free and open to both, which it did until they set a boundary in 1846. Meanwhile, both nations tried to solidify their claims. The United States received help on this front from Protestant missionaries. In the fall of 1831, four Indians from the Pacific Northwest arrived in St. Louis. Some versions of the story say they were Flatheads, but more likely three of them were Nez Percé and the fourth half Nez Percé and half Flathead. Among other things, they told William Clark – the same Clark of Lewis and Clark fame, now Superintendent for Indian Affairs – that they hoped a missionary could be sent to their people to teach them about the Bible, which they called "the book of Heaven." What exactly they wanted remains a bit of a mystery, but word of their visit traveled back east in a way that brought Protestant missionaries to Oregon country and that shows the intimate links between religion and US expansion.

William Walker, a white Ohioan, wrote an account of the four Indians' visit that included interesting claims. According to Walker's version, a white visitor to the Northwest told the Indians that their religion displeased God. Not to worry, the visitor told them, back East whites had a book that would explain how to please God and, thereby, be welcomed to God's country when they died. The Indians met in a "national council" and decided to send the four emissaries to St. Louis to get the book. A Methodist publication with the revealing title *Christian Advocate and Journal and Zion's Herald* printed Walker's version of the story.[1] Other religious publications quickly reprinted it. Preachers included the story

---

[1]   Elliott West, *The Last Indian War: The Nez Perce Story* (New York: Oxford, 2009), 35.

in their sermons. Soon, missionaries eager to rectify this dire situation stood ready to take the gospel to the Northwest.

What *did* those four Nez Percés want? At face value, they sought religious instruction and, presumably, help in converting to Christianity. But was it that simple? Almost certainly they wanted to discuss trade relations. Whites who had been coming into the Northwest brought interesting things such as guns, metal goods, and blankets, and the Nez Percés wanted access to that inventory. But to Nez Percés, trade did not exist in a vacuum; neither did any other aspect of life as the stories in Chapter 1 illustrate. As the Nez Percés saw it, the interesting things that whites possessed indicated they also had "impressive supernatural connections," in historian Elliott West's phrase. In all likelihood, those four Nez Percés aimed to improve trade with Americans operating out of St. Louis and to tap or at least curry favor with the whites' supernatural influence. Today we might see economic and religious motives as separate matters, but the Nez Percé did not.

Methodists responded first with a party led by Jason Lee. Lee's party arrived in the Willamette Valley in what is now Oregon in 1834. Additional recruits arrived to support the mission in 1837 and the Great Reinforcement of 1840 added more than 50 to the region's Methodist population. By that point, mission families had established a Methodist presence from the Columbia River to Puget Sound.

These missionaries probably accomplished more as secular colonists than as evangelizers. They established communities, farmed, and advertised Oregon to easterners as they sought more settlers. Jason Lee preached at a camp meeting in the fall of 1841 where he claimed 130 baptisms of local Indians and 500 people partaking in the sacrament. Those numbers might seem promising, but contemporaries reported the Indians who participated lacked the depth of commitment and understanding the missionaries would have preferred. For example, the Indians expected to be paid to attend services. For another, the Indians ignored what missionaries considered "religious duties" and instead focused on their seasonal economic activities, such as gathering berries.

Lee's move into Oregon Territory provided an example of the empire of Christianity moving faster than the US empire, although the two often worked as a team and toward similar goals. Lee, for example, urged the United States to add Oregon to its territory.

In 1839, five years after his arrival in the territory, he wrote to a US congressman urging action. Lee saw in Oregon "the germ of a great state" and believed the United States should grab it before another nation did. One of Lee's settlers, Elijah White, departed in 1841 under a cloud of accusations of immorality. White returned, though, the next year. He brought with him more than 100 new immigrants. White also had been named an Indian subagent, which meant that this man who had come west to join a religious settlement would be acting as an agent of the US government, the first US official assigned to Oregon.

Other missionaries followed closely on Lee's heels. Two years after Lee's arrival, another group of Protestant missionaries representing the American Board of Commissioners for Foreign Missions (ABCFM) came to Oregon. This group included Henry Spalding, whose mission to the Nez Percé at Lapwai (near present Lewiston, Idaho) is regarded as the most successful of the Protestant missions in Oregon Country. The ABCFM group also included Marcus and Narcissa Whitman, whose mission to the Cayuse sparked one of several Indian conflicts in the region and ended in death for the Whitmans. Catholic priests also joined the competition with a contingent arriving in 1838 to serve Oregon's French–Canadian population. More Catholic missionaries, Jesuits led by Pierre-Jean De Smet, arrived in 1840.

This diversity of faiths and their competition with each other affected early political affairs in Oregon and contributed to Jason Lee's interest in seeing US jurisdiction extended to Oregon. When a growing population concerned about defending itself from Indian attacks formed a provisional government in 1843, Lee and many Methodists opposed it. They feared the provisional government might endanger their land claims, the foundation of their evangelizing endeavors. They also feared the provisional government might somehow favor Catholic missionaries, which would give the Catholics the upper hand in the competition for converting Indians. For the Methodists, immediate US jurisdiction offered the best solution for governing Oregon and for promoting their evangelical agenda.

The Whitman mission, located on Cayuse land along the Walla Walla River, illustrates the goals and frustrations of the mission to Oregon and how mission work could lead to tragic results. Dr Marcus Whitman and his wife, Narcissa, established their mission to convert the Cayuse Indians to Christianity and to transform them culturally. For their part, the Cayuses had serious reservations about these strangers, but allowed the Whitmans to live on Cayuse land in the hope of gaining spiritual power and access to technology and material goods. Each party grew increasingly frustrated with the other. The Whitmans registered dismay that the Cayuse seemed not to make spiritual progress and instead clung to "sinful" customs such as gambling, adultery, and polygamy. The Cayuses failed to realize benefits of trade and other concrete manifestations of divine favor they expected from the missionaries. They resented the Whitmans' attempts to change their culture, and the farms the missionaries established to support themselves at the mission interfered with their highly valued horse pasturage. Furthermore, many Cayuses may have seen farming as practiced by the Whitmans as a violation of mother earth.

Tensions escalated during and after 1843 as traffic on the Oregon Trail increased and brought more outsiders into Cayuse lands. The Whitman mission provided food and services for wagon trains and the mission grew into a small village of about 80 people. Among other services, the Whitmans adopted children, both mixed-blood children from the area and white children orphaned when their parents died along the Overland Trail. By the 1840s, Narcissa Whitman seemed to be withdrawing from missionary work to the local Indians, but in her domestic work she performed what missionaries considered a vital role. As missionaries saw it, Christian family life provided a valuable role model for heathens to follow. Narcissa wrote that local Indians got "great pleasure" from seeing so many children growing up at the mission. But, she probably missed some important cultural differences. For one thing, Narcissa placed strict limits on her children's contact with the Cayuse. Her children did not learn to speak Nez Percé; nor did they attend the Cayuse Sabbath service. These segregating practices would not have escaped the notice of the Cayuses but were typical of missionaries at this time. The Cayuses, who placed great value on children, also would have noted Narcissa's style of discipline, which included beating unruly children. These Indians did not do this. Instead, they relied on example and the fear of shame to affect behavior. In all likelihood, they viewed Narcissa as a savage for beating children. So while the Whitmans congratulated themselves for providing an example of a

Christian family, that very example may well have horrified the Cayuse audience.

The increase in settler traffic through their territory brought both problems and opportunities for the Cayuses, but the bad outweighed the good. "The poor Indians are amazed at the overwhelming numbers of Americans coming into the country," Narcissa Whitman observed. "They seem not to know what to make of it."[2] Some Cayuse seized opportunities to trade horses with the travelers. Probably most important and most disturbing, increased settler traffic brought more diseases such as measles and scarlet fever that devastated the Cayuse population. Even though Dr Whitman cared for both white and Indian victims of these diseases, many Cayuses died. Cayuse leaders came to believe that Whitman was using medicine to fatally poison Indians. Some Cayuses believed he possessed spiritual powers and that he used them to bring harm to the tribe. The Cayuses divided over whether to support the mission or to get rid of it. When a Cayuse leader became ill in 1845, his son blamed Dr Whitman and threatened to kill him. Other death threats followed. The balance of tribal opinion and power remained with the pro-mission faction, though, and the Whitmans appeared safe for the time being.

Cayuse frustration mounted during the harsh winter of 1846–1847, which brought more Indian deaths. The summer of 1847 brought an outbreak of dysentery. At about the same time a new group of emigrants arrived at the mission, a measles epidemic erupted. Whites sickened and died, but in much smaller numbers than the Cayuse. Whitman's medicine did little for the Indians and their traditional sweat baths made matters worse. The Cayuses faced a grim situation. In their eyes, their spiritual powers had failed them and the outsiders practiced a powerful, deadly witchcraft. Tribes in the area killed shamans who practiced witchcraft and the mounting death toll of 1847 prompted the Cayuses to act. Fear, anger, and frustration erupted in violence when Cayuse leaders killed the Whitmans and a dozen other missionaries in November 1847 (Figure 3.1).

The Waiilatpu massacre brought an end to the ABCFM missionary program in Oregon. Protestants saw the Whitmans and the other slain

---

[2]   Quoted in Julie Roy Jeffrey, *Converting the West: A Biography of Narcissa Whitman* (Norman, OK: University of Oklahoma Press, 1991), 203.

Figure 3.1   Massacre of Rev. Dr Whitman of the Presbyterian Mission.
Source: Oregon Historical Society, Negative #1644.

missionaries as martyrs. One of Narcissa Whitman's biographers suggests that history could see the Cayuses as the martyrs. The years after
1847 brought the Nez Percé violent reprisals by settlers and the US military, reservation life, and the loss of tribal identity, which Jeffrey calls
"the unanticipated fruits of the ABCFM missionary endeavors at
Waiilatpu."[3] These dramatic events in Oregon demonstrate the close
association of religious and national interests in US westward expansion.
Efforts meant to spread civilization and to bestow benefits and progress
on the people and places of the West produced some achievements
worth celebrating. At the same time, they had often dire consequences
for people and societies already in place.

The history of the Santee Sioux illustrates another confluence of
US Indian policy and Protestantism. The Santees, also known as
Dakotas, belonged to a larger group known as Sioux and lived mostly
in what is now Minnesota. Treaty obligations required the United
States to provide goods and services, namely education, to the Santee
Sioux. The difficulty of getting funds to provide those services as well
as the difficulty of finding teachers willing to work for the low wages

3   Jeffrey (1991), 221.

offered by the government left the Indian agent in a bind. In the 1830s the agent found a solution in the form of Protestant missionaries. The missionaries, who volunteered or had financial support from missionary organizations, agreed to teach the Santees about farming *and* about Christianity. They cost the government very little and helped the agent in his twin goals of "civilizing" and "Christianizing" his charges.

For most of the next three decades, the Santee–Protestant interaction changed agriculture in the region, but did little on the religious front. Some of the Santees adopted "American" farming techniques. But, with the exception of a small congregation here or there, few Santees showed much interest in Christianity. The missionaries' great accomplishment in these years came in creating a written form of the Dakota language. As missionaries, they needed language skills to communicate complicated ideas to the Dakotas. As Protestants, they believed it critical to present the Bible in Dakota so Santees could build their own understanding of scripture and establish as direct as possible a relationship with God. The missionaries produced Bibles, hymnals, and schoolbooks in Dakota, which helped spread literacy. More important for this story, it provided the foundation for a boom in Santee Christianity during the 1860s.

Protestantism also played an important role in establishing European immigrant communities in the West. The availability of agricultural land in Missouri lured a range of settlers in the 1830s and 1840s, including Germans who wished to establish a religious colony based on principles of a conservative brand of Lutheranism. Sometimes called "Old Lutherans," they disliked the theological direction they saw Lutheranism taking in Germany. They left Germany and settled in Missouri and other Midwestern states. In 1847 they formed the Lutheran Church-Missouri Synod, with headquarters in St. Louis. Religion provided the organizational foundation for Missouri Synod settlements, which dedicated themselves to preserving German language and customs and "pure doctrine." To Missouri Synod Lutherans, that meant divinely inspired, inerrant scripture. They found American liberalism and secularism every bit as threatening as events in Germany. To protect and promulgate its values, the Missouri Synod created an ambitious and far-reaching educational system that started with elementary schools and continued to junior colleges, colleges, and seminaries. Until World War I, the Missouri Synod ran the largest American Protestant educational system. It also ran a publishing company, Concordia Publishing House, to provide educational and other literature to serve the synod. From its inception, the Missouri Synod looked West and it used this developing institutional machinery to serve existing and new German settlements, several of which will be discussed in the next chapter.

Roman Catholicism

Although obviously not part of a "Protestant Empire," Roman Catholicism retained influence in the West established prior to the region joining the United States. In the US era, which commenced at different times, depending on the location, Roman Catholic missionaries worked to spread Christianity. French and Spanish missionaries had established Catholic institutions in parts of the West. Despite the fact that they were all Catholics, the French and Spanish missionaries operated within different administrative hierarchies and in the context of competing nations. The transition to US control of areas previously under French or Spanish jurisdiction brought additional national and religious complications. For example, when Louis William DuBourg became bishop of Louisiana and the Floridas in 1815 the new bishop took over a post that had been ignored for years and inherited parishes and people marked by lasting French and Spanish influence. Spanish Catholics in east and west Florida continued to follow the bishop of Havana. In New Orleans, French Catholics ignored the American-appointed DuBourg. In fact, they treated DuBourg so poorly he chose to reside in St. Louis. This points to the continuity of Roman Catholic influence in important Mississippi Valley cities and the ongoing significance of national rivalries within Catholicism.

DuBourg attacked what he perceived as the West's religious problems. Notably, he recruited Jesuits, the order discussed at length in Chapter 2 and known for its members' dedication to overseas missions including long experience with Native Americans in North America, to work among the West's Indian tribes. Pierre Jean DeSmet, a Jesuit, answered DuBourg's call and built a remarkable career establishing Roman Catholic missions in the West. De Smet's first mission effort did not go well. In 1838, De Smet went with a team to western Iowa, near present-day Council Bluffs, to open a mission for the Potawatomis. The Potawatomis, recently removed from their homeland, as a result of US expansion and the policy of removing Indian tribes living east of the Mississippi River to lands west of the Mississippi, proved unrecep-tive. De Smet left after 18 months and the mission struggled before closing in 1841. After this rocky start, De Smet fared better.

Beginning in 1840, De Smet made many trips through the West and established a string of missions. With five other missionaries, he founded St. Mary's Mission among the Salish near Missoula, Montana. De Smet lived in Montana for about a year before returning to St. Louis. For most of the 1840s, he traveled widely. He went to New Orleans, Boston, and Europe promoting Indian missions and seeking money to fund them. He also traveled extensively through the Pacific Northwest, helping to establish and administer missions. All told, the peripatetic De Smet covered more than 180 000 miles in his lifetime, distinguishing himself more as a founder and promoter of missions rather than a resident missionary.

De Smet also distinguished himself from many whites, including many missionaries, by noting and praising positive characteristics of the tribes to which he ministered. For example, De Smet described the Flatheads as honest, trustworthy, hospitable, and good-humored. The Flatheads had not "learned the vices of the whites," he added. De Smet challenged popular opinion of his day by asking, How could such people be considered "savages"?[4] That open-minded attitude helped earn De Smet the respect and trust of many tribes, some of which adopted him as a relative.

De Smet used that trust in his work as a diplomat for the US government, helping it broker important treaties in the 1850s and 1860s. The US government asked him to attend the 1851 Fort Laramie Peace Council as a "pacificator." The US Army invited De Smet to serve as a chaplain for several expeditions in the West, including an expedition to Utah in 1858 in response to the Mormon rebellion (see below). The government also recruited him to accompany peace missions to the northern plains in 1864, 1867, and in 1868 when he

[4] Edwin Gaustad and Leigh Schmidt, *The Religious History of America: The Heart of the American Story from Colonial Times to Today, Revised Edition* (New York: HarperCollins, 2002), 170.

helped convince the Sioux to accept a peace treaty. De Smet usually refused to travel with the military, fearing that would destroy the trust he had established with many tribes. He would travel ahead of the army to persuade tribal delegations to meet with representatives of the United States. De Smet generally encouraged tribes to accept reservations and treaties, which he saw as tragic compromises necessary for peace and assimilation of American Indians into US society. De Smet thus can be seen as both a champion of American Indians and as an agent of American expansion. His career shows the intimate relationship between religion and state policy and how Catholic missionaries shaped the West. It also offers yet another example of how the separation of church and state in the United States was not by any means complete in the development of the West. This ambiguous position has been a common one among missionaries and secular reformers alike, in the United States and imperial contexts around the world from the sixteenth to the twentieth century.

Ethnic diversity in the West, not just among Indians but also Mexicans and European–American settlers, challenged Roman Catholicism in the United States and the West offered unique challenges. Catholic communities in the United States included Germans, Irish, and French and none particularly cared to be under the supervision of priests, or brothers or sisters in religious orders, from a different ethnic group. In the Southwest, a large Hispanic Catholic population further complicated ethnic politics. Incorporating former Mexican territories into the United States after the US–Mexican war in 1848 presented challenges for Roman Catholics. Would US authorities respect their rights?

The career of Jean Baptiste Lamy, a native of France who became the first bishop of New Mexico, demonstrates the problematic progress made by the Catholic Church in the Southwest in the years after the US–Mexican War. On one hand, Lamy built an extensive infrastructure that expanded Catholicism's influence in the Southwest. On the other, he did it in a way that created tension between the church leadership and its largely Hispanic membership that would take generations to heal.

Lamy used his leadership position to Europeanize the church in New Mexico from the appearance of its buildings to the ethnicity of its staff. He bragged that he was making a little Auvergne, referring to the province in France where he was born. He directed construction of a cathedral in Santa Fe that was French in architecture and built by French artisans imported for the task. He appointed some Hispanic priests, but generally preferred Frenchmen, which killed a tradition of developing a Hispanic priesthood that began to develop during the period Mexico controlled New Mexico. By the end of the century, Hispanic Americans in the Southwest would have no institutional voice in the church.

In northern New Mexico, a Catholic group called the Penitentes engaged in severe self-mortification (self-flagellation) and other practices (carrying huge crosses, for instance) that dated to late medieval Spain. Horrified Protestant missionaries labeled the practices "barbarities" and "ignorant superstitions."[5] Even other Catholics, namely Bishop Lamy, condemned the practices and tried to get the Penitentes to stop and to practice Catholicism as done in northern Europe and eastern America. The Penitentes continued. In an echo of a broader western theme – the power of outsiders (namely easterners who financed economic development from the nation's economic capital in New York City or easterners who governed from the seat of power in Washington, DC) in the region – Hispanic Catholics in the West found themselves in a church governed from the East, be it the Vatican in Rome or the US church hierarchy. As some westerners saw themselves living in a colony of economic and political forces in the East, so did Hispanic Catholics in the West see themselves governed by a church hierarchy located in the East and dominated by Irish, French, and German leaders. Not until after World War II would Mexican Americans become a significant presence in the Roman Catholic Church leadership.

Judaism

Jews constituted a much smaller portion of the US population in the nineteenth century than did Roman Catholics and Protestants, but Jews expanded west with the nation and the experience shaped them and their religion. Unlike Roman Catholics and Protestants, Jews did not seek to convert American Indians. In terms of religion, Jews focused on maintaining and building their own communities and they contributed to building western communities. Because Jews and

[5]   Gaustad and Schmidt (2002), 174.

Christians share core ethical standards that spring from the Ten Commandments, their community-building efforts often worked in concert. German Jews, especially, associated the US and the American West with opportunity and freedom. Rabbi Isaac Mayer Wise, who moved to Ohio in the middle of the nineteenth century, argued American Jews should change to accommodate new times and new settings. Wise believed technological advances such as the steamboat and the railroad signaled the arrival of modern times that called for the modernization of Judaism. According to Wise, "The Jew must be Americanized ... in order to gain the proud self-consciousness of the free-born man."[6]

The California gold rush brought significant Jewish settlement to the trans-Mississippi West in 1849 and after. Some Jews went to the gold fields, but most earned a living as merchants or wholesalers in San Francisco, the instant city whose merchants supplied the miners. By the mid-1850s, Jewish merchants operated supply houses in Los Angeles and Portland. Perhaps the most famous Jewish supplier of the mining boom was the tailor Levi Strauss, whose success with denim work pants allowed him to transform his small shop into a large clothing factory and helped Strauss become a leader in San Francisco's Jewish community.

San Francisco's booming population included the critical mass of Jews necessary to open Temple Emanu-El in 1850, making it the oldest Jewish congregation west of the Mississippi (Figure 3.2). From its start, the Emanu-El congregation worked to improve lives of San Franciscans. Many congregants helped found the Eureka Benevolent Society, which developed into Jewish Family and Children's Services and became the largest Jewish organization in the West. The temple, itself, quickly became an important landmark and its rabbis shaped Reform Judaism in the West. It should be noted that Jews participated in early pioneering, especially in California, and that despite religious differences with Christians, they pursued largely the same goals and served the same purposes as Protestants and Roman Catholics, with the notable exception of missionary work. Jewish migrants brought their religion with them and Jewish religious institutions developed to support faith communities and contributed to the development of societies built on a Judeo-Christian ethic.

---

[6] Quoted in Gaustad and Schmidt (2002), 176.

Figure 3.2 Temple Emmanu-El, 1867. Source: San Francisco History Center, San Francisco Public Library.

Asian religions

Chinese laborers came to the American West in droves during the middle decades of the nineteenth century and they brought their religion with them. The discovery of gold in California in 1848 sparked the immigration boom, and railroad construction and other job opportunities sustained it. Unfortunately, we know little about the religious practices of Chinese in the West in the mid-nineteenth century. Chinese–Americans tended not to define their religiousness with an easily identifiable exclusivity. For example, their religiousness often included elements of Buddhism, Confucianism, Taoism, and folk religion. Furthermore, most Euro-Christian observers of the day, the people most likely to have left us information, would probably not have described what they saw among Chinese as "religion." More likely, they would have described Chinese religion as "superstition" or "occult science." The fact that no one kept reliable membership statistics for Chinese–American Buddhism also complicates the task.

We can say with near certainty that Chinese have practiced Buddhism and other elements of their religiousness in the West since the 1840s and we can pinpoint the establishment of the West's first Buddhist temple. Buddhism traces its origins to what is now India and a man named Siddhartha Gautama, the son of a warrior-king, who lived about 500 BC and went on a spiritual quest to understand and overcome suffering. After reaching this understanding, Gautama became known as the Buddha or "Enlightened One." Buddhism came to the United States as early as 1789, but existed in small pockets with limited influence well into the twentieth century. Chinese merchant organizations, which also functioned as social organizations for Chinese immigrants, became primary sponsors of religious life in Chinese–American communities. One of the merchant organizations, the Sze Yap Company, sponsored the first Buddhist temple in San Francisco in 1853. In 1854, a rival company founded the second. In each case, the temple was located on the top floor of the company's headquarters building. More Asian immigrants would arrive in the West in the second half of the century and they would expand the footprint of Asian religions established by those who arrived earlier.

Religion and Manifest Destiny

People moving into the West and the imperial contests associated with the region inspired US leaders and intellectuals to think about what was happening and how to justify US expansion. The attitude or ideology known as "manifest destiny" flowered in the 1840s and it reveals important things about a nation with a complicated and contentious relationship between church and state. At its core, advocates of manifest destiny claimed that divine providence gave the American people a continent and blessed the expansion of their domain and with it their institutions. The idea's American roots extend at least to the colonial period. The Puritans believed God had led them to North America, and they built a community they hoped would serve as a "city upon a hill," an example of righteous living for the rest of the world to follow. Benjamin Franklin expressed a similar idea, if not by the same name, demonstrating the continuity of the concept to the revolutionary period. In 1811, John Quincy Adams, who would later become president of the United States, wrote, "The whole continent of North America appears to be *destined by Divine Providence* to be peopled by one nation, speaking one language, professing one general system of religious and political principles, and accustomed to one general tenor of social usages and customs."[7] The people and politicians of the United States have embraced this "chosen-ness" from the nation's creation through the speeches of Ronald Reagan and politicians today, who resurrected the image of the United States as a nation that could serve as a model and a beacon for the rest of the world, especially in contrast to the model of godless communism offered by the Soviet Union, America's chief rival in Reagan's time. But the idea is not uniquely American. Similar ideas can be found in the histories of most powerful nations and empires.

The US story of its national destiny developed through the early 1800s. Though the American invasion of British North America (now Canada) failed, the War of 1812 demonstrated the United States' ability to maintain its independence from Britain and solidified its hold on the continental interior. In its wake, expressions of what could be called proto-manifest destiny appeared with increasing frequency. In all likelihood, the demonstration of the nation's viability strengthened nationalism and pointed to an increased likelihood of expansion, which, in turn called for a rationale or justification. In the expansionist fervor of the 1840s, a newspaper editor named John L. O'Sullivan coined the exact phrase "manifest destiny" in the *Democratic Review* in 1845.[8] The phrase came up in O'Sullivan's support for the US annexation of Texas as part of an international competition west of the Mississippi. He feared foreign interference that aimed at "checking the fulfillment of our manifest destiny to overspread the continent allotted by Providence for the free development of our yearly multiplying millions." Manifest destiny meant many things and had no precise definition, but virtually all its proponents saw US expansion and success as a result of their nation's God-given moral superiority. American institutions, another concept not precisely defined, were unquestionably good and superior and would benefit and uplift all under their sovereignty. Those peoples who resisted or stood in the way were seen as evil. All told, "manifest

[7] Quoted in Amanda Porterfield and John Corrigan, eds, *Religion in American History* (Oxford: Wiley-Blackwell, 2010), 212.

[8] *Democratic Review* 17 (July–August 1845): 5–10.

destiny" was most closely associated with the annexation of Texas, the acquisition of the Oregon Territory, and the conquest of much of northern Mexico in war between 1846 and 1848.

The US–Mexican War of 1846–1848 encouraged expressions of manifest destiny and pointed out tensions between mainstream Protestant America and Catholicism, which was the dominant religion of Mexico and a force among immigrants to the United States. Virulent anti-Catholicism ran through American society as witnessed by anti-Catholic riots in northeastern cities in the 1830s and 1840s. Protestant–Catholic schisms plagued the Army, too. A significant number of enlisted men were Catholic immigrants, but most officers were Protestants. Soldiers of all faiths knew through orders or "suggestion" that they should attend Protestant worship services conducted by Army chaplains. President James Polk knew about these religious tensions and made at least token efforts to counter the perception that the war was not a crusade against Mexican Catholicism. In 1846 Polk commissioned two Jesuit priests as Catholic chaplains in the Army. Neither priest spoke Spanish, but one, a native of Ireland, spoke Gaelic fluently and the other spoke German. Polk might, indeed, have hoped to convince Mexicans that the United States did not wish to overthrow their religion, but these priests' linguistic abilities suggest Polk was concerned more with stemming the tide of desertions by disgruntled Catholic immigrant soldiers.

For their part, Mexican officials sought to exploit Protestant–Catholic tensions, especially the poor treatment of Catholics in the United States and especially the poor treatment of Catholic soldiers in the US Army. For example, Juan Soto, governor of Veracruz (a Mexican state), issued in 1847 a handbill calling the US war effort unjust and immoral, and emphasizing religious differences separating Mexico and the United States. Soto, appealing to US soldiers, argued they should not fight against "a religious people" (Roman Catholic Mexicans) and should not fight for a nation (the United States) that supported the institution of slavery. Mexico had already ended slavery. Furthermore, Soto argued "religious" men should not fight to acquire territories that do not belong to them. Finally, Soto urged US Catholic soldiers to desert, to leave the US Army and fight with the Mexicans. A grateful Mexican government would offer US deserters equality and the opportunity to become farmers in Mexico. Soto's handbill made this impassioned plea: "Catholic Irish, French, and German!! Long live liberty!! Long live our holy Religion!!"[9]

Despite Polk's efforts to appeal to Catholic soldiers, an Irish immigrant named John Reilly and about 150 other US soldiers, many of them Irish and German Catholic, accepted Mexico's offer and deserted. Ironically, General Winfield Scott, commander of the US expedition to take Mexico City, went out of his way to maintain good relations with local Catholics his force encountered. Still, Reilly and others deserted to the enemy. Formed into the San Patricio (St Patrick's) Battalion, they fought tenaciously for Mexico hoping to cash in on promises of land bounties and glory. They also fought hard because by deserting they had become traitors to the United States and surrender would have meant execution for their crime.

Why did those soldiers turn their backs on the United States and "the American dream" to fight for Mexico and "the Mexican dream"? There were probably as many answers as there were soldiers, but religious reasons probably contributed to many desertions. Recent immigrants made up about 40 percent of the US Army. Many of them had not formed a strong bond with their new nation. Many of them also practiced Roman Catholicism. Those who arrived in the United States during the 1830s and 1840s found virulent and violent anti-Catholicism in the United States. Catholics who enlisted in the US army often found themselves commanded by Protestant officers. A number of those officers, not to mention Protestant enlisted men, believed in manifest destiny or held similar sentiments. Some of those soldiers claimed "that the present war is favored by the Almighty, because it will be the means of eradicating Papacy, and extending the benefits of Protestantism."[10] If that were not enough to make a Catholic soldier question his loyalty, many found themselves advised or required to attend Protestant worship services and, frequently, banned from attending Catholic mass. In another ironic twist, Reilly was able to desert because his commander in the US Army granted him a pass to attend Catholic services outside camp. Reilly's pass aside, the US–Mexican War demonstrates the not so subtle Protestant influence at

---

[9]   Quoted in Amy S. Greenberg, *A Wicked War: Polk, Clay, Lincoln, and the 1846 U.S. Invasion of Mexico* (New York: Knopf, 2012), 204.

[10]   Quoted in Greenberg (2012), 203.

Figure 3.3   George Caleb Bingham, *Daniel Boone escorting settlers through the Cumberland Gap*, 1851–52, oil on canvas. Source: Washington University, St. Louis, USA/The Bridgeman Art Library.

work in US expansion and gives insight to the decision of some US soldiers to desert and to fight for a friendlier and more hospitable Mexico.

The notion of manifest destiny circulated beyond politicians, journalists, and soldiers. Painters embraced the notion in the middle of the nineteenth century and created deeply symbolic images of manifest destiny that could be understood even by an illiterate audience and that show how deeply the concept penetrated popular culture. Artistic depictions of US expansion flourished amidst expansionist fervor and contain obvious references to divine favor and to the meeting of savagery and civilization. George Caleb Bingham, for example, brought overtones of manifest destiny to *Daniel Boone Escorting Settlers through the Cumberland Gap*, which he painted in 1851 (Figure 3.3). The painting depicts a dramatic moment from Boone's life, leading settlers through the Cumberland Gap in 1775. A heavenly light shines on Daniel Boone as he walks through a dark wilderness with his wife Rebecca astride a white horse. Rebecca

Boone marks the apex of a pyramid formed by the divinely lighted figures. Bingham's rendering of the Boone family quotes other artists' depiction of the Holy Family emphasizing the message that US expansion brought Christianity and civilization to a howling wilderness. William Ranney, another painter known in the mid-1800s for his historical scenes, made similar references in *Advice on the Prairie* (1853). *Advice* depicts a guide or a mountain man dispensing advice to overland migrants encamped in front of their covered wagons. Ranney draws the viewer's eye not only to the guide, but also to a prominently placed mother and child that quotes the Holy Family of the baby Jesus, Mary (the Madonna), and Joseph. This artistic device carried into the twentieth century, as did the notion of manifest destiny. William H. D. Koerner produced *Madonna of the Prairie* in 1921. Koerner's title makes his intention clear, but most viewers would be hard pressed to miss the halo distinguishing the female overlander in the painting. One of the most familiar, in its own day and ours, images depicting manifest destiny is John Gast's *American Progress* (sometimes known as *Westward Ho*), which Gast painted in 1872. The Goddess of Liberty, floating majestically in the sky, holds the focal point. Illuminated by a heavenly glow and holding a book (variously identified as a school book or book of laws) and paying out telegraph wire, she leads a veritable parade of civilization westward. Miners, farmers, a covered wagon, a stagecoach, and trains advance westward with her. Bison, bears, and Indians flee westward into the retreating darkness of wilderness and savagery.

Manifest destiny had a prominent place in US culture by the middle of the nineteenth century and flourished into the twentieth century. As Benjamin Franklin's ideas and John Quincy Adams' words show, the idea did not come out of nowhere in 1845. In fact, the very next year brought the dramatic exodus of Mormons from Illinois – the scene described at the beginning of this chapter – a migration about which swirled a competing version of manifest destiny.

Mormons and the Quest for Zion

The Church of Jesus Christ of Latter-day Saints, commonly known as Mormons, operated both within and in tension with the Judeo-Christian boundaries of dominant US society and culture in the nineteenth century. Other than Indian peoples, no group discussed in this book has had a more intimate and meaningful connection with the American West than the Church of Jesus Christ of Latter-day Saints. One could even argue that no other religious group has a more important relationship with US history. Mormonism's unique and intimate ties to the nation and the West justify an extended discussion here.

Shortly after the religion's founding in upstate New York, early Mormons made the first of a series of westward migrations that took them to Ohio, Missouri, Illinois, and ultimately to the Mountain West where they established Salt Lake City. Simply on the basis of their westward migration, the Mormons participated in and could be said to personify US expansion and conquest of the West. On a symbolic level, Mormons, like many others in the nineteenth century, looked to the West as a place where they could build ideal lives and practice their religion freely. One historian has likened the Mormons' westward migration to the Exodus of the ancient Israelites from Egypt and argued that the Mormon exodus, as much as their belief system, made them a distinctive people. Mormons' distinctive beliefs, though, clashed with those of mainstream Americans and produced a clash with the US government that circumscribed Mormon practice and narrowed the possibilities for what the West could become.

Joseph Smith founded Mormonism in upstate New York in 1830. As a boy and young man, Smith experienced a profound crisis of faith as the religious tumult of the Second Great Awakening, a wave of religious revivals that swept the United States and aimed at kindling religious fervor in a population perceived as increasingly concerned with worldly (rather than spiritual) matters, seethed around him. As he sought answers to his questions about faith, he had a number of visions throughout the 1820s. As Smith told it, God and Jesus Christ appeared to him and told him that all then-current religions had fallen away from the true path and that he would receive subsequent revelations about religious practice. He produced a text that would become the Book of Mormon, the basis of a new religion Smith founded in 1830.[11]

The story in the Book of Mormon gave North America a special place in religious history. It tells of peoples who lived in the Americas before Christopher Columbus arrived in 1492. The tale begins in the

---

[11]   *Book of Mormon* (Palmyra, NY, 1830).

Holy Land in 600 BC with a group of Hebrews escaping Jerusalem before an invasion of Babylonians. With divine guidance, the people made their way to the Indian Ocean where they built boats and sailed to the west coast of the Americas. Disagreements led them to splinter into two groups, the Nephites and the Lamanites. Over the course of centuries they built elaborate cities. After his crucifixion, Jesus Christ appeared in the Americas and organized his church, which led to two centuries of harmony. Conflict between the Lamanites and Nephites reemerged, plunging the groups into warfare. About 421 AD the Lamanites destroyed the Nephites, but not before Moroni, the last of the Nephites, recorded his people's story on the golden tablets, which he buried in what is now upstate New York. The Lamanites mixed with Asians and Europeans to produce American Indians.

Mormonism's creation in upstate New York and its migration history inextricably link the religion to westward expansion and to the important idea of the frontier. Frederick Jackson Turner, an influential historian of the late nineteenth and early twentieth century, argued that the existence of an area of free land and its continuous recession westward explain American development. Turner identified the edge of European settlement as the frontier. At that point, he argued in the dated language of his time, civilization met savagery and prompted people to abandon the old ways of Europe and to develop innovative new ways of living. Turner saw in this process the origins of a uniquely American people. Turner and his supporters could point to Mormonism as evidence to support this frontier hypothesis. In the 1820s and 1830s, Mormonism's upstate New York birthplace could be considered the American West and Mormonism's creation could be linked to the dynamism of frontier society. Even if that interpretation links the religion only marginally with the West, Mormonism's subsequent history fits securely into frontier--western paradigms. As Mormonism and Mormons moved west with the US frontier they produced a series of innovations as the religion developed.

The first Mormon move west took the group to Kirtland, Ohio. In Kirtland, Mormon missionaries converted enough local residents to form the critical mass of what would become an important Mormon center during the 1830s. By 1835 the Mormon population in the Kirtland area climbed above 1500 and might have reached as high as 2000. This migration had a uniquely religious component. Mormons began to conceive themselves as engaged in a Hebrew-like gathering of a unique people defined by their religion. In Kirtland, Mormons took significant steps toward building a community in which religious matters intertwined with secular ones to the point where distinctions blurred or vanished. Mormons built their first temple, which still stands and functions as a museum, an important landmark as well as a sacred space to perform new rituals or "ordinances" being revealed to Joseph Smith. Mormons devised economic experiments that helped solidify the community and separate Mormons from their non-Mormon neighbors. For example, Smith founded the United Firm, a communal property owning system controlled by the church. The order did not last long, but it set a precedent for cooperation and communal forms of settlement that would prove critical in establishing Mormon communities in the Great Basin, a region between the Rocky Mountains and the Sierra Nevada. Smith also founded an Antibanking Society, named so as to avoid banking regulations and which issued currency and otherwise functioned much as a bank. The Antibanking Society's collapse and the hostility it inspired in non-Mormons contributed to their decision to leave Kirtland for Missouri.

In its Kirtland phase the church reached out in several directions foreshadowing its expansive designs. The church sent missionaries to northwestern Europe. This effort yielded converts willing to migrate to the United States as part of the gathering of "saints," a term Mormons use to describe themselves. Smith, inspired by revelation and practicality, also sent followers to settle in western Missouri where he believed the Garden of Eden had been. Here Smith's vision intersected with the myth of the West as an Edenic paradise – more generically speaking – that had been developing in the American mind, although the two visions differed in their theological particulars. Non-Mormons saw the undeveloped West as a land of opportunity and abundant resources waiting to be harnessed, while Mormons saw that as well as the place they would gather as a people to build a new Zion.

Western Missouri proved more hellish than Edenic for Mormons, who once again found themselves conflicting with non-Mormon neighbors over a variety of issues, all related in some way to religion. They also found themselves the target of a state-sponsored extermination order in what has been called the Mormon War. Problems started soon after Mormons arrived and both sides engaged in vigilantism over the years. Tension escalated during 1838 when the arrival of refugees from Kirtland swelled the number of Mormons in Missouri. Non-Mormons, fearing increased Mormon economic and political power, reacted with hostility. Mormon leader Sidney Rigdon, in a sermon preached on the symbolically important July 4, responded by calling on Mormons to wage a war of extermination against Missourians. The conflict reached a bloody boil in late summer and early fall, and on October 27 Missouri governor Lilburn W. Boggs ordered that Mormons "be exterminated, or driven from the State if necessary for the public peace."[12] Three days later Missouri soldiers killed 18 Mormons at the Haun's Mill settlement. Missouri forces surrounded Joseph Smith and a large group of Mormons two days later and forced the Mormons to surrender. About 15 000 Mormons fled Missouri that winter enduring remarkable suffering on their way to their next destination, which they hoped would be their promised land.

The Mormons escaped the danger and disappointment of Missouri by trekking east to Illinois, a state carved from the Old Northwest. Illinois officials had recruited Mormons to live in a sparsely settled region on the east bank of the Mississippi River. Here the church entered one of its most dynamic – and tragic – phases. Here, too, the church's history offers evidence in support of Turner's frontier hypothesis. Smith named the Illinois settlement Nauvoo, a term Smith said meant "a beautiful plantation" in revised Hebrew. The Mormons laid out Nauvoo on a grid system similar to that being used by many contemporary new settlements, especially in newly settled western lands. Unlike any other US city, Nauvoo held the distinction of being Mormonism's capital. It would be a new Jerusalem for a new Zion Smith envisioned in the heart of America. Mormons built their second temple in Nauvoo and Smith continued to add ritual and doctrine to Mormonism based on continuing revelations. Also, the liberal charter granted by Illinois allowed establishment of a militia, the Nauvoo Legion, staffed with Mormon officers and soldiers. Given their experiences, many Mormons surely saw this as an important and welcome development.

[12] Quoted in Leonard J. Arrington and Davis Bitton, *The Mormon Experience: A History of the Latter-day Saints*, 2d edn (Urbana and Chicago, IL: University of Illinois Press, 1992), 44.

Non-Mormons in the area felt differently. By 1844 Nauvoo counted about 10 000 residents, which made it the second largest city in Illinois. At the frontier of US settlement, Mormons had established a large, well-armed, theocratic city-state marked by bloc voting and "peculiar" ways inspired by religion. Once again, Mormons made their neighbors uneasy.

Politics created tension between Mormons and their Illinois neighbors almost from the time the Saints arrived. Lyman Wight, a Mormon apostle, published letters in the Quincy, Illinois, *Whig* (a newspaper affiliated with the Whig political party) blaming Missouri, and by implication national, Democrats for Mormon persecutions in Illinois. Subsequent Whig denunciations of Mormonism led Joseph Smith to urge his followers to support the Democrats. Whigs and anti-Mormon Democrats responded in 1841 by establishing an Anti-Mormon party. In a subsequent election Hyrum Smith, Joseph's brother, announced a revelation indicating Mormons should support a Democratic candidate for the state legislature. When that candidate received 629 votes in Nauvoo to his Whig opponent's 71, the church's bloc voting power became clear. Whigs and some Democrats reportedly decided the Mormons had to be driven from the state.

Conflict over church–state relations and politics contributed heavily to one of the most tragic episodes in Mormon history. In 1844 Joseph Smith announced he would run for president of the United States. Smith supported a theocratic form of democracy, which Mormon enemies saw as further confirmation that Mormons mixed religion and politics in dangerously un-American ways. A conflict over the bedrock value of freedom of the press brought even more trouble. A group of Mormon dissidents, including a man who suspected Smith had romantic designs on his wife, founded a newspaper called the Nauvoo *Expositor* in which to air their grievances. In the *Expositor*'s inaugural, and only, issue they printed volatile allegations about the sex lives of Mormons and their leaders. To fight the dissidents and to silence the *Expositor*, Smith, Nauvoo's mayor, his brother, the vice-mayor, and the city council passed a libel law, charged the paper with being a public nuisance, and Smith ordered the press destroyed. The Mormon dissenters, citing defense of freedom of the press, filed charges against Smith and other Mormon leaders. Smith ended up in the Carthage,

Figure 3.4   Brigham Young, circa 1849. Source: Courtesy of the Library of Congress Prints and Photographs Division (LC-DIG-cwpbh-01671).

Illinois, jail. On June 27, 1844, an anti-Mormon mob stormed the jail and murdered Smith and his brother Hyrum.

The leadership vacuum created by the prophet's death led the Mormon community to splinter. The largest group chose to follow the Twelve Apostles, a council of the church's top leaders, led by Brigham Young (Figure 3.4). During a period of relative calm, this group continued missionary work, continued construction of the Nauvoo Temple, and refined the church's internal structure to strengthen it. Conflict with neighbors resumed in the fall of 1844 and through the summer of 1845 as raiders burned Mormon homes and crops outside Nauvoo. By fall of 1845, Young and the other leaders saw maintaining Nauvoo as impossible and looked to the West. That fall Young read the just-published John C. Fremont's *Report of the Exploring Expedition to the Rocky Mountains* and decided to send a 1500-man expedition to the Great Basin as the vanguard of yet another Mormon exodus. This time the Saints hoped isolation in the Mountain West would protect them from outsider persecution and allow them to establish their Zion, a gathering place for God's people. For the first time in their history, they would be the first to settle an area and they could truly start from scratch.

Brigham Young engineered the Nauvoo exodus and led his church and its people into their quintessentially western phase. Young's leadership in this period of Mormon history has inspired some to label him "the American Moses." Among contemporary Mormons, Young's success leading the exodus confirmed his legitimacy as president. The Mormon migration at once placed the Saints in the main current of US westward expansion and separated them from it. Most overlanders traveled on the south side of the Platte River; the Mormons traveled on the north. Most overlanders planned to stop in Oregon or California; the Mormons stopped in the Great Basin in what would become Utah. Most overlanders traveled as individuals, a family, or in an ad hoc arrangement of families; the Mormon migration marked the permanent flight of an entire people. Mormons traversed the overland trails continuously from 1847 until the completion of the transcontinental railroad as a united, sober, disciplined group unlike any other. Most overlanders sought economic betterment and other secular opportunity in the West; the Mormons, too, sought opportunity, but hope for realization of their religious aspirations, and religion permeated everything they did.

The flight from Nauvoo could have degenerated into chaos, but Young and other church leaders organized the migrants into an orderly procession. Top leaders, including Young himself, led companies of 400–500 wagons. Leaders subdivided each company into groups of 10s, 50s, and 100s, often along family lines. Specialized guards and experienced pioneers accompanied the groups of 50. The leadership also set regulations to prevent Mormon migrants from bidding against each other for food and supplies along the trail. This centralized organization further distinguished Mormons from other overlanders.

The outbreak of the US–Mexican War turned the refugee Mormons into reluctant allies of the United States, the very country they believed had failed them and that they sought to escape. Mormons offered to help fight Mexico in exchange for financial support. The offer came with a veiled threat. The church wished to relocate thousands of recent British converts to the West. If the United States would not assist this process, the Mormons would request help from the British.

President Polk, needing help with the war in the West and worried about Britain expanding its influence in the West, offered to help the Mormons. Polk approved the formation of what came to be known as the Mormon Battalion, a unit of Saints 500 strong.

The Mormon Battalion embodied an alliance that served both church and state. The United States secured Mormon loyalty in the war and a force that aided the military in the Southwest and in California. The US Army gained a peculiar unit. Most battalion members deeply resented being asked to serve a nation they believed had turned its back on their religious freedoms. They served not out of patriotism, but in response to a call by church leaders and in obedience to their faith. The church demonstrated service to the nation and, much more importantly, gained a critical subsidy for its exodus. Hundreds of Mormons – the members of the battalion – moved to California at government expense. This freed church resources to support other migrants. Even better, from the Mormon perspective, the soldiers' pay provided a badly needed infusion of cash into church coffers. Unlike the Catholic members of the San Patricio Battalion who abandoned the US cause to ally with Mexico, the Mormon Battalion, despite rampant American anti-Mormonism, sided with the United States.

For the overwhelming number of Mormons who remained civilians, the difficulties of overland travel and the tough winter of 1846–1847 tested them and produced more evidence of what they perceived as divine intervention and, perhaps, evidence that manifest destiny came in more than one shape. Winter halted travel with the Saints scattered across Iowa. An advance party had crossed the Missouri River and established Winter Quarters near present-day Omaha, Nebraska. About 200 Mormons died during their stay that season at Winter Quarters. There and elsewhere along the trail quarrels erupted and circulation of counterfeit money led to problems in camps and with Indians. On January 14, 1847, Brigham Young announced a revelation – "The Word and will of the Lord" – aimed at the Saints' situation.[13] It affirmed the pyramidal organization adopted the previous year and called on leaders to organize travel for the coming season. It urged the Saints to share their resources with each other. It also contained a code of conduct for the travelers urging

---

[13]   Arrington and Bitton (1992), 100.

them, for example, to repay debts to each other, to keep their promises, and to avoid arguing, speaking ill of each other, and drunkenness. The revelation also endorsed singing, dancing, and music in praise of the Lord. The experience of receiving divine revelation distinguished Mormons from other groups on the overland trails.

A carefully selected party resumed the journey in April 1847 and by late July had reached the Salt Lake Valley in present-day Utah, which would become the end of the Mormon Trail. The so-called pioneer party, 148 members of the pioneer party (143 men, 3 women, 2 children) traveled on the north side of the Platte River Valley, which kept them from contact with most other overland travelers, who kept to the south side. The distance also kept the groups from competing with each other for scarce natural resources along the trail. Brigham Young, ill with Rocky Mountain (tick) fever and traveling at the rear of the pioneer party, arrived in the Salt Lake Valley on July 24, a date still celebrated by the Saints as Pioneer Day. By the end of the 1847 travel season about 1700 more Saints had arrived and the foundation for a new community was in place. Young and other church leaders saw the Saints' safe arrival in the Salt Lake Valley as fulfillment of Old Testament prophesy.

Immediately the pioneer company began building their Zion and preparing, in a distinctly religious way, for those who followed. The day after his arrival and again on July 28, Brigham Young preached sermons outlining plans for the community. Young demanded all settlers be industrious and that none labor on the Sabbath. He also called on the Saints to become industrially self-sufficient so that their kingdom of God would not be dependent on outsiders.

After arriving in the Salt Lake Valley the Saints continued to struggle. Clawing for survival in their harsh new home led some to believe they might have to move on … again. Crops planted immediately on the arrival of the pioneer party produced little food. As new crops emerged in the spring of 1848, masses of crickets descended and threatened to eat the lot. Seagulls swept in from the Great Salt Lake to feast on the crickets, which saved some of the crop and gave Mormons hope for remaining in the valley. Some saw divine intervention at work. More unlikely help arrived in the form of Argonauts, gold seekers bound for California beginning in 1849. The gold rushers – an estimated 5000–8000 passed through Salt Lake City in 1849 – bought or traded for Mormon goods and services, providing what amounted to a revenue stream for the fledgling settlement. Gold rushers who discovered they had brought too many things with them decided to lighten their loads in Salt Lake City before tackling the Sierra Nevada. They flat-out abandoned some items and others they traded away to Mormons (and others, but in Utah primarily Mormons) at fire sale rates for food, livestock, services, and other items they needed for their journey. These items amounted to a windfall for the Mormon settlement. As with the seagull incident, some Mormons saw the hand of God at work.

The westward trek also helped the Saints establish a foothold in an inhospitable, remote environment and reflected the church's enormous influence in this colonization effort. Within 10 years of arriving in the Salt Lake Valley, pioneer-missionaries had founded 96 communities fanning out in all directions from Salt Lake City. As more settlers arrived, Young organized the Salt Lake stake, referring to the settlement as one stake in the tent of Zion. A presidency, consisting of a president and two counselors appointed by Young, governed the stake. Young also appointed a 12-man high council to formulate policy, arbitrate disputes, and provide leadership on religious and secular projects. By the end of the nineteenth century Mormons had established more than 500 communities in the West.

In 1848 Young modified the system to include 19 wards. Each ward, the equivalent of a congregation, contained 70–100 families. The ward dated to the Nauvoo period and represents a case of civil organization influencing ecclesiastical organization. The demands of assisting the swelling numbers of indigent Saints entering the young city outstripped the abilities of a single organization. The city had been organized by municipal wards and to spread the burden of indigent assistance the church created a parallel ecclesiastical system with its units also labeled "ward" and supervised by an appointed bishop. The bishop, who had to be confirmed by the ward's residents, provided voluntary leadership as part of his religious commitment. Bishops supervised construction and operation of schools and other infrastructure projects and led worship services. They found aid for the poor, integrated new arrivals into the community, collected tithes, supervised common fields and herds, and managed conflicts among ward members. Within a year of arrival the settlers learned irrigation would be critical to their farming success and they began building dams and canals. Each bishop served as water master for his ward and had the responsibility for constructing adequate ditches and distributing water equitably. In Utah and throughout the West and other areas of Mormon colonization, the ward served not only as the basic ecclesiastical unit, but also as an important political unit and as a social unit surpassed only by the family in significance. This type of intimate church–state relationship led some non-Mormons to view the Saints as a threat to the nation's republican organization and values.

The concept of gathering as a people also set the Saints apart and the practice escalated with the establishment of the Utah settlements. Almost immediately on settling in the Salt Lake Valley, Brigham Young began church assistance to Saints bound for Utah. The windfall from gold rushers prompted Mormon leaders to extend their planned assistance to Saints emigrating from Britain. The church's plan incorporated in 1850 as the Perpetual Emigrating Company. By 1870 the church had subsidized the immigration of more than 38 000 converts from the British Isles and another 13 000 from continental Europe.

The Mormon exodus contributed to Mormon identity. Brigham Young and other leaders self-consciously compared their movement to the exodus of the Jews from Egypt led by Moses and referred to their lead party as the Camp of Israel. They interpreted their passage across the frozen Mississippi and events such as the appearance of flocks of quail to the starving migrants as miraculous blessings. Outsiders such as non-Mormon historian Jan Shipps also liken the Mormon migration to the Biblical exodus of the Jews. According to Shipps, Brigham Young not only led his followers from persecution but also "backward into a primordial sacred time."[14] Like the Israelites, the Mormons crossed a wilderness (the Great Plains and the Rocky Mountains) to arrive in a holy land (the Great Basin) as a chosen people who set about building God's kingdom on earth. This migration landed them in the heart of the West and the isolation they found in the Salt Lake Valley bought them time todevelop themselves and the West according to their divine plan.

Their divine plan included – for a time – a theocratic state to be called Deseret. Deseret, a term for honeybee drawn from the Book of Mormon and probably meant to symbolize industry and cooperation, would have been massive. Geographically it encompassed almost all of what would become the states of Utah and Nevada and portions of what would become California, Oregon, Idaho,

[14] Jan Shipps, *Mormonism: The Story of a New Religious Tradition* (Urbana and Chicago, IL: University of Illinois Press, 1985), 122.

Wyoming, Colorado, New Mexico, and Arizona. Church leaders drafted a constitution and proposed a slate of officers, all Saints, including a governor and a lieutenant governor, and submitted the plan for approval in an election. In some respects Deseret fit the American political model, but ultimately it provided an instrument for a Mormon theocracy. Congress, facing rumors of Mormon polygamy and disloyalty and in the midst struggling with the nation's slavery crisis, organized a territory named Utah after the Ute Indians as part of the Compromise of 1850. The territory, much reduced from the proposed 200 000-square mile Deseret, would remain under federal jurisdiction until 1896.

Despite Deseret's fate, the Mormon faithful continued to gather in Utah. Not all migrants shared the same level of devotion to the church. Some wished to devote most of their energy to the worldly pursuits of establishing their homes with little involvement in the church. Some arrived with zeal for the group's religious vision, but backslid. In 1856 and 1857 Brigham Young's counselor Jedediah M. Grant directed a program to "wake up the saints." The resulting "Reformation" resembled religious revivals in other parts of the country, but demonstrated the nature of church control in territorial Utah. Grant dispatched reformation missionaries to the wards where they organized meetings that included fiery sermons to remind participants of their sinful natures and to reinforce ties to the church. The meetings might include rebaptisms, visions, and speaking in tongues, manifestations of the spirit that made some Mormons uncomfortable. Grant urged bishops to continue the programs until they had achieved a boiling heat of enthusiasm. In some areas gangs of zealots intimidated those suspected of spiritual weakness or apostasy. Despite the drawbacks, Brigham Young saw good results. Financial support for the church increased as did polygamous marriages, a visible sign of observance that dominated conflict with the United States for the rest of the nineteenth century.

The Mormon Question, 1852–1860

Despite Mormon achievements and success settling the West, the Saints found themselves struggling with the United States in a contest over how the West and American society should be shaped. Specifically, the struggle centered on what role religion and religiously inspired behavior could play in shaping society and moral values. Perhaps the very success that the Mormons enjoyed in settling the West contributed to this struggle; the institution of plural marriage, which the church openly announced in 1852, certainly did. Mormons for years had idealistically hoped the federal government would protect them from persecution and violence. Mormons saw the United States, especially the Constitution's first amendment guarantees, as a beacon of hope and an indication that this place (the United States) would allow them opportunity and freedom to develop. In their Ohio, Missouri, and Illinois periods, local conflicts and opponents had driven them from their homes and Mormon pleas to the United States for assistance went unanswered. The Mormons fled the United States for what they hoped would be unfettered freedom in the wide-open space of the West. In the West, though, competing visions of manifest destiny and family, a remote location, and an increasingly powerful federal government led to a new era of conflict. Rather than facing opposition from local non-Mormon Americans, as they had in Ohio, Missouri, and Illinois, Mormons now faced opposition from the institutional embodiment of all Americans: the federal government.

Various factions had struggled for the new nation's soul since its creation. The slavery question challenged bedrock definitions of what it meant to be American and what the new nation stood for. Women played important roles in the abolition movement and by the mid-1800s womanhood and definitions of family intertwined with the debate about slavery and the meaning of freedom and nation. Plural marriage, which might be considered Mormonism's "peculiar institution" (a phrase often attached to race slavery) became a foundational element of Mormonism and debate over it entered the national dialogue about society and social order early in the new religion's young life. After years of avoiding the issue publicly, the Latter-day Saints Church openly acknowledged its practice of plural marriage in 1852 from its stronghold in Utah Territory. The nation added "the Mormon Question" to its debates and national leaders began seeking answers to this question, an increasingly vexing one considering Mormons' growing power and their Zion's location astride important transcontinental transportation routes in the remote mountain West.

The fledgling Republican Party attacked polygamy on two fronts in 1856. In that year's presidential campaign the party platform promised to eradicate the "twin relics of barbarism": slavery and polygamy. The Republicans failed to win the White House, but James Buchanan, the Democrat who won the presidency in the 1856 election, would act on the Mormon Question. On another front, a Vermont Republican senator named Justin Morrill attacked plural marriage and, by extension, Mormonism by sponsoring an anti-bigamy bill. The bill died, but it marked the first legislative effort to answer the Mormon question. It also demonstrated the Republican Party's dedication to moral social reform in both the South and the West.

Conflict between Mormons and the United States came to a head in 1857. In Utah, the Mormon Reformation had put much of the population on edge. The Republican Party's attacks on polygamy in 1856 added to tension in the territory. Meanwhile, in Washington, DC, newly elected President James Buchanan heard reports from disaffected Utah Territory officials that the Mormons effectively ignored federal authority and stood in a state of rebellion. The eastern press called for action. The *New York Times* recommended in May, 1857 that Buchanan replace Brigham Young with a new territorial governor to be installed by force, if necessary. With the recently completed election fresh in his memory, Buchanan decided to avoid acting on the slavery issue and instead to act on Utah and the other relic of barbarism, polygamy. Buchanan asserted federal authority by naming a new slate of territorial officials and ordering the US Army to escort them to Utah, a mission that came to be known as the Utah Expedition. This chain of events showed how the Mormon Question held the nation's attention even in the East and how it united Republicans and Democrats interested in answering the question.

In Utah, Mormons braced for war. At face value, at least back east, the Utah Expedition amounted to a secular exercise of power by the United States. One need not scratch very deeply, though, to find religiously related undercurrents. From Utah, the expedition looked like a crusade, or worse, a federally supported mob on its way to continue persecution of Mormons or even to destroy them. Brigham Young declared martial law and recounted for the Saints their history of persecution in the United States. To Young, the US Army's approach promised more of the same. In his proclamation, Young accused the federal government of using "prejudice existing against us, because of our religious faith, to send out a formidable host to accomplish our destruction."[15] Wilford Woodruff, a leading Mormon who would later become church president, wrote much the same in his diary on August 25, 1857. Woodruff viewed non-Mormon Americans as wicked enemies of God determined to prevent the establishment of God's kingdom on earth. News of the army's approach fueled emotional fires ignited by the reformation. The highly charged atmosphere erupted in a disaster in Utah's "zealous south."

Into this emotionally toxically charged environment came a wagon train of emigrants, Missourians and Arkansans known as the Fancher train, headed for California through Utah. Mormons throughout Utah feared and were preparing for the army's arrival. Settlements began conserving food, ammunition, and other supplies. Overland travelers found themselves either unable to buy or trade for supplies or charged exorbitant prices for goods and services. Frustrated, they lashed out with insults, which increased tension with the settlers. Some Mormon officials wished to charge members of the Fancher train with blasphemy and public intoxication. When that plan failed, others sought to chasten the overlanders by organizing an Indian attack. That plan went off prematurely and with deadly results as several emigrants died and the remainder circled their wagons and established an impressive defensive position. Now facing a bigger, messier problem Mormon leaders in southern Utah looked for a solution and opted to eliminate those who might incriminate them.

Mormon militia from southern Utah settlements and Paiutes killed more than 120 men, women, and children from the train on September 11, 1857, in what became known as the Mountain Meadows Massacre. Seventeen children, spared because the murderers considered them too young to tell tales that could incriminate the perpetrators, survived. The perpetrators later cited motivations including suspicion that the emigrants might be allied with the army bearing down on Utah, a desire to avenge wrongs committed against Mormons in Missouri and Arkansas, and a desire by those in the poor southern settlements to loot the wagon train. Controversy surrounds the event to this day. Some have charged that Brigham Young ordered the massacre and its subsequent cover up. Recent research indicates that was

[15] Utah Territory, Governor, 1850–1858 (Brigham Young), proclamation by the governor, August 5,1847, broadside, Western Americana Collection, Beinecke Rare Book and Manuscript Library, Yale University, New Haven, CT.

unlikely. Young excommunicated three men for their roles at Mountain Meadows. One of them, John Doyle Lee, a loyal supporter of Young, who was tried, convicted, and executed (by firing squad at the site of the massacre) for his role, bore the brunt of the legal consequences and denounced the pragmatic Young for what he saw as personal betrayal.

Meanwhile the army continued its advance on Utah. Mormon raiders harassed the army by attacking its supply trains. Those actions and the army's late start prevented it from reaching Utah in 1857 and the troops wintered in southwest Wyoming. Brigham Young decided not to fight and instead began an evacuation of Salt Lake City. Thousands of Mormons fled south to Provo as Young emptied the city for the troops' arrival. Circumstances changed in Washington, too, where lawmakers expressed concern over the Utah Expedition's huge cost. To avoid war, which would be even costlier, President Buchanan sent a peace commission to join the soldiers and, hopefully, head off a fight. In the end, the army marched through an empty Salt Lake City and established Camp Floyd about 40 miles to the south. New territorial officers took their places with the occupying army nearby to ensure continued federal control. Salt Lake's Mormon residents returned to their homes and eventually profited from supplying the army. Peaceful, if tense, coexistence resumed between the Saints and their nation. It would not last for long.

Conclusion

Between 1803 and 1860, the United States acquired and began to exert control over a massive territory stretching from the Mississippi River to the Pacific Ocean. The United States saw itself transforming this region by "civilizing" it, which included bringing the perceived benefits of Christian society with notable Protestant overtones. Many prominent Americans subscribed to the principles embedded in manifest destiny, which provided a short-hand description for the process and included a justification for it. For them, the continent had been a gift from God, and civilization and religious conversion went hand in hand. Religious people and religious institutions contributed to the social and cultural infrastructure the United States built in the West. In a broad sense, this can be seen as a taming of a wilderness. For much of this period, the line separating church and state remained blurry as the US government and Christian missionaries worked as partners extending US control over the West. The Mormon exodus and settlement of the Great Salt Lake Valley complicated the situation further. For Mormons of the time, the line separating church and state wasn't blurry, it barely existed. They saw the West as their Zion and worked, at least for a while, to establish a theocratic kingdom of God on earth. Their efforts brought Mormons into direct conflict with the United States over how the West and society should be organized and religious principles undergirded each side's thoughts and actions. By 1860, the West's religious landscape remained a work in progress.

Suggested Reading

Berkhofer, Jr, Robert F. 1965. *Salvation and the Savage: An Analysis of Protestant Missions and American Indian Response, 1787–1862*. Lexington, KY: University of Kentucky Press.

Bigler, David L. and Will Bagley. 2000. *Army of Israel: Mormon Battalion Narratives*. Logan, UT: Utah State University Press.

Botham, Fay and Sara Patterson, eds. 2006. *Race, Religion, Region: Landscapes of Encounter in the American West*. Tucson, AZ: University of Arizona Press.

Higham, C. L. 2000. *Noble, Wretched, and Redeemable: Protestant Missionaries to the Indians in Canada and the United States, 1820–1900*. Albuquerque, NM: University of New Mexico Press.

Johansen, Dorothy O. and Charles M. Gates. 1957. *Empire of the Columbia: A History of the Pacific Northwest*. New York: Harper and Brothers.

Merry, Robert W. 2009. *A Country of Vast Designs: James K. Polk, the Mexican War, and the Conquest of the Continent*. New York: Simon and Schuster.

Seager, Richard Hughes. 1999. *Buddhism in America*. New York: Columbia University Press.

Tweed, Thomas A. 1992. *The American Encounter with Buddhism, 1844–1912: Victorian Culture and the Limits of Dissent*. Bloomington, IN: Indiana University Press.

Tweed, Thomas A. and Stephen Prothero, eds. 1999. *Asian Religions in America: A Documentary History*. New York: Oxford University Press.

Wheelan, Joseph. 2007. *Invading Mexico: America's Continental Dream and the Mexican War, 1846–1848*. New York: Carroll and Graf.

Woodworth, Stephen E. 2010. *Manifest Destinies: America's Westward Expansion and the Road to the Civil War*. New York: Knopf.

4

The West and Religion in the Era of the Civil War and Reconstruction, 1860–1890

Dawn gave way to bright sunshine on December 29, 1890. For scores of Miniconjou Lakotas in Big Foot's band, it would be their last day. For many who survived, it would be the worst day of their lives. They had gone to sleep the night before with their camp in southwestern South Dakota surrounded by soldiers of the Seventh US Cavalry. Big Foot's people had embraced a new religious movement called the Ghost Dance. The soldiers, implementing the US policy of suppressing the Ghost Dance, had been sent to escort Big Foot and his people to the government agency at the Pine Ridge Reservation.

Tensions in Lakota Country had reached fever pitch thanks in large measure to the Ghost Dance's arrival. Government Indian agents and non-Indians living near the Lakota reservations misunderstood the Ghost Dance's peaceful message. Many non-Indians interpreted the movement as a threat and saw the ceremonial dances as evidence that an uprising and, maybe, a new outbreak of Indian warfare was brewing. Lakotas had been the major players in defeating Lt. Col. George Custer and the Seventh Cavalry at the Little Bighorn in 1876. Sitting Bull, widely known and feared for his opposition to

Inspiration and Innovation: Religion in the American West,
First Edition. Todd M. Kerstetter.
© 2015 John Wiley & Sons, Inc. Published 2015 by John Wiley & Sons, Inc.

US expansion, was a Lakota, too, and he had submitted to reservation life only nine years earlier. In late 1890 he wanted to learn more about this new religion. Thanks to recent US–Lakota relations and condescending attitudes about Indian religions, whites in the Dakotas considered the arrival of the Ghost Dance as very bad news.

Indian agents sought to suppress the Ghost Dance and Christian missionaries took great pains to convince Lakotas that the new religion was incorrect and that they should ignore it. In November, President Benjamin Harrison dispatched soldiers to Pine Ridge to stop the Ghost Dance and to maintain order. In mid-December, the Indian agent at the Standing Rock Reservation, where Sitting Bull lived, ordered Indian police to arrest the influential leader. The arresting officers, Lakotas themselves, said a Christian prayer before entering Sitting Bull's property. The arrest went horribly wrong. Sitting Bull, his arresting officer, and several others died that day. Sitting Bull's death sent fear through the Ghost Dance community, including Big Foot's band, which had been visiting Sitting Bull's people at Standing Rock. Big Foot led his followers away from Standing Rock toward Pine Ridge, where they intended to turn themselves in to US officials. Before they could get there, the Seventh Cavalry intercepted them.

The details of what happened on the morning of December 29 might never be known with certainty because eyewitness accounts conflict. We know that a firefight broke out between Big Foot's band of Ghost Dancers and the US soldiers. We also know that the shooting left hundreds of Ghost Dancers dead and wounded and dozens of soldiers dead and more soldiers wounded (Figure 4.1). The Lakota holy man Black Elk recalled witnessing the aftermath of the shooting and what it meant to him: "I can still see the butchered women and children lying heaped and scattered all along the crooked gulch as plain as when I saw them with eyes still young," he said later. "And I can see that something else died there in the bloody mud, and was buried in the blizzard. A people's dream died there. It was a beautiful dream."[1] Another Lakota offered a blunt assessment of what happened to Ghost Dancers at Wounded Knee Creek: "The dance was our religion, but the government sent soldiers to kill us on account of it."[2]

[1] John G. Neihardt, *Black Elk Speaks* (New York: Morrow, 1932), 270.
[2] Quoted in James Mooney, *The Ghost-Dance Religion and the Sioux Outbreak of 1890* (Washington, DC: Government Printing Office, 1896. Reprint. Lincoln, NB: University of Nebraska Press, 1991), 1060.

Figure 4.1   Big Foot's camp three weeks after the Wounded Knee Massacre. Source: Courtesy of the Library of Congress Prints and Photographs Division, (LC-DIG-ppmsca-15849).

Between 1860 and 1890 the United States experienced astounding upheaval. The nation tore itself apart during the Civil War (1861–1865). Reconstruction, which lasted roughly from 1865 through to 1877, saw the national government set the terms whereby states that had seceded could rejoin the union. In a phase called Congressional or "radical" Reconstruction, the Republican-dominated Congress set terms that punished secessionist politicians and attempted to reform southern society and politics to end slavery and provide civil liberties for former slaves. States that met these terms could rejoin the union and resume governing themselves, a process completed by 1877.

The period 1860 through 1890 also witnessed stunning developments in the trans-Mississippi West. The dispossession of American Indians and the settlement of the West by non-Indians quickened. As of 1890, the US Census Bureau reported that it was impossible to distinguish the frontier of settlement in the West. Historian Frederick Jackson Turner seized on this development in 1893 in his now famous essay, "The Significance of the Frontier in American History."[3] He argued that a frontier process, a meeting of "savagery" and "civilization," made possible by the existence of an area of free land and its continuous recession westward created a unique people and explained American history. With the end of the frontier in 1890, Turner said, a chapter in the nation's history had closed.

The West's religious history reflected these dramatic events. Pioneer missionaries and church folk moved into sparsely or newly settled areas to serve their fellow religionists or to convert new members. Generally, they sought to impose a particular type of religious order in what Turner would have called a frontier setting. Eastern politicians also had a hand in shaping the West's religious history, although that story often gets obscured by the seemingly secular master narrative of Reconstruction and westward expansion. Northern Republicans, left in control of Washington, DC, thanks to secession by southern states passed legislation that encouraged settler colonialism in the West. The best-known examples of these laws include the Homestead Act, the Morrill Act, and the Pacific Railroad Act, all passed in 1862. After the war, Republican lawmakers supervised Reconstruction, the reintegration of the seceded southern states into the nation. The nation also remade the West in the late 1800s and historian Elliott West argues that we should think of this period as "Greater Reconstruction" that remade both the the the South and the West. This chapter borrows the idea of "Greater Reconstruction" to argue that from 1860 to 1890 US government policies and settlement of the West by non-Indians amounted to a crusade to remake the region in the image of a Protestant-dominated eastern establishment. The United States followed in the footsteps of France, Spain, and Russia in trying to impose a Christian monoculture on its territory, but partial success left the West a multi-religious region without a dominant religious tradition.

Protestantism in the West

The people who poured into the trans-Mississippi West during the second half of the nineteenth century brought with them a wide range of religious beliefs and created or tapped existing religious communities.

---

[3] See Frederick Jackson Turner, *The Frontier in American History* (New York: Holt, 1920).

The most important religious events of this time and era involved Mormons and American Indians whose stories appear later in this chapter. Before considering those dramatic events, an impressionistic sample of activities by Protestants, Catholics, and Jews in the West will illuminate the region's diversity and how members of those faiths contributed to westward expansion. Each group tried to carve a space for itself and to serve its members' spiritual needs in what has been called the "pioneer phase of western European–American religious history."[4]

Denominations with roots in Germany (such as Lutheranism) when transplanted to new settlements in places such as Nebraska and Kansas depended for support on a steady stream of new immigrants. To ensure that steady stream of believers, members of the clergy encouraged and shaped immigration. The process often started in Germany, where a minister would advise a migrant to settle in a place where a congregation had already been established. The migrant, facing a difficult and potentially frightening relocation, often welcomed the prospect of settling among people who spoke a familiar language and preserved a familiar culture, including worship. Churches thus became the center of ethnoreligious settlements in the West.

The community of Block, Kansas, shows how important religion could be in the lives of people who settled in the nineteenth-century West. The German Lutherans who established and populated Block, located in east-central Kansas about 70 miles southwest of Kansas City, organized their lives around Trinity Lutheran Church and its affiliated school. This example uses Missouri Synod Lutherans (introduced in Chapter 3) in Kansas as a case study, but its general contours suggest the importance of mainline Protestant institutions in building community. Block's parochial (church-affiliated) school likewise shows how religion and education worked together for denominations such as Lutherans and Roman Catholics as they built and maintained communities. In Block's case, the church and its school transmitted German language and values and Lutheran doctrine to the town's founders and generations of descendants.

The first German Lutherans arrived in what would become Block in about 1860. By 1863 the community had enough members to

---

[4] Ferenc M. Szasz and Margaret Connell Szasz, "Religion and Spirituality," in *The Oxford History of the American West*, Clyde A. Milner II, Carol A. O'Connor, and Martha A. Sandweiss, eds (New York: Oxford University Press, 1994), 373.

justify a Missouri Synod mission. The community established Trinity Lutheran Church in 1868 and called a permanent minister. Once Block established a stable core population that could sustain a German church and school, it became more attractive as a destination for other similarly minded German immigrants who continued to arrive for decades to follow. As the community grew, it added facilities: a church/school building in 1870, a separate parsonage in 1875, and an expanded 400-seat church in 1884. Just as Missouri Synod belief organized community life, the church building acted as a visual and physical anchor. The bell tower, for example, reminded immigrants of the central place of the church in their home country.

Missouri Synod values shaped Block's social life. For example, the church followed a strictly patriarchal structure. Men ran the church and were expected to rule in homes. The church valued women as wives and mothers, but they were to remain silent in church and to obey their husbands at home. A woman who challenged this system questioned God's order. The pastor's wife acted as a model of German-Lutheran womanhood for the entire community. As wife of the community's spiritual leader, she had a high profile in the town and along with her husband and children had to live according to exemplary standards.

Religion shaped community life in Block as the Missouri Synod fought to protect family, school, and church from corrosive or "sinful" outside influences. The church discouraged or tried to flat-out prohibit contact with non-Lutherans, for example. The synod bent this rule when it came to economics and politics, but did its best to assure compliance on social and religious matters and events. Members of the church observed and discussed people's public (as well as what we would likely consider private) behavior and sought to impose morality. In 1878, for example, the pastor learned that a young man had been seen drunk at a dance hall. The pastor said the young man had dishonored his pious, deceased parents and went so far as to accuse him of ruining the entire congregation. The pastor's comments led to an angry confrontation at a church meeting. Some members of the congregation criticized the pastor for "going too far," but others said he had been too easy on the young man. So, the pastor did not exercise power unchallenged, but this shows he could set a community's agenda and that everyone's behavior could be scrutinized and discussed. This also suggests that even recently formed western communities could have a religiously influenced social order that ran counter to the myth of the wide-open West.

The synod also shaped communities through its parochial schools, which played important roles. Students daily studied and memorized Lutheran doctrine and beliefs. They also learned moral values and German language and culture. In many new communities, the pastor also served as the school teacher. When a community could support both a teacher and a pastor, both individuals served as important role models and guardians of Lutheranism and morality in the community. Furthermore, starting in the 1870s the synod's publishing company provided school books to ensure doctrine and beliefs were taught consistently. The company also printed materials for adults that contained advice on how to think and behave as well as the synod's position on both religious and secular matters.

As religion supplied organization and cultural familiarity in new settlements, it could also insulate communities and isolate individuals. German Lutherans, especially Missouri Synod Lutherans, considered themselves the only group to understand and practice Christianity properly. Every other group, they thought, held an erroneous understanding of religion. So, German Lutherans typically had little to do with members of other denominations and, as you might guess, outsiders wanted little to do with German Lutherans. This isolated entire communities.

Religion could isolate individuals, too. A German-born Protestant farmer who settled in a German Catholic community in Cuming County, Nebraska, in 1867, found himself socially shunned when his Catholic neighbors discovered his religious identity. His Catholic neighbors even refused to sell him the grain he needed to begin farming. A group of Catholic families from Germany found the tables turned in 1883 when they settled in among German Protestants in Sutton, Nebraska. The new arrivals found Sutton so unwelcoming that they moved again, this time to a community dominated by Catholics.

For American Protestants, the West presented both problems and opportunities. Josiah Strong, an influential Congregationalist minister, expressed Protestant concerns in *Our Country: Its Possible Future and Its Present Crisis*, a widely read book published in 1885. He argued that in its first century the United States had achieved prosperity and developed a "pure spiritual Christianity."[5] But, he warned, the nation

---

[5] Edwin Gaustad and Leigh Schmidt, *The Religious History of America: The Heart of the American Story from Colonial Times to Today*, Revised Edition (New York: HarperCollins, 2002), 225.

faced a "present crisis" in the forms of a rising tide of worldliness (people focusing on material things rather than on spiritual matters) and self-indulgence and the rising influence of non-Protestants. Changing immigration patterns brought more Catholics and Jews from southern and eastern Europe to the United States, and people like Strong worried about how that might affect American culture and society. He worried about Roman Catholic immigrants moving to the West. He feared Catholic immigrants populating the West with communities loyal to their church and the Pope rather than to the United States. He worried about the steady influx of European Mormons, who owed their primary allegiance to their church rather than to the United States. Strong feared that the United States was being "foreignized" and that the unformed West was a critical battleground.

Pioneering American churches moved into the West with fears like Strong's in mind, but also with increasing enthusiasm. Protestant missionaries had been fighting to convert and "Americanize" the West for decades. That work continued, of course; but, representatives of many Protestant denominations also worked with determination to attract members from the settler population and to stake a claim in new communities they hoped to serve. These church folk found valuable allies in railroad corporations and civic booster organizations, which gave away building lots for church construction to virtually any denomination that asked. Railroad executives and town boosters saw church buildings as symbols of stability and order, which they hoped would attract more settlers thereby improving their businesses. In addition to churches, pioneer church folk with denominational support built a significant part of the western urban infrastructure. For example, they often led the way in providing hospitals, orphanages, old-age homes, and schools, both public and parochial, and colleges, both denominational and secular state colleges and universities. In other words, religious groups tended to the social needs as well as the spiritual needs of pioneer communities. Their work, with Indians and with settlers, continued through the close of the nineteenth century and took them to new frontiers such as Alaska.

In Alaska two New Yorkers demonstrated the tight relationship between churches and the expansion of the US nation. Sheldon Jackson, a short, near-sighted graduate of Princeton Theological

Seminary and an ordained Presbyterian minister, brought ambition, energy, and administrative genius to the mission field. After working among the Choctaws in Oklahoma, Jackson in 1870 became supervisor of Presbyterian missions in the Rocky Mountain District, which included Montana, Wyoming, Utah, Colorado, New Mexico, and Arizona. In 1877, he accompanied a group to Alaska to establish the Fort Wrangell Presbyterian mission and school for Alaska natives. What Jackson saw convinced him that Alaska had a dire need for missionaries and he became a tireless advocate. Several denominations shared mission work in Alaska with territories set by an informal arrangement. Jackson worked to obtain federal funding for the schools and in 1885 the US secretary of the interior appointed him general agent for education in Alaska. That arrangement reflected the cozy relationship between church and state that existed during much of the late 1800s, especially in US Indian policy. Jackson's close friendship with politicians such as Senator Benjamin Harrison (later president), who served on the Committee on Territories, and his ability to stir public opinion made him Alaska's most powerful and effective lobbyist in the nineteenth century. Jackson supported Alaska's legal organization as a territory and a number of laws beneficial to its development.

Jackson also played an important role in the "Presbyterian hierarchy," a group of prominent churchmen with great influence in Alaska. In addition to their work with Alaska's natives, Jackson and the Presbyterian hierarchy advocated moral reform, namely sobriety and chastity. These reforms alienated a large segment of the territory's population, predominantly single young men lured to Alaska by a gold rush and who often held decidedly different views about drinking and prostitution. The "Presbyterian hierarchy" and Jackson's roles as both a churchman and a civil official point to religion's influence on US expansion.

Another New Yorker, John Green Brady, dedicated his life to reforming society and spreading Presbyterian Christianity in Alaska. Brady spent part of his childhood as an orphan on the streets of New York City. The Children's Aid Society shipped young Brady to rural Indiana, where he was adopted by a judge who boosted the young orphan's prospects. Brady earned a bachelor's degree from Yale University in 1874 and prepared for the ministry at Union Theological Seminary in New York. His background led him to work with street missions in New York City and to try to start a school for disadvantaged boys in Texas. After the Texas plan failed, Brady accepted an invitation to work for the Presbyterian Board of Home Missions as a teacher in Alaska.

Brady arrived in Sitka, Alaska, in 1878 to teach Christianity to local natives. He wanted to develop an industrial school (a school where students learn a trade, craft, or skill and also known as a vocational school), too, but when the mission rejected that plan he abandoned it to pursue business opportunities in Sitka. Brady and Sheldon Jackson, who had hired him for the mission, remained friends. Brady prospered in business. He hired native graduates of the Presbyterian school to work in his lumber mill and store with the intention of giving them additional training that would prepare them to prosper in "Americanized" Alaska. President Chester Arthur appointed Brady a commissioner of the US land office in the mid-1880s. Brady served as governor of the District of Alaska beginning in 1897. As governor, Brady worked to protect native rights in ways he hoped would speed their assimilation into American society. His native rights advocacy, attempts to regulate alcohol sales and settlement, and his friendship with Sheldon Jackson caused Brady to be lumped with Alaska's "Presbyterian hierarchy," which brought political enemies. By 1906, Alaskans favoring more wide-open development and enemies of the Presbyterian ring began organizing a recall effort. Facing that and controversy related to a conflict of interest with a mining company Brady invested in, the governor resigned in 1906.

In Alaska, as had happened in frontier settlements in the contiguous United States, Protestant churchmen traveled in the vanguard of US occupation. These figures sought to spread their religion among other settlers and among non-Christians, including American Indians. They considered Protestant Christianity a civilizing and uplifting force that would improve the lives, and afterlives, of individuals, and a force that operated inseparably from the expansion of the US political and economic system. Indeed, their efforts helped establish an American presence on distant frontiers such as Alaska, helping ensure that the new territory remained American. These Alaska stories also echo themes of manifest destiny and Greater Reconstruction. As the United States assumed control of new territory, it sought to impose a familiar social and religious order.

Catholicism in the West

Catholics experienced these decades of western history differently. They lived outside the mainstream of American religious experience. Many American Protestants viewed Catholics as unAmerican and, in fact, as a threat to American values. For example, the Catholic Church's hierarchical organization and loyalty to the Pope led outsiders to suspect Catholics' primary loyalties tied them to Rome and the Vatican rather than to Washington, DC, and the American nation. Would Catholics be good citizens of the United States and vote according to their consciences, or would they cast ballots as directed by the Pope? Would they think for themselves or blindly follow orders from their church leaders? Catholics also faced a challenge in the form of ethnic diversity among Catholics in the United States, particularly among Catholics west of the Mississippi. Facing these challenges, Catholics continued a centuries-old religious conquest of the West that often competed with that of mainstream American Protestants.

Catholic conquest was especially complicated in the Southwest where the religion had been in place for centuries. In fact, it might make more sense to consider Catholic activity there a *reconquest* fraught with racial and ethnic conflicts. Catholicism had been brought to the region by Spain in a time of national rivalry with France and those nations practiced slightly different versions of Catholicism. The Spanish-based Catholicism that developed in the Southwest reflected American Indian and folk influences. Mexico's independence from Spain influenced church administration and brought republican ideals (favoring overthrow of monarchy and giving people more say in their government) of revolutionary Mexico into the church. When the US–Mexican War transformed approximately half of Mexico into the American Southwest, the shift had profound consequences for Catholicism in the region.

Despite suspicion of Catholics held by people such as Josiah Strong, Catholics such as Padre Antonio Martínez of Taos supported republican ideals – republican Mexico before US conquest, and the republican United States after. He preached on July 4, 1860, celebrating American independence, and praising the US constitution for its protection of fundamental liberties, including freedom of religion. He told his audience that freedoms of thought, speech, writing, and communication were critical to a population being able to adopt a religion of its choice. He praised the spirit of religious toleration that flowed from the US Constitution and urged his audience to celebrate the divinely inspired government that protected their liberties and made it possible for them to pursue happiness. As directed to a largely Hispanic audience in Taos in 1860, Martínez' sermon could be interpreted in many ways. At face value, though, it can be seen as a religious figure supporting US expansion by extolling the virtues of the regime that had recently taken control of the Southwest.

But control of the Southwest involved more than just politics; it also involved an expanding Catholic Church bureaucracy rife with ethnic conflict. After the United States took control of the territory known as the Mexican Cession, the Catholic Church added eight new dioceses (a diocese is an administrative territory supervised by a bishop and divided into smaller units called parishes) in the West in 50 years. The bishops named to lead these dioceses in Texas, New Mexico, Arizona, Colorado, and California, all of which had large Hispanic populations were French (six bishops), Irish, and Spanish. All but one of these bishops had been born in Europe and they sought to replicate churches they knew there. The European newcomers took control of a territory that had developed unique regional practices and in which a native clergy had begun to develop. The new bishops worked to erase regional practices and replaced native Hispanic priests with non-Hispanics. These actions created divisions within the church and between the largely Hispanic church membership and the increasingly non-Hispanic church leadership that would take generations to heal.

Bishop Jean Baptiste Lamy, the French bishop of New Mexico introduced in Chapter 3, continued to build Catholic infrastructure in the West after 1860 in ways that demonstrated ethnic divisions within the church and its strong ties to Europe. Lamy directed Catholic expansion in Arizona and Colorado. He successfully attracted missionaries to the Southwest, including a group of nuns from the Sisters of Charity in Cincinnati in 1865 and Jesuits from Naples, Italy, in 1867. In 1860, he dispatched Joseph Machebeuf, a fellow Frenchman and trusted lieutenant, to Denver to serve Catholics in Colorado, which was then mostly a mining district.

Machebeuf not only served Colorado's Catholics but also contributed significantly to the territory's settlement and economic and social development. Displaying business acumen, he bought cheap land on which to build churches and to farm. In so doing, he established churches and showed that Colorado, thought by many to be suitable only for mining, had agricultural potential. He oversaw construction of churches in Central City, Golden, and Trinidad by 1865 and in a number of smaller communities. He also helped Catholic religious orders build hospitals and schools in Central City, Pueblo, and Denver. In 1888, a year before he died, Machebeuf helped establish the College of the Sacred Heart (later Peter Regis College) in Denver, the first Catholic college for men in Colorado.

Machebeuf's efforts served Catholics and non-Catholics and made Colorado an increasingly desirable destination, but they also inflamed religious competitors. A Protestant clergyman in Colorado complained in 1865 about Catholic schools in Denver, which he saw as part of a "Romish" conspiracy to control the region. Roman Catholics, he contended, aimed to establish the best schools in newly settled areas, which would compel even Protestants to enroll their children. It should be noted that the clergyman was trying to shock his own denomination into sending money to support a competing school in Denver. Still, his words reflect the reality of denominations competing for supremacy in the burgeoning West. And, it should be noted, religious agendas cut many ways. The first Catholic priest in Utah wrote in 1876 that Ogden, where Catholic children attended either Mormon or Protestant schools, badly needed a Catholic school. Without one, he warned, those children would certainly be lost to Catholicism. Machebeuf's achievements and the reaction they inspired point to the importance of religious figures and institutions developing infrastructure in the West, and they reveal how interdenominational competition inspired institution building.

In this period, Hispanics in the Southwest from Texas to California saw their influence in the Catholic Church diminish. In Texas, immigration from Europe placed Hispanics in the minority during the nineteenth century and church leaders looked to Europe to staff the ranks of clergy and the religious. California had some influential Spanish bishops during the nineteenth century, but by the century's end all its bishops came from Ireland. By the end of the century most Hispanic priests in the Southwest had either been removed or had died and, in either case, replaced by priests from northern Europe, and Hispanics had virtually no institutional voice in the Catholic Church in the West.

In areas of the West where non-Indians moved in to build new settlements, lay Catholics often preceded priests and responded eagerly to the presence or prospect of having one in their community. In June 1860, Father Emmanuel Hartig, visited a new community near Atchison, Kansas. The town had built a church and a new house for a priest, despite not having one. The buildings reflected optimism for the community's future prosperity and showed the importance the residents placed on adding religious life to their world. Father Hartig wrote that the people did not want him to leave. He also reported three more nearby congregations that had gathered building materials for churches yet lacked priests to operate them. When a priest finally arrived to serve the three towns, he had to cover an area 100 miles in circumference that included parts of three counties. Although he was stretched thin, the priest provided much welcomed services to his followers and contributed to building the social order of the frontier communities. The presence of a church building brought a sense of permanence to a community. When a priest led familiar services in that church building, the West seemed, perhaps, less remote and felt more civilized.

Five years later, residents of the Virginia City mining boom town in Montana Territory showed their hunger for the cherished traditions of Christmas worship. When a priest arrived in town a few days before Christmas, he found neither a church nor a home awaiting him. He struggled to find a place to conduct a Christmas service until word of his search fell on receptive ears of young, rough-hewn bachelor miners. They commandeered the theater, the largest venue in town, and converted it into a makeshift church. The quick, dramatic remodeling and the tender, spirit-filled Christmas service it housed left the visiting priest overwhelmed with emotion and showed the importance these miners attached to religion and the familiar hominess and comfort it could convey.

Sustaining these missionary efforts required money and labor, and in the late 1880s the Catholic cause received a windfall in both thanks to Katharine Drexel, heiress to a Philadelphia banking fortune. Drexel and her two sisters grew up in a devoutly Catholic household and one dedicated to public service. When the Drexel sisters' parents both died by 1885, the girls inherited an estate estimated to be worth at least US$14 million. In early twenty-first century numbers, that would be at least $250 million. The inheritance generated for each daughter an annual income of more than $350 000. The sisters donated money for a mission building named in honor of their father at the Rosebud Reservation in South Dakota. Their success at Rosebud inspired them to expand their efforts to educate American Indians and to develop a robust Catholic spiritual life on reservations throughout the West.

Katharine Drexel wanted to do more than donate money. By the spring of 1889, she decided she would become a nun and dedicate her personal life to advancing her spiritual goals. That year she began preparations to join the Sisters of Mercy. The Mercy sisters designed an exceptional novitiate, or training regimen, for their wealthy new member. She followed a different prayer and work regimen than did her fellows and she got fresh fruit with her breakfast, a luxury not enjoyed by others. More important, Drexel retained control of her money, eschewing a vow of poverty made by nuns in virtually every other order, which she continued to spend on her Indian projects. In order to ensure she could continue devoting her labor and money to her pet projects, which also included works to benefit African Americans struggling to find footing in American society after the abolition of slavery, she considered founding a new religious order while she was in training. Katharine Drexel shows the importance of eastern capital (investment money) in sustaining the spiritual and social development of the West, and how the West's unique population and spiritual needs inspired one influential woman to dedicate her fortune and her life to remaking western religion.

From 1860 through 1890 Catholics continued to build their religious infrastructure in the West both to serve existing Catholics and to make new ones by converting non-believers. In settled areas, the church continued to serve an existing population. From those centers, leaders dispatched clergy and missionaries to serve newly arrived settlers and to help them build Catholic communities. The geographic remoteness of some settlements and the desire to reach American Indian populations prompted innovative approaches. The nature of Catholic work in the West in this era continued to echo the competition with Protestantism that characterized earlier periods, but the dominance of the United States, the nation's republican ideology, and the affiliation of the nation's leadership with Protestantism complicated the story.

Judaism in the West

The West's Jewish history has often disappeared into the shadows even though Jews played important roles in establishing western communities, especially cities on the West Coast. From 1860 through 1890 western Jewish communities grew more populous and influential, and operated more or less in orbit around San Francisco, the most important city for western Jews in the late nineteenth century. By 1870, San Francisco had the United States' second largest Jewish community and served as the hub for a distinctive western Jewish community that pushed the relationship between Jews and America in new directions.

Thanks to explosive and diverse growth resulting from the gold rush, San Francisco developed in ways beneficial to its Jewish settlers. To observers in the 1850s, San Francisco seemed more diverse than any place on earth. No dominant culture emerged, and mobility and exposure to different societies made San Francisco and gold rush country singular. By 1864, San Francisco had four Jewish congregations. When Rabbi Max Lilienthal's train pulled into Sacramento, California, on a Sunday in 1876, he noted, "No traces of a Puritan-Sunday; people and land are cosmopolitan in the Far West."[6] Lilienthal spent much of his life advocating Reform Judaism, a democratic form of Judaism that conducted services in English, allowed choral singing, and gave women a more prominent place than did Orthodox Judaism. He enjoyed friendly relations with Christian clergymen in Cincinnati where he spent the last decades of his life and fought to exclude religious teaching from public education. His comment about Sacramento suggests he saw a strong Protestant (Puritans practiced an intense brand of Protestantism with Sundays reserved for spiritual pursuits and, by the late 1800s, evangelical Protestants supported that cause as well as a strict code of morality) influence in other parts of the country. Lilienthal apparently found Sacramento refreshingly free of restrictive Protestant influence and a pleasantly diverse and open place. In the absence of a Protestant hegemony, Jews and other groups outside the mainstream enjoyed cultural

---

[6] Quoted in Ellen Eisenberg, Ava F. Kahn, and William Toll, *Jews of the Pacific Coast: Reinventing Community on America's Edge* (Seattle, WA: University of Washington Press, 2009), 19.

acceptance and could achieve middle class status. By the 1870s, San Francisco not only had the nation's second largest Jewish population, but also had a society in which Jews counted as 7–8 percent of the city's inhabitants, a sizeable minority.

Rabbi Jacob Voorsanger, who joined San Francisco's Temple Emanu-El in 1886 and became its senior rabbi in 1889, became one of the leading Jewish figures on the West Coast. Voorsanger came to the United States from Holland and held his first rabbinical post in Houston in 1878. Voorsanger rejected many tenets of Orthodox Judaism and worked to remake Judaism into a modern, enlightened religion. As if foreshadowing San Francisco radicalism to come, Voorsanger pursued radical reform within Judaism. He conducted most of his services in English. He prayed bareheaded and without wearing a traditional prayer shawl. He performed marriages between Jews and gentiles (non-Jews). With his brother, Voorsanger cofounded in 1895 *Emanu-El*, a 20-page weekly that contained fiction, philosophy, and international news of Jewish interest that made the publication one of the most influential Jewish publications on the West Coast. Voorsanger also extended Temple Emanu-El's community outreach by founding organizations to assist Eastern European Jews settling in the West and by organizing a boarding home for San Francisco's Jewish working girls.

Not all Jews ended up in western cities; some came to the West for the opportunity afforded by cheap land and open space and settled in rural agricultural communities. Members of Russia's Am Olam movement, for example, fled pogroms in their native Russia for opportunity in the United States. More than 60 Am Olamites arrived in New York City in 1882. Scouts for the group recommended Oregon as an ideal settlement site and they received encouragement from railroad magnate Henry Villard, who was then building the Oregon and California Railroad and wanted people to settle along its route to generate revenue. In this sense, the Am Olamites followed in the steps of immigrant settlers who followed railroad promotions into the West. The Am Olamites founded the New Odessa community in Oregon in 1882. The constitution the group adopted in 1883 prohibited members from working outside the colony and limited members' economic activity to selling colony products. It also called for equal rights for men and women. Very few women joined the colony, which created tension among the many young men. Furthermore, the colonists, many of whom had grown up in cities, had trouble adapting to the rural, agricultural lifestyle. These and other problems plagued the colony, which met its demise in a bankruptcy foreclosure in 1888.

Vast spaces and isolation challenged other western Jewish communities, too, and opportunity tempted Jews (and members of other denominations) to lose sight of their traditions. Men formed burial societies, volunteer organizations who prepare the deceased for proper Jewish burial, as a way to maintain religious obligations in pioneer communities. Those societies often developed into synagogues. Still, spiritual leaders in the East worried about Jews who settled in smaller cities or in remote areas. Rabbi Isaac Leeser traveled around the West and tried to help Jews remain obedient to the Torah and to retain their traditions. Leeser saw wide-open western society as a threat to maintaining Jewish faith communities, not unlike the Presbyterian hierarchy. He worried especially about California and its booming economy, which tempted people to focus on making as much money as quickly as possible and to disregard or overlook their religious obligations and community. That threat to Jewish stability motivated Leeser in his work and led him to dream of a West that would one day hold many synagogues anchoring stable, observant Jewish communities. Leeser and other Jewish leaders shared this concern with Protestants and Catholics as discussed earlier. By the end of the century, Leeser's dream had come true not only in San Francisco, but in places such as Denver, which boasted the national Jewish Hospital for tubercular patients. Denver's hospital shows how people of faith helped build western infrastructure and also shows how expansion into the West allowed Jews to tap the region's distinctive climate and elevation for health benefits. Poor Jews suffering from tuberculosis in eastern cities came to Denver for treatment joining the stream of migrants who went west for their health. Around the West, but particularly on the West Coast, pioneer Jews contributed to building cities and establishing the social order and governance of areas being brought into the United States.

In the general outline of their goals and acts, Protestants, Catholics, and Jews pursued similar ends in the West, even if it meant competing with each other from time to time. Jewish leaders wished to provide religious infrastructure and social services for Jews who moved to the West. San Francisco served as a hub for the West Coast Jewish community. Jews did not engage in missionary work to convert members of other faiths. But the West harbored other religious groups.

If Protestants thought of themselves as genuine Americans and Jews and Catholics as outsiders, then Mormons and Indians presented a different kind of competition, which, in both cases, led to dramatic and even violent confrontations that demonstrated the limits of religious tolerance in the United States.

Asian Religions in the West

Buddhism and other Asian religions developed in a limited fashion during the late 1800s in the American West. By 1875 San Francisco claimed eight Chinese Buddhist temples. By the end of the nineteenth century, one estimate counted more than 400 temples scattered across the West. Many of these small "shacks" and home temples have since disappeared. The people who worshipped in these temples combined elements of Confucianism, Taoism, and Buddhism typical of popular religion in China. This complicated mix of religions defies easy or exclusive categorization. Furthermore most Euro-Christian observers of the day, the people most likely to have left us information, would probably not have described what they saw among Chinese as "religion." More likely, they would have described Chinese religion as "superstition" or "occult science." The fact that no one kept reliable membership statistics for Chinese–American Buddhism also complicates the task. We can say that Buddhism played a significant role in the religious lives of thousands of Chinese in America in the nineteenth century. The Chinese Exclusion Act of 1882 dramatically reduced Chinese immigration and with it the flow of Chinese Buddhists.

The Mormon Question and the Mormon Answer, 1862–1890

The most profound religious issues to emerge in the West from 1860 to 1890 involved Mormons and American Indians. Broadly speaking, the issues involved conflicts between those groups and the Protestant-dominated US mainstream, and support the assertion that the nineteenth-century frontier was fundamentally Protestant. Relations between the United States and its Mormon and American Indian populations in the late nineteenth century highlight the limits of religious freedom in the United States. Ironically, these events unfolded in the West, a region mythically associated with freedom and opportunity. These events show the dynamic and innovative nature of religious belief and practice, and reinforce the argument that the West inspired change and creativity and that religion influenced US policy in developing the West.

In the wake of the Mountain Meadows Massacre, the United States had dispatched soldiers to install non-Mormon territorial officials and to restore US authority in a territory perceived to be in rebellion. An occupying force remained in Utah at Camp Floyd. The outbreak of the Civil War prompted the United States to withdraw troops from Camp Floyd and saw the resumption of Republican anti-polygamy measures. Senator Justin Morrill, who had proposed antibigamy legislation in 1856, led the charge again in 1862 (Figure 4.2). This time,

Figure 4.2   Hon. J[ustin] S. Morrill, circa 1855–1865. Source: Courtesy of the Library of Congress Prints and Photographs Division, (LC-DIG-cwpbh-01802).

with the White House and Congress in the hands of the Republican Party, he succeeded and the Morrill Antibigamy Act became the law of the land. This act accompanied a barrage of legislation aimed at imposing a Republican vision on the American West. Better-known legislation from 1862 includes another Morrill Act, which paved the way for land grant colleges, the Homestead Act, and the Pacific Railroad Act. The "other" Morrill Act banned polygamy in the territories and divested the Latter-day Saints Church of all assets in excess of $50 000. The Civil War and the remoteness of the territories made enforcement difficult and, in fact, non-existent for decades. Some questioned whether it violated First Amendment religious protections. Still, it stood as the first of three laws passed to kill Mormon polygamy. These actions sat squarely at the heart of Greater Reconstruction, policies aimed at defining geographic, political, social, and cultural boundaries to make the West and its people, down to their religion, American.

Meanwhile, the Mormon leadership pursued policies designed to build a unique and strong faith community. In addition to strictly spiritual matters, Brigham Young, the president of the church, sought to strengthen the social and economic fibers of the Mormon community. Young wished to keep Mormon economic affairs independent from those of the United States. This goal followed policy pioneered by Joseph Smith and made for a distinctive social and economic settlement in Utah. As in many things, concern for the Church's survival drove Young's actions. He believed, or at least stated, that while American armies could never conquer Utah, American merchants could by making Mormons dependent on manufactured goods. So, the Mormons experimented with economic ventures that ranged from the radical to the conventional with all aimed at ensuring the survival of the uniquely religious Mormon community.

At the radical end of the spectrum, the Church organized home-grown industries and cooperative enterprises. Mormons in the West tried to supply their own needs by producing sugar beet, iron, and textiles. The Brigham City cooperative issued stock to 400 individuals, virtually the entire community, who pooled their resources and tried to cut or reduce ties to the outside world. The experiment worked well enough to breed a system of other cooperatives. The Church established the United Order of Enoch in 1873 at St. George. This system of Mormon cooperatives functioned in a variety of ways. Some took a form as simple as a cooperative joint stock company. Others, like the Orderville community, which functioned from 1875–1885, held all property in common. Generally members pooled their resources, including land, labor, and property, and were governed by elected leaders. They pledged not to import goods and to do business only with other members of the Order. At its high point, the system boasted as many as 150 communities. This system conflicted with mainstream US ideals of private property and individualism, but it served the Mormons well.

Young also spearheaded more conventional Church-centered enterprises in railroads, banking, and merchandising conditioned by the desire to attain economic self-sufficiency and to promote economic development in Mormon areas. Mormon laborers helped build portions of both the Union Pacific and Central Pacific transcontinental railroads. Under Young's leadership the Church also built railroads (Utah Central, Utah Southern, and Utah Northern) to connect outlying settlements with Salt Lake City. The church-sponsored cooperative Bank of Deseret, later Deseret National Bank, began operations in 1871 and was the first Mormon bank in the Great Basin, where it was the leading bank well into the twentieth century. Zion's Savings Bank & Trust Company, established in 1873 under Brigham Young's direction, took over the savings department of Deseret National. Church officials dominated the officers and directors of both organizations and the Church owned about half the stock in each. Decades of conflict with non-Mormons and the desire to develop a strong community that would not be dependent on – and thus beholden to – outsiders contributed to the Church's economic policy.

In merchandising, Young sought to maintain Mormon independence and to counter what he perceived as price gouging by Mormon and non-Mormon merchants alike by proposing the people become their own merchants. Young's proposal spurred the creation in 1868 of Zion's Cooperative Mercantile Institution (ZCMI), directed by Brigham Young and the Quorum of the Twelve Apostles, the Church president's top advisory council. Claimed by some to be the nation's first department store, ZCMI acted as a wholesaler, with retail outlets in Salt Lake City and other Mormon settlements. It would undercut prices charged by non-Mormon merchants. Leaders let it be known that Mormon merchants should merge with the co-op and trading with the firm became a religious obligation intended to preserve social and economic unity. Mormon merchants would earn lower profits, but would keep wealth within the community. Storefronts displayed signs showing the Lord's "All-Seeing Eye" and the phrase "Holiness to the Lord: Zion's Cooperative Mercantile Institution." These efforts show the development of a religiously guided economy and society in the Mormon West and one that outsiders might consider at odds with mainstream US values. One can find some similarities between Mormon community development and that in non-Mormon areas, but the Mormon Church played a larger, more pervasive role. Also, in the late 1800s, Mormon development can be seen as an effort to build Zion, a religious community within but apart from the United States.

Economic issues contributed to "the Mormon Question," but plural marriage drove the debate, which intensified in the late 1870s. Approximately 200 non-Mormon women anti-polygamists met in Salt Lake City on November 7, 1878, and issued an appeal to "the Christian women of the United States" to petition Congress to act. They counted Mrs Rutherford B. Hayes, the first lady, as a supporter and they sent a circular letter to clergy nationwide requesting they read the Salt Lake resolution from their pulpit and send petitions to Congress. A week later, about 2000 Mormon women gathered in a Salt Lake City theater in a counter demonstration. The Mormon women passed resolutions supporting polygamy as a religious practice and claiming First Amendment protection. John M. Coyner, an anti-Mormon journalist working in Salt Lake City at the time, attended both meetings and wrote that he saw "an irrepressible conflict between the Mormon power and the principles upon which our free institutions are established." Coyner predicted that if the United States did not "stop the development of this law-breaking, law-defying fanaticism [Mormonism]," either free institutions would erode, or, "as with slavery, it must be wiped out in blood."[7] While women demonstrated in Utah, lawyers in Washington, DC, argued in the nation's highest court about what might be done.

The US Supreme Court addressed those questions in its 1879 ruling in *Reynolds* v. *United States*. Mormons decided to test the constitutionality of the Morrill Antibigamy Act and settled on George

[7] Coyner quoted in William Mulder and A. Russell Mortensen, eds, *Among the Mormons* (New York: Knopf, 1958), 407–408.

Reynolds, Brigham Young's polygamous secretary to enter the legal system. The Court ruled that religious practitioners could believe whatever they wished, but that when it came to practice, certain behaviors remained out of bounds. In this case, the Court found that plural marriage and the ills perceived to be associated with it so threatened the nation's social fabric that the behavior could be outlawed. Put another way, the government's compelling interest in protecting women, children, and the institutions of marriage and family outweighed the Mormons' right to practice a component of their religion. Of course, this implied a certain type of marriage and a particular family structure favored by the mainstream of US society. Mormons found the Constitution did not protect them as thoroughly as they had hoped and that even in the remote mountain West, America did not keep its promise of freedom and independence. The *Reynolds* decision paved the way for more aggressive restrictive legislation aimed at solving the Mormon Question permanently.

In 1882 Congress passed the Edmunds Act, which carefully adjusted the noose designed to strangle polygamy. Despite the *Reynolds* decision, enforcement of the Antibigamy Act had remained difficult. Senator George F. Edmunds (R-Vermont) aimed to ease enforcement and to create a tool more precise than the 1862 act for rooting out and destroying polygamy. The Edmunds Act made polygamy a felony, disfranchised polygamists, and barred them from jury duty and holding office. It created the Utah Commission to supervise territorial elections with instructions to certify only non-polygamous candidates. Finally, to discourage one technique some polygamists used to hide in the open, the act carefully defined unlawful cohabitation and made it a misdemeanor. Edmunds intended to put polygamists behind bars and to strip political power from those who could not be jailed. Some observers interpreted these acts as evidence that Congressional Republicans were establishing the same kind of control in Utah that they had exercised in the defeated South in the 1860s and 1870s. In other words, this amounted to federal reconstruction of the West, exactly the type of policy historian Elliott West had in mind when he coined the term Greater Reconstruction. In Utah, though, federal policy intended to remake society extended into shaping the practice of Mormonism.

Some people thought Congress had gone too far. For example, a sympathetic Senator Joseph E. Brown of Georgia decried the

Edmunds Act. Brown's state had recently experienced Congressional Reconstruction and he saw the Edmunds Act as a betrayal of the Constitution with respect to religious liberty. Popular vengeance aimed at the Mormons for the moment, he remarked in a speech in February 1882, but, he warned, might be aimed at another sect or denomination in the future. Brown also saw the act, as he did Radical Reconstruction, as a manifestation of New England's moral and social vision expressed in federal policy. Brown, in other words, expressed concern about the same lingering Puritan influence in American society that Rabbi Lilienthal named in his comment about Sacramento. Lilienthal saw Sacramento as a place free of that encumbrance, but Brown saw threats of its expansion.

Armed with the Edmunds Act, federal officials attacked polygamists with new zeal and tangible results during the mid-1880s. Arrests and convictions increased (Figure 4.3). The courts convicted four for unlawful cohabitation in 1884, 55 in 1885, 132 in 1886, and 220 in 1887. Given that most Mormons did not practice polygamy and those who did tended to be well-off and high-ranking officials, the polygamy prosecutions amounted to an attack on Mormon leadership. Some leaders fled to Hawaii, Canada, and Mexico. Some received convictions and served terms of six months or more in

Figure 4.3 Polygamists in prison. Source: Courtesy of the Library of Congress Prints and Photographs Division (LC-USZ62-80399).

the territorial prison. Still others remained in the West but went underground. Their number included President John Taylor, who died in 1887 while in hiding. To Mormons Taylor became a "double martyr" as he had been injured in the fatal assault on Joseph Smith in the Carthage jail and because they attributed his death to strain from what they perceived as the harassment of the Edmunds persecution. The Church presidency passed to Wilford Woodruff, who, like Taylor, administered the Church while in hiding. Woodruff would eventually steer his followers out of this conflict, but by 1887 outsiders, namely federal officials, saw evidence of continued Mormon resistance.

Congress tightened the noose further in 1887 by passing the Edmunds–Tucker Act. Edmunds–Tucker supplemented the Edmunds Act with a provision dissolving the Corporation of the Church of Jesus Christ of Latter-day Saints. The act called for Church assets in excess of $50 000 to be applied to financing non-Mormon schools in Utah Territory. The Church challenged these attacks, but found no help from the US Supreme Court, which upheld disfranchisement of *all* Mormons, not just those who believed in or practiced polygamy, and the dissolution of the Church corporation. Nearly 600 Mormons had been imprisoned or fined by 1889. Furthermore, during the summer of 1890 both houses of Congress had bills pending that would disfranchise all Mormons in federally administered territories, all of which were in the West.

Facing this situation, President Woodruff saw his church's very existence threatened and took drastic action credited with saving the Church but compromising its beliefs. On September 25, 1890, Woodruff issued a statement, known as the Manifesto, which acknowledged the attacks against the Church and the principle of plural marriage and announced his intention to comply with federal law. While the manifesto promised obedience to the law, it did not explicitly renounce plural marriage, which disturbed some outsiders. Some insiders also found the manifesto troubling and continued to practice plural marriage without the Church's institutional support.

Woodruff kept the Church alive and took a significant step in the Americanization of Mormonism and on the path to statehood for Utah. By joint resolution, Congress restored the Church's property by the mid-1890s. In 1894 Congress signaled an end to its anti-Mormon crusade by passing legislation enabling Utah to form a state government. In 1896 Utah achieved statehood under a constitution that prohibited plural marriage. The reconstruction of the Mormon West came to an end.

After being born on the frontier of New York and participating in migrations that took them to successive frontiers in Ohio, Missouri, and Illinois, Mormonism found a home in the mountain west frontier of Utah. Mormons' westward movement placed them simultaneously in and apart from the main currents of US nineteenth-century history. They found a home and a place isolated enough to allow them to develop in ways they could not have elsewhere in the nation. But they also found the arm of the federal government extended to Utah and that Reconstruction did, indeed, extend beyond the South.

American Indian Religious Experiences

Like Mormons, American Indians in the West experienced religious innovation and felt the hand of federal policy in their religious experiences during the era of Greater Reconstruction. Some Indian peoples continued to practice religion as they had for as long as they could remember. Some Indian peoples exposed to Christianity found it appealing and converted. Still others embraced both elements of traditional religion *and* Christianity.

The Dakota–US War in 1862 resulted in remarkable religious developments. The war began with desperate Dakota warriors attacking American settlements in southern Minnesota and killing hundreds of settlers. Four main factors led the Dakotas to go to war in August 1862. Three of these might be considered secular factors: white settlement and the reduction of the Dakota land base; late payment of goods promised by treaty that left the Dakotas starving; and the reduction of hunting and fishing grounds that left Dakotas dependent on treaty goods promised by the government. Pressure to adopt Christian ways and values, which eroded Dakota culture and religion, provided a fourth factor.

American troops defeated the Dakotas and took prisoner about 1700. Protestant and Catholic missionaries visited the incarcerated Dakotas, including dozens who had been condemned to die for war crimes. Many accepted Christian baptism. On the day after Christmas 1862, 38 men, to be hung in the largest mass execution in US history, ascended the scaffold singing. Some observers claimed the men were singing their "death songs," a ritual performed by some American Indians as they prepare to die. Others said they were singing hymns. The missionaries saw this mass conversion as an example of good resulting from evil.

The passage of time would provide more evidence to support such a conclusion. In addition to the condemned men, hundreds more Dakotas remained incarcerated in what could fairly be called concentration camps. Missionaries preached to them every Sunday, held nightly prayer meetings, and ran what amounted to a religious academy where men learned to become preachers and to play the piano and organ. They also taught many of the prisoners to read and write. The disastrous results of the conflict and the mass execution seem to have shaken the Santees' faith in their religion and led many to consider or reconsider Christianity. Hundreds professed faith in Jesus and received baptism. Some became Roman Catholic, but overwhelmingly they became Protestants. A number of them became Christian missionaries themselves and spent the rest of their lives working to convert other Indians.

Eventually the Dakotas relocated to reservations, including the Santee Agency in northeastern Nebraska, where Protestant missionaries established the Santee Normal Training-School. The school trained native teachers and became a center of Dakota-language teaching and publishing. The school published a bilingual newspaper (English and Dakota) called *Iapi Oaye* or *The Word Carrier*. The school's press also published Dakota-language Bibles, hymnals, and secular materials such as translations of *Aesop's Fables* and the life of Abraham Lincoln. Missionaries used those texts in their twin-pronged campaign to Christianize and "civilize" not only at the Santee Agency, but also elsewhere among the Sioux.

The use of the Dakota language for instruction at Santee points again to the complicated nature of missionary efforts. On one hand, the missionaries played a critical role in developing a written form of the language. Whether written or spoken, Dakota proved effective in both secular and religious education. On the other hand, US Indian policy, especially by the 1880s, pushed heavily for English-only education. The missionaries at Santee resisted this policy until 1887 when the commissioner of Indian Affairs wrote that instruction in native languages not only did not help Indians, but also hindered their education and the "civilization" process. The commissioner ordered the exclusive teaching of English at all schools on Indian reservations. At Santee, that meant suspension of theological classes, all of which had been taught in Dakota. Government agents also tried to eradicate native-language Christian worship. This shows yet again the close relationship between church and state that existed at the time and reflects the ethnocentrism and Christo-centrism of white America.

Meanwhile, among the Lakotas, also known as the Teton or Western Sioux, the story of Black Elk, an Oglala Lakota holy man, reminds us that traditional Indian religions continued to thrive in a rapidly changing world in which the United States, as a matter of policy, tried to eliminate Indian religions and replace them with Christianity (Figure 4.4). Born in 1863 in what is now Wyoming, Black Elk came

Figure 4.4   Black Elk and Elk in Dance Costume, 1880. Source: National Anthropological Archives, Smithsonian Institution NEG 72-7016.

of age in a Lakota world similar to the one described in Chapter 1. People interacted daily with the spiritual forces they believed actively influenced events. At age nine, Black Elk had a remarkable experience in which the Thunder-beings, embodiments of the powers of the West, visited him and imparted a vision that would lead him to become a powerful healer and spiritual guide for his people. Over time, he would interpret his vision as a mission to help not just his own people, but all humankind.

When he was 17, Black Elk sought help interpreting his vision by sharing it with experienced medicine men. The power and scope of Black Elk's vision astounded the elders. They advised him to perform a public ceremonial demonstration of his vision, which he did in the spring of 1881. This ceremony announced his spiritual calling to the Oglalas and opened the chapter of his life in which he became an important healer and spiritual leader of the reservation era. During the 1880s, Black Elk continued to seek visions according to Lakota custom. He also experienced a spiritual crisis. The hardships he saw on the reservation – the demise of the bison herds and his people's dependence on government rations, for instance – made him wonder if Lakotas ought to abandon their traditions and adopt the ways of whites. As he pondered this question, Black Elk joined Buffalo Bill's Wild West show, which he saw as an opportunity to earn money, to travel, and as a chance to learn more about whites and their customs.

Black Elk's showbusiness career included significant religious education. He underwent Christian baptism, probably in the Episcopal Church. All Indians in the show had to belong to the same religious faith so that Buffalo Bill could hire a representative of that faith to travel with the show to supervise the Indians' moral welfare. This contractual requirement reflects US Indian policy aimed at "civilizing" Indians, partly by religious means, as well as concern about allowing "savage" Indians to leave reservations, the crucibles of the government's civilization program. Black Elk used this opportunity to learn about Christianity, which he found impressive. His exploration was consistent with the Lakota (and shared by virtually all tribes) philosophy of exploring widely to understand the spiritual world. He also reported that while in Europe his own spiritual power disappeared, which might have strengthened his interest in Christianity. When Black Elk returned to Pine Ridge, his powers resumed. He resumed his role as a successful healer and traditional religious leader at Pine Ridge, roles he would continue into the twentieth century. This part of Black Elk's life emphasizes the importance of place in indigenous religion and also reveals dynamic and innovative facets of indigenous religion.

Elsewhere in Indian Country, people embraced new religious forms known as revitalization movements. Such movements often emerge in a time of great stress and involve an organized effort to create a more satisfying culture based on familiar practices and are usually led by one or more prophets or charismatic figures. The reservation era inspired Indian spiritual leaders to explore paths other than Black Elk's and to develop religious innovations that revealed the influence of Christianity and other European ideas and practices. At the same time, the movements represented a reaction against US expansion. Anglo-American responses to revitalization movements provide more examples of the close ties between religious and state (US) values. Three prominent American Indian revitalization movements attracted followers in the years 1860 to 1890.

The Dreamer movement of the Pacific Northwest appeared earliest. In late 1860, the *Olympia (WA) Pioneer and Democrat* reported a "mysterious prophet" stirring "religious fanaticism" among American Indians in the Columbia River Valley.[8] The prophet, a shaman of the Wanapam tribe named Smohalla ("Dreamer" or "Preacher" in English), had disappeared for a time and on reappearing claimed he was, in fact, returning from the dead. Smohalla also reported he had been given the basics of a new religion by divine power. As Smohalla spread his teachings he gained followers who became known as Dreamers – they received messages from the Creator through dreams and trances.

The Dreamers believed the earth sacred and that it had been perfect as humans first found it. Humans should live lightly and respectfully on the land. As Smohalla and his followers saw it, whites injured and offended the earth when they plowed it when farming or dug in it when mining. Instead, Smohalla urged his followers to practice traditional subsistence living off the earth's natural bounty. Picking berries or digging roots did no harm. Smohalla saw harm in virtually everything whites did and he blamed them for the decline of the region's indigenous population. And yet, like other

---

[8] Quotations in Elliott West, *The Last Indian War: The Nez Perce Story* (New York: Oxford, 2009), 81.

revitalization movements, his also revealed white influences. Services happened on Sundays and participants entered a hall with flags, recited tenets of their faith, and ate a ceremonial meal.

Smohalla offered hope through his religion. If his followers would reject the white lifestyle, maintain traditional lifestyles, and perform certain rituals, the Creator would bring back deceased family members and restore the game and abundance that had existed before whites appeared. The great tide of life would force out, or maybe destroy, whites and the problems they had brought with them. These characteristics of Dreamer belief made it a "millenarian movement," or one that emphasized an apocalyptic transformation guided by the supernatural.

Smohalla's vision inspired mixed responses. Some whites saw it as a threat. The *Olympia* newspaper feared the Dreamers were preparing for a race war. Some Indians subscribed to it; others did not. Some Nez Percés, for example, signed on to resist changes associated with white settlement and, almost certainly, for a variety of other reasons. For example, Christianity became more popular during the 1870s. Missionaries intensified their work. Also, as white settlement continued and it became clear the newcomers were there to stay and becoming more powerful, it made sense to many Nez Percés to tap white spiritual power, Christianity. The religious experiences of the Nez Percés in the 1860s and 1870s demonstrate the cultural complexities related to the westward expansion of the United States. Some Nez Percés, faced with the challenges posed by US expansion chose to embrace a revitalization movement that promised a return to the good old days and which had both strong ties to traditional religion and elements of imported religion (Christianity). Other Nez Percés chose to embrace Christianity wholeheartedly.

Another important Indian religion, peyotism, took shape during the late 1800s. Unlike the Dreamer religion, peyotism does not include an apocalyptic world transformation. Native American use of peyote, a hallucinogen derived from a spineless cactus, dates at least to the Aztecs. Indians used peyote as medicine and to facilitate visions by people seeking supernatural power. In the 1870s, Mescalero Apaches, Kiowas, and Comanches embraced peyotism. Western tribes such as the Caddos, Otoes, and Winnebagoes also embraced peyotism and blended traditional religious practices with elements of Christianity to create a religion that would be organized as the Native American

Church. In a key component of the religion, followers eat peyote, which they recognize as a sacrament, as part of a night-long ritual. The peyote helps induce a state that facilitates communion with God and native spirits. Christian missionaries and US government officials saw peyotism as a threat to their civilization agenda and tried to suppress the religion. Ironically, government boarding schools, which brought students of various tribes together to strip them of their Indian identity, served to spread peyotism, as did the expanding railroad system, which increased the mobility of people and ideas.

The best-known of the late-nineteenth-century American Indian revitalization movements, the Ghost Dance, emerged in Nevada in 1869 or 1870 and spread across the West in two waves during the last decades of the nineteenth century. Tävibo, a Northern Paiute from the area of Virginia City, Nevada, preached that whites would be swallowed up by the earth and that dead Indians would return to enjoy a better world. Tävibo said he communicated with the dead during trances. He also learned special songs and ceremonies, which he taught to his followers. The ceremonies and belief system came to be known as the Ghost Dance. The movement spread in Nevada and to Oregon and California. When Tävibo's prophecies failed to materialize, many followers abandoned the Ghost Dance. The movement would enjoy a stunning resurgence in 1889 and would play a central role in the tragic violence at Wounded Knee in 1890. To understand Wounded Knee, though, we need to know more about US Indian policy and how religion figured into the nation-state's plans for expansion and for solving "the Indian problem."

US officials aimed to reform or "reconstruct" American Indians into "civilized" people. This transformation would involve erasing indigenous people's "Indian-ness," including spiritual practices, and replacing them with hallmarks of civilization, including the practice of Christianity. An early and blatant example of this came when President Ulysses S. Grant adopted an Indian policy designed "to conquer by kindness."[9]

In the aftermath of the Civil War, the public and many elected officials had little desire to see more bloody conflict related to the nation's

[9] *Report of the Indian Peace Commissioners. Message From the President of the United States, Transmitting Report of the Indian Peace Commissioners, January 14, 1868,* H.Exec.Doc. 97, 40th Cong., 2nd sess., Serial Set 1337, 11: 4.

westward expansion. As the federal government turned its attention to the "Indian problem" in the late 1860s, it focused on the Great Plains. Two treaties, Medicine Lodge (1867) and Fort Laramie (1868), aimed to concentrate Plains tribes on two reservations. In theory, this would get Indians out of the way of US expansion and simultaneously expedite assimilation. The reservations would facilitate assimilation by making it easier for the government to provide education to Indian children, provide agricultural and trade education for Indian adults, and to provide support for Indian communities until they became self-sustaining under the new "civilized" regime. Washington politics interfered. Congress delayed ratification of the treaties and failed to appropriate money to support the assimilation campaign. President Grant responded with what became known as the "peace policy" or Quaker policy, named for the Society of Friends, or Quakers, a religious movement that advocated reform of US Indian policy. Quakers and members of Protestant denominations would dominate the policy.

Grant took an experimental step toward the peace policy by placing Quakers in charge of Indian agencies in Kansas, Nebraska, and Oklahoma. He and his advisers hoped these "Christian gentlemen" could "civilize" Indians by making them into cultural copies of white Americans. Grant and his advisers also hoped upstanding churchmen would perform better than their corrupt predecessors who got their jobs by political appointment. In 1870, when Congress made it illegal for members of the military to hold civil posts, Grant extended the experiment in faith-based administration of Indian affairs. The government assigned supervision of Indian agencies based on existing missionary work and the ability of churches to support the program. For example, the Methodists took control of 14 agencies where 54 500 Indians lived. The next four largest assignments went to Baptists (five agencies with 41 000 Indians), Presbyterians (nine agencies with 38 000 Indians), Episcopalians (eight agencies with 26 900 Indians), and Roman Catholics (seven agencies with 18 000 Indians). The denominations recommended an agent for each agency and, generally, the president followed their suggestions when making appointments.

Despite good if paternalistic intentions, the peace policy struggled and ultimately failed. Grant's reforms alienated politicians and appointees who lost positions. They made life difficult for administrators, and turnover plagued the Department of the Interior and the Indian Bureau. As if these problems were not enough, on several reservations "shared" by different churches, the Christians argued among themselves about who should have the right to establish missions. Furthermore, the denominations often lacked resources to support adequately the difficult and demanding conditions they faced on most reservations. President Grant lost interest in the reforms and without his attention Indian affairs again suffered administrative problems. In the West, religious leaders held authority on reservations, but relied on the military for enforcement. Military leaders resented having been removed from control of Indian affairs and criticized the religious appointees for their inexperience and naïveté. Indians had mixed reactions. Many distrusted the government and had no interest in living on reservations no matter who administered them. Others, including prominent opponents of US policy such as Sitting Bull, a Lakota, and Quanah Parker, a Comanche, recognized the need for Indians to adapt and sent their children to get a "white" education and help their people adapt to a rapidly changing world. Violent conflicts with Indians on the Great Plains led many settlers to clamor for protection. The Battle of the Little Bighorn in 1876 pushed public opinion to favor a tougher, more militant Indian policy. Insufficient allocations from Congress made it difficult for the religious agents to do their jobs and low pay tempted even some of the religious appointees into corruption. When Grant left office, the experiment in religious administration of Indian policy ended. Missionaries and religious reformers remained active on reservations, but not in the same capacity. The change in leadership, though, did not change most goals for Indian policy, which continued to reflect strong similarities in state and Christian interests and shows that understanding US Indian policy requires an appreciation of its religious undercurrents.

Even as the Peace Policy went into decline, the federal government and major church organizations cooperated to spread Christianity through education. Those in charge of Indian policy could not imagine Indians becoming "civilized" while maintaining pagan ways. To them, being Christian was a vital part of being American. Nearly every reservation had at least one mission school affiliated with a Christian denomination. Some had day schools, but administrators preferred boarding schools, where pupils would spend days, weeks, or months at a time away from the "corrupting" influences of their families and communities. Educators came to prefer off-reservation boarding schools, which could put hundreds or even thousands of miles between pupils and their families and therefore, their cultures. That would give educators even more power to remake Indian students.

Carlisle Indian School in Pennsylvania, founded in 1879, took this approach to the extreme. Indian students came to Carlisle from around the country for complete immersion in white society. The first students came from the Rosebud and Pine Ridge Sioux reservations in what is now South Dakota. After a long train ride, Carlisle students had their clothes replaced with European–American ones, had their hair cut, and were required to speak English only. The formal curriculum trained boys for farming or trades and girls to become housekeepers and wives. Lessons also included fundamentals of reading, writing, and arithmetic as well as religious instruction. As Richard Henry Pratt, Carlisle's founder, put it, "Kill the Indian in him, and save the man."[10] Carlisle and other schools like it aimed to destroy Indian ways of life in order to save individual Indians, who might adapt to modern life. Although located in Pennsylvania, Carlisle influenced the West because many students such as those from Rosebud and Pine Ridge returned home and took with them lessons learned in the East.

The United States also used the legal system to promote Christianity in Indian Country. In 1878, Congress approved money to hire nearly 500 Indian policemen on reservations. This innovation gave Indian agents an alternative to the US Army for maintaining order on the reservations. The legislation creating Indian police called for them to be used "for the purposes of civilization of the Indians" and Indian agents hired officers they could trust to oppose "heathenish" practices. Indian police could have only one wife, forsook face paint, cut their hair short, and wore European–American clothing. Among other things, they enforced school attendance and opposed the work of medicine men, which represented a continuation of

---

[10] *Official Report of the Nineteenth Annual Conference of Charities and Correction* (1892), 46–59. Reprinted in Richard H. Pratt, "The Advantages of Mingling Indians with Whites," *Americanizing the American Indians: Writings by the "Friends of the Indian" 1880–1900* (Cambridge, MA: Harvard University Press, 1973), 260–271.

traditional spirituality. When one Indian police officer summoned a medicine man to treat his sick children, the agent removed him from the force. Most Indian police officers came from tribal factions that favored, at least to some extent, accommodation and cooperation with the United States. Many converted to Christianity and acted to suppress ceremonies such as the Sun Dance and the Ghost Dance.

In 1883, the US government established courts of Indian offenses, staffed by Indian judges, which added another layer of cultural coercion and enforcement of Christian values on reservations. Indian judges represented "the civilized or Christian" segment of Indian society. They followed many of the same practices required of Indian police and were often Christians. For example, the three judges on the Cheyenne River Reservation's court of Indian offenses in 1890 were Roman Catholic and Episcopalian. The courts most often heard cases involving adultery, rape, polygamy, cohabitation, licentiousness, bastardy, and fornication. Indians might also find themselves in court for infidelity to marriage vows, illegal marriage, and participating in or encouraging religious ceremonies such as funeral rites and the Sun Dance. The courts hit their peak activity in the 1890s. Allotment and the assumption of more law enforcement duties by counties and states put most of the courts out of business in the first decade of the twentieth century. While the courts operated, they acted in tandem with Indian police and the federal government's bureaucratic machinery to discourage native spirituality in an attempt to coerce Indians to become "civilized" Christians.

Against this backdrop of oppression and in a world of breathtakingly rapid and dramatic change, the Ghost Dance movement enjoyed a resurgence beginning in 1889. Another Paiute, Wovoka (also known to non-Indians as Jack Wilson), reported that in the midst of a fever during a solar eclipse he had an encounter with the Supreme Being (Figure 4.5). Wovoka predicted that soon all Indians, living and dead, would be reunited on a regenerated earth to live a life of happiness and plenty free from death, disease, and poverty. The white race, and the evils it brought to the Indian world, would disappear forever, probably during an earthquake or some other natural disaster that would not harm Ghost Dancers. The Supreme Being gave Wovoka instructions for a ceremony to teach Indians and told Wovoka to encourage his people to work hard, be honest, and to love

Figure 4.5   Charcoal drawing of Wovoka. Source: National
Anthropological Archives, Smithsonian Institution NEG01659 B.

one another, even whites as long as they were around. Ghost Dance
teachings also encouraged followers to turn their backs on war and to
embrace peace. Wovoka taught his followers to perform a five-day
dance ceremony. If Indians did these things, which to outside
observers represented a syncretic blend of traditional indigenous
religious practices and Christianity, whites would disappear and
Indians would be reunited with the dead in a golden age, a key
element in many Native American religions.

Wovoka's Ghost Dance found little foothold among people who
had been disappointed by Tävibo's message, but spread across the
Rocky Mountains and onto the Great Plains. Segments of many
tribes embraced the Ghost Dance, but the best-known Ghost
Dancers were the Lakotas. Lakota leaders sent emissaries to Wovoka
to listen to his message, to learn the Ghost Dance, and to bring back
details of his vision. The return of these Lakota Ghost Dance

apostles in the spring of 1890 inspired excitement and experimentation with the ceremony for the rest of that year.

Indian agents and non-Indian neighbors feared the Ghost Dance, which they saw as fanaticism and labeled "the Messiah craze" because Wovoka was often referred to as the Indian Messiah. To non-Indians, it appeared Lakota Ghost Dancers were rejecting Christianity and civilization and embracing their savage past. Worse, they feared resistance leaders such as Sitting Bull planned to use the Ghost Dance to inspire an uprising.

As 1890 wore on, US government officials became increasingly concerned about the Ghost Dance and its influence among Lakotas. As the Ghost Dance spread east, it evolved. As new tribes encountered and embraced the ceremony, they sometimes added to it. The Lakotas wore "ghost shirts" during the ceremony. Lakota Ghost Dancers believed these ceremonial garments, usually made of white muslin, protected them from harm – even, perhaps, from being wounded by bullets. These developments added to the perception that the Lakota Ghost Dance had a militant character and might be part of a budding uprising. Something had to be done.

Meanwhile, at the Standing Rock reservation, which straddles the border of North and South Dakota, Sitting Bull, one of the most prominent leaders of Lakota resistance to US political and cultural expansion into Lakota country, expressed interest in the Ghost Dance. Sitting Bull, a great warrior in his youth and a *Wichasha Wakan*, or holy man, held great status among Lakotas. In early October 1890, Sitting Bull invited Kicking Bear, a Miniconjou Lakota and one of the Lakota Ghost Dance apostles, to visit Standing Rock and speak about the Ghost Dance. Kicking Bear delivered an electrifying sermon that promised a bright future for Indians – if they danced all winter, the Ghost Dance millennium would come in the spring of 1891.

Government officials deployed an array of tools to try to stop the Ghost Dance. Courts of Indian offenses punished people who encouraged the Ghost Dance. One agent threatened to withhold government rations from those who refused to stop performing the Ghost Dance ceremony. The agent at Standing Rock, James McLaughlin, sent Indian police to remove Kicking Bear, whom they escorted to the reservation's boundary. Another agent panicked and cabled a request for soldiers to suppress the dance. "Indians are dancing in the snow and are wild and crazy," read the agent's frantic cable. "We need protection now."[11] The government dispatched troops to South Dakota.

At Standing Rock, McLaughlin's efforts came too late. Sitting Bull's people had taken up the Ghost Dance. Ghost Dance converts abandoned their cabins and pitched tipis near Sitting Bull's home. Parents pulled their children from the new government school so they could "go to church," that is, to participate in Ghost Dance activities. To Agent McLaughlin and Christian missionaries of the day, these actions demonstrated the failure of civilization programs. By abandoning their frame houses for tipis, the Ghost Dancers stepped *backwards*. Likewise, removing their children from the government schools amounted to rejecting civilizing education for the next generation. Teaching the children Ghost Dance values moved them in exactly the opposite direction to that intended by agents and missionaries. Then there was the matter of Sitting Bull.

Sitting Bull's history of resistance and his association with both the Little Bighorn and the advent of the Ghost Dance put US officials on edge, even though no one was certain he truly believed in the Ghost Dance. On one hand, he never danced and he expressed some skepticism about the Ghost Dance. On the other hand, he promoted the Ghost Dance, encouraged his followers to participate, and, in his capacity as a *Wichasha Wakan*, interpreted the visions of Ghost Dancers. He also defied all efforts by government officials, school teachers, missionaries, and skeptical tribal members to convince him to reject the Ghost Dance and to halt the ceremonies at his home. What did this mean? Agent McLaughlin feared the worst.

In mid-December, McLaughlin ordered Indian police to arrest Sitting Bull. The arrest turned into a deadly shootout, which left Sitting Bull dead. This episode can be interpreted in a number of ways. One perspective reveals a US government agent enforcing law and order in his jurisdiction and implementing policy aimed at "civilizing" his charges. Another angle shows a *Wichasha Wakan*

[11] D. F. Royer to Commissioner of Indian Affairs, 15 Nov. 1890, Record Group 75, Office of Indian Affairs, Special Case 188 (The Ghost Dance, 1890–98), National Archives and Records.

confronting tribesmen who had embraced Christianity and joined the Indian police force to become agents of US policy, which included suppressing the Ghost Dance and reconstructing Indians.

Sitting Bull's death shocked the Ghost Dance community. A group of Ghost Dancers followed a leader named Big Foot (also known as Spotted Elk), in a flight toward the Pine Ridge reservation. Soldiers of the US 7th Cavalry intercepted them, which led to the tragic episode at Wounded Knee Creek described at the beginning of this chapter.

The holy man Black Elk avoided the Ghost Dance at first, but embraced it when he discovered similarities with his own spiritual vision. It inspired him to help his people maintain their traditional Lakota ways and gave his life a new sense of meaning. When he heard gunfire on December 29, he knew immediately what was happening and he rode to defend the Ghost Dancers. The death and destruction at Wounded Knee turned the Ghost Dance into a cruel disappointment for Black Elk. A missionary observed that the tragedy left many Lakotas numbly indifferent toward religion in general. Despite his disappointment, Black Elk continued his work as a healer and as a Lakota religious leader, but his spiritual journey was far from over.

Many factors complicate consideration of Wounded Knee, but it cannot be separated from the process of conquest and policy of civilization in which government officials and religious figures worked in partnership to strip Indians of their identities and turn them into Christianized Americans. The words of a Protestant missionary offer stark insight to how the dominant culture viewed Wounded Knee: "They were not permitted (or encouraged) to do the [Ghost Dance]. But they did not listen and, thus, they died."[12] Another urged consolation of Wounded Knee's widows and orphans, but warned survivors that they should heed Jesus' teachings and go to church, for otherwise their souls would be in peril. A missionary newspaper went so far as to find "a providential aspect" in the episode and to claim the tragedy was a "blessing" to the rebellious Lakotas.[13] These comments reveal the dark side of the relationship between religion and Greater Reconstruction.

---

[12] See "*Wowapi Maqupi* [Letter They Gave Me]," *Iapi Oaye* (Santee Agency, Nebraska), February 1891.

[13] Untitled article, *The Word Carrier* (Santee Agency, Nebraska), January 1891.

Conclusion

Church, state, and conquest came to a bloody confluence in December 1890 with the death of Sitting Bull and the tragedy at Wounded Knee Creek. These events can be seen as watershed moments in several ways. The US Census Bureau and historian Frederick Jackson Turner pointed to 1890 as the year the frontier closed. In the sense that Sitting Bull embodied Lakota resistance to the US expansion and dedication to Lakota spirituality and nationhood, his death marked the end of an era. The death of hundreds of Lakota Ghost Dancers at the hands of the US Army at Wounded Knee marked a low point in US–Indian relations and one of the most violent spasms of religious violence in US history. For a time, even the fuzzy line that separated church and state disappeared completely in Indian policy. Turner and others might argue that Wounded Knee marked not only an end to the frontier, but also marked a tragic achievement in Reconstruction. That the Church of Jesus Christ of Latter-day Saints abandoned plural marriage only months earlier in 1890 only reinforces those notions. One might argue that a frontier period of Mormon history had ended and that Mormon-dominated Utah had been reconstructed in such a way that it would be fit to join the union, which it would in 1896 with a state constitution that prohibited polygamy.

These dire episodes should not obscure broader themes evident in this chapter of the West's religious history. The tragic violence at Wounded Knee should not overshadow the innovative development of the Ghost Dance in all its incarnations, which inspired hope for the future among American Indians who practiced the ceremony. The crusade against Mormonism should not obscure the dynamic path Mormons followed to survive. As the nineteenth century drew to a close, Christianity had a larger footprint in the West thanks to efforts of Protestants and Catholics discussed in this chapter, but so did Judaism and other religions. Despite the best efforts of missionaries, the West's religious landscape, relative to other US regions, lacked a norm. Whatever watershed moments occurred in 1890, the West's religious history continued in glorious complexity.

Suggested Reading

Arrington, Leonard J. and Davis Bitton. 1992. *The Mormon Experience: A History of the Latter-day Saints*, 2nd edn. Urbana and Chicago, IL: University of Illinois Press.

Butler, Anne M. 2012. *Across God's Frontiers: Catholic Sisters in the American West, 1850–1920*. Chapel Hill, NC: University of North Carolina Press.

Butler, Anne M., Michael E. Engh, S.J., and Thomas W. Spalding, C.F.X., eds. 1999. *The Frontiers and Catholic Identities*. Maryknoll, NY: Orbis.

Canku, Clifford and Michael Simon. 2013. *The Dakota Prisoner of War Letters: Dakota Kaśkapi Okicize Wowapi*. St. Paul, MN: Minnesota Historical Society Press.

Coburn, Carol. 1992. *Life at Four Corners: Religion, Gender, and Education in a German-Lutheran Community, 1868–1945*. Lawrence: University Press of Kansas.

Emmons, David M. 2010. *Beyond the American Pale: The Irish in the West, 1845–1910*. Norman, OK: University of Oklahoma Press.

Gordon, Sarah Barringer. 2002. *The Mormon Question: Polygamy and Constitutional Conflict in Nineteenth Century America*. Chapel Hill, NC: University of North Carolina Press.

Kerstetter, Todd M. 2006. *God's Country, Uncle Sam's Land: Faith and Conflict in the American West*. Urbana and Chicago, IL: University of Illinois Press.

Luebke, Frederick C. 1969. *Immigrants and Politics: The Germans of Nebraska, 1880–1900*. Lincoln, NE: University of Nebraska Press.

Meyer, Roy W. 1967. *History of the Santee Sioux: United States Indian Policy on Trial*. Lincoln, NE: University of Nebraska Press.

Milner II, Clyde A. 1982. *With Good Intentions: Quaker Work among the Pawnees, Otos, and Omahas in the 1870s*. Lincoln, NE: University of Nebraska Press.

Richardson, Heather Cox. 2010. *Wounded Knee: Party Politics and the Road to an American Massacre*. New York: Basic.

Riggs, Thomas Lawrence as told to Margaret Kellogg Howard. 1997. *Sunset to Sunset: A Lifetime with My Brothers, the Dakotas*. Pierre, SD: South Dakota State Historical Society Press.

Sandoval, Moises. 2006. *On the Move: A History of the Hispanic Church in the United States*. Maryknoll, NY: Orbis.

Shipps, Jan. 1985. *Mormonism: The Story of a New Religious Tradition*. Urbana and Chicago, IL: University of Illinois Press.

Steltenkamp, Michael F. 2009. *Nicholas Black Elk: Medicine Man, Missionary, Mystic*. Norman, OK: University of Oklahoma Press.

Strong, Josiah. 1885. *Our Country: Its Possible Future and Its Present Crisis*. New York: American Home Missionary Society.

Utley, Robert M. 1993. *The Lance and the Shield: The Life and Times of Sitting Bull*. New York: Holt.

Wallace, Anthony F. C. 1956. "Revitalization Movements." *American Anthropologist* 58: 264–281.

5

Religion in the Modern West, 1890–1945

At Skillman Grove, a high-mountain pasture about 19 miles outside Fort Davis in west Texas, William B. Bloys offered a camp meeting for cowboys in 1890. Bloys, a US Army chaplain, had come west for his health and had helped to start Presbyterian churches in the west Texas communities of Alpine, Marfa, and Fort Davis. He had also performed religious services for area ranchers, one of whom suggested Bloys hold a camp meeting for cowboys. That 1890 event, popular enough to become an annual affair, grew into an interdenominational gathering known by 1900 as the Bloys Camp Meeting. Bloys presented Jesus as a role model for his cowboy audience. He told the cowboys that God was available to anyone who would have Him and that there was nothing weak or unmanly about declaring one's faith and living it. The Bloys Camp Meeting thrives after more than a century and inspired the construction of a tabernacle that seats about a thousand at the "Spiritual Hitchin' Post of West Texas." Locals say that no boy "raised up at Bloys ever landed in Jeff Davis County Jail."[1] Writers have called

[1] Quoted in Ferenc M. Szasz, *Religion in the Modern American West* (Tucson, AZ: University of Arizona Press, 2000), 45.

Inspiration and Innovation: Religion in the American West,
First Edition. Todd M. Kerstetter.
© 2015 John Wiley & Sons, Inc. Published 2015 by John Wiley & Sons, Inc.

it the greatest thing that ever happened to west Texas and a vital source of stability on the Texas frontier. Bloys' innovative cowboy ministry served as a model for similar camp meetings in other western cattle centers, including Valentine, Nebraska, Prescott, Arizona, Nogales Mesa, New Mexico, and Elko, Nevada.

When the Bloys meeting was in its 14th year, the Lakota holy man and healer Black Elk received a call to doctor a gravely ill young boy near Manderson, South Dakota, on the Pine Ridge Reservation. When we left Black Elk in the previous chapter, he had returned to Pine Ridge from his travels with Buffalo Bill's Wild West show and, after exploring Christianity, had resumed practicing traditional Lakota spirituality. He had been close enough to Wounded Knee to hear the gunfire and he witnessed the gory results. Many Lakotas abandoned the Ghost Dance after Wounded Knee, which some non-Indians used to symbolize the end of the frontier. Black Elk evidently turned his back on the Ghost Dance, which he had considered a source of hope, but continued observing Lakota religious practices that many US political and Christian religious leaders of the day would have considered a relic of frontier "savagery." When he received the call for help in 1904, Black Elk gathered his medicine and walked to the young boy's home. He found the boy lying in a tent and he immediately began his treatment. He sang healing songs and beat his drum as he appealed to spirits for their cooperation.

As Black Elk immersed himself in his work, a Catholic priest arrived and boldly interrupted. The priest gathered Black Elk's medicine and threw it into the stove. He grabbed Black Elk by the neck and as he roughly escorted him from the tent said, "Satan, get out!" The priest returned to the boy, whom he had baptized some time earlier, to give Communion and last rites.

When the priest emerged from the tent, he found Black Elk sitting outside, looking lonely and dejected, as if he had lost all his powers. The priest invited Black Elk to accompany him to Holy Rosary Mission and Black Elk accepted. He had been considering Catholicism for some time and had been advised by a Lakota friend to give up his traditional ceremonies and healing practices. Jesuit brothers at Holy Rosary welcomed Black Elk and gave him some clothes – underwear, shirt, suit, tie, shoes, and a hat. Black Elk stayed with them for two weeks and, on December 6, accepted the Catholic faith and underwent baptism. For the rest of his life – he lived until 1950 – Black Elk practiced Catholicism.

Black Elk's daughter told this story of his conversion to Catholicism to a biographer, who concedes that the details might not be completely accurate. What matters, he says, is the spiritual transformation Black Elk experienced and that we understand that Black Elk's spiritual life did not screech to a halt in the aftermath of the 1890 Wounded Knee tragedy. Black Elk went on, as did life in the West after the close of the frontier.

These anecdotes about Bloys and Black Elk suggest several things about the West in the decades following the purported close of the frontier in 1890. For one thing, cowboys and Indians didn't fade into the mists of history; they thrived past the turn of the twentieth century and in ways we might not have expected. Religion came to cowboys at remote settings. Indians not only did not disappear, their population began to increase and they continued to practice age-old Indian spiritual traditions. At the same time, Indians such as Black Elk explored spiritual innovations such as converting to Christianity. Stepping back from these specific examples, we can see a region developing economically, politically, and socially. In many respects, the West had not "matured" and still functioned as a colony of the East. But that was changing. By the end of World War II, the West would have millions more people than it did in 1890. It would boast a much bigger and more diversified economy than existed in 1890.

Culturally, the West changed from a raw region that the nation sought to reconstruct and transformed into a developed, "mature" region that would produce its own ideas to influence the rest of the nation. Religious people in the West confronted impulses bred by the social gospel and faced challenges of modernity, as did the rest of the nation. The period 1890 to 1945 had less to do with European–American religions rushing west to convert natives and to establish congregations and infrastructure than it did with building on foundations established earlier. The period also saw the birth of the modern West and the conflicts that came with it, as religious diversity expanded and in which religious conservatives reacted against modernization in ways that shaped national religious developments for the rest of the century.

Mormonism

Mormonism continued to play a prominent role in the West's religious history from 1890 through 1945. Plural marriage remained a source of conflict into the early twentieth century, but by the end of World War II Mormons and their church had become a more respected religious community, less persecuted and feared than in the past. They had moved "from the margin toward the mainstream."

Despite the Manifesto of 1890 and the Utah state constitution of 1896 that prohibited polygamy, the issue continued to fester. There was no way that a fundamental tenet of Mormonism – one critical to salvation some Mormons continued to insist – could be erased quickly and easily. Church authorities continued to authorize and perform polygamous marriages covertly. The issue surfaced dramatically in 1898 with the election of Brigham H. Roberts as congressman from Utah. Roberts, an avowed polygamist, encountered sharp opposition from Republicans in the House of Representatives and from the US population at large. The opposition resulted in Roberts being denied his seat in the House. Anti-Roberts petitions containing seven million signatures arrived in Washington, DC. Protestant religious organizations and women's groups led the opposition. They saw Roberts' continued practice of plural marriage and the willingness of Utah's Mormon electorate to send him to Congress as evidence that the Latter-day Saints Church did not take seriously its repudiation of polygamy. In fact, anti-Mormons saw evidence that the Woodruff Manifesto amounted only to window dressing.

The renewed controversy prompted Latter-day Saints President Lorenzo Snow to respond publicly. The *Deseret News* of January 8, 1900, published an article by Snow reaffirming the church's full endorsement of the Woodruff Manifesto, stating that the church would not sanction new plural marriages, and promising that the church would discipline members who did not comply with US law.[2] Despite Snow's clear stand, some church officials ignored it along with the Woodruff Manifesto. Plural marriage still had a heartbeat and ties to the mainline church.

---

[2] Lorenzo Snow, "Polygamy and Unlawful Cohabitation," *Deseret News* (Salt Lake City) 8 January 1900, p. 4.

The 1902 announcement that Church Apostle Reed Smoot (the Quorum of the Twelve Apostles is the church president's highest advisory board) would be a candidate for the US Senate and his subsequent election that year brought renewed interest in church–state relations in Utah and in the doctrine and practice of plural marriage. Although Smoot himself was not a polygamist, the fact that he sat on the Quorum of the Twelve Apostles raised suspicions among outsiders. Would his loyalty to his church supersede his loyalty to the United States and its constitution? The church's apparent unwillingness to abandon completely the practice of plural marriage fueled this suspicion. A group of Salt Lake City leaders, including businessmen, lawyers, and ministers (Presbyterian, Congregationalist, Methodist, and Episcopalian) protested Smoot's election. The protest initiated a thorough Congressional investigation of the Latter-day Saints Church, possibly the longest and most thorough investigation of a religious body in the history of the United States.

Church President Joseph F. Smith responded in 1904 with what has been called the Second Manifesto. In it, Smith denied that new polygamous marriages had occurred "with the sanction, consent or knowledge of the Church" and stated that violators would be excommunicated.[3] The Church continued to wrestle with an issue that some Mormons still considered a critical matter of divine revelation. Two members of the Quorum of the Twelve Apostles resigned in late 1905 and officials who ignored Church policy, or were confused by it, continued to perform plural marriages. Satisfied that the Church was heading in the right direction, and that Smoot's dual roles as Mormon Apostle and US Senator would not conflict, the Senate concluded the investigation with a vote of support for Smoot in 1907. But the issue still had legs.

By 1910, the Church leadership deemed unofficial plural marriages a threat to the Church and ordered local leaders to discipline those performing them. Church courts excommunicated dozens of offenders over the next few decades indicating a clear, decisive shift away from plural marriage by the mainstream Church. In 1935, the Church excommunicated a group of polygamists who had settled in Short Creek, Arizona. The mainline Latter-day Saints Church had

[3] James R. Clark, ed., *Messages of the First Presidency of the Church of Jesus Christ of Latter-day Saints*, 6 vols. (Salt Lake City, UT: Bookcraft, 1965–75), 4: 84.

moved convincingly away from plural marriage and toward the mainstream of American life, but the Short Creek polygamists, who became known as fundamentalist Mormons, continued to practice "the principle" into the twenty-first century. In the sense that making a hard break with polygamy in the early twentieth century ended a distinctive practice considered barbaric by outsiders, Mormons left their pioneer phase behind and entered the modern era along with the rest of the West.

Catholicism

Between 1890 and 1945 Roman Catholicism in the West showed signs of both the persistence of the old colonial or imperial order, in which influence and a desire to civilize flowed from the East to the West, and of a new order, in which innovation in the West spread outward. The church's relationship to the West's Hispanic communities vividly illustrates those issues, especially an ongoing ethnic tension within the church, and shows how in these decades the West's Hispanic population contributed to changes in church policy and practice. Stories of Catholics in the West during this period also reflect the strong influence of the social gospel movement, which sought to channel spiritual energy to cure or mitigate social problems.

The Catholic Church continued to prioritize Anglo Americans and European immigrants over Hispanics in this era, but a new awareness of Hispanic Catholics touched church leaders starting around 1900. By 1945 Hispanics would hold an improved place in American Catholicism, but that development occurred gradually. During the last half of the 1800s the Hispanic population of the Southwest grew in absolute numbers, but shrank in terms of percentage thanks to substantial immigration by Anglos and Europeans. The church continued to serve Hispanics, but bishops and clergy seemed to treat this service as temporary and to think the Hispanic population would continue to decline in importance. Western church leaders saw the dominant society (Anglos) as their main responsibility. They went so far as to curtail elements of the Hispanic ministry that might offend Anglos. For example, many Hispanic Catholics revere and celebrate Our Lady of Guadalupe, an icon of Mary that commemorates a Mexican peasant's vision of the Virgin Mary in 1531. In the 1930s Charles Buddy, the first bishop of San Diego, called feasts and dances such as those celebrating Our Lady of Guadalupe scandalous. He feared they might weaken people's faith and he canceled some celebrations. Buddy's attitude and policies demonstrate the disdain non-Hispanic church leaders had for Hispanic Catholicism into the twentieth century.

In Texas, the church relied heavily on foreign clergy rather than on cultivating native Hispanic clergy, and a separate Hispanic ministry (churches and church-sponsored institutions such as hospitals) developed. This situation reflected the demographic influence of European immigration. It also likely reflected Texas' hybrid identity as southern and western. As a southern state, Texas developed a segregated society because the Anglo majority wished to avoid mixing with African Americans and Hispanics, even in church. "Mexican" churches proliferated, especially in the decade of the 1910s. For example, two priests with Spanish surnames in 1915 established St. Joseph Parish in Fort Worth to serve Spanish speakers. In the 1920s St. Paul Hospital opened a free clinic in the Mexican section of Fort Worth.

The Catholic Church in California followed a trajectory similar to that in Texas. Irish bishops dominated during this period and they catered to what might be called "mainstream" Catholics. Exceptions included Archbishop John Cantwell of Los Angeles, who built clinics and spent more than half of his social welfare budget to serve Mexican Americans and priests in Oakland and Anaheim who built chapels to serve migrant workers. On the other hand, Archbishop Edward Hanna of San Francisco (1915–1935) projected hostility toward Mexican Americans by urging California's congressional delegation to limit immigration from Mexico in terms that suggest racist motives. More evidence of antipathy toward Mexican Americans can be found in the city of San Jose, which had a large Hispanic population but no Mexican or Mexican American pastor from 1852 through 1962.

The Catholic commitment to mission work and the social gospel as well as the West's ongoing dependence on the East can be seen in the career of Katharine Drexel, the Philadelphia banking heiress who became a nun and used her fortune to support Catholic Indian missions. Drexel completed her novitiate (training to become a nun) as the frontier allegedly closed, and in February 1891 took her vows as the first Sister of the Blessed Sacrament for Indians and Colored People. By the end of 1891, 28 novices had entered the order. Drexel, now known as Mother Katharine, built the order's headquarters outside Philadelphia. As the sisters reached out to African Americans and Native Americans, most of whom lived in the South and West, respectively, the order's work contributed to nation-building in the sense that reform and assistance efforts would emanate from powerful centers of religious influence in the East.

Organizing and training took years, but in 1894 Mother Drexel sent four sisters to open St. Catharine's School in Santa Fe, New Mexico. In subsequent years, she would use her money to support the Sisters of the Blessed Sacrament in opening convents and schools throughout Indian Country, including Arizona, the Dakotas, Montana, Washington, and Wisconsin. Although Drexel plowed more and more of her money into the Sisters of the Blessed Sacrament, she continued to fund, sometimes at a reduced level, other Catholic projects with which she had been involved. In 1935, for example, she used both her money and personnel from her order to support seven Sioux women in South Dakota who wished to start a congregation to support work among their own tribe.

In addition to Drexel's work, the use of railroad "chapel cars" suggests that what many easterners would consider "frontier" conditions continued to exist in the West and religious groups created innovative measures to confront them. Chapel cars, or railroad cars fitted with a pulpit, a lectern, an organ, and maybe even stained glass windows, could be attached to trains and hauled to remote areas not served by a church. The cars came into existence in the late 1800s and functioned into the twentieth century. Several denominations used the cars and until 1913 railroad companies did not charge to pull them, a corporate subsidy perhaps intended to generate favorable publicity and that also reflected the corporate desire to promote religion in the West. Catholics had a chapel car called the *St. Anthony* in service by 1907 and Father Alvah Doran, who served on it, kept a diary describing his work.

Father Doran's description of the *St. Anthony*'s tour through Idaho in 1909 tells us about the nature of religious life in the rural and predominately Mormon West at the turn of the century. In Oxford, Idaho, a town located three miles from the train station where the *St. Anthony* came to a temporary rest in July 1909, the local Mormon community shared its meeting house with Doran and a companion priest. The Mormons held services on a Sunday morning and afternoon and the Catholics held their service that evening.

Doran wrote that Oxford had not a single Catholic and that his entire audience consisted of Mormons. This type of interdenominational cooperation typified religious life in remote and recently settled areas of the West. In St. Anthony, Idaho, Doran found a small, but dedicated Catholic community that had dug a foundation for a church building, but had not yet completed the structure. One Catholic family lived 12 miles from town, yet drove in twice each day during the *St. Anthony's* stay so the family could attend both the morning masses and the evening services offered by the itinerant (traveling) priests. Nearly a decade into the twentieth century, the remote, rural West still looked like a religious frontier, at least to some denominations, and both settlers and denominations sought expanded services and a greater institutional presence.

The years between 1890 and 1945 saw the West produce one of the century's most famous Roman Catholics, who gained renown by revolutionizing juvenile institutions, taking new approaches to child care and development, and becoming the subject of a Hollywood movie about his work with troubled boys. Whether or not the West's environment influenced this work, Father Edward Flanagan and Boys Town demonstrate the West produced an innovative social development that influenced the nation and even the world.

A native of Ireland, Edward Joseph Flanagan came to the United States in 1904 when he was 18. He earned a bachelor's degree and a master's degree from Mount St. Mary's College in Maryland and studied at St. Joseph's Seminary in New York before traveling to Europe in 1907. In 1912 he became an ordained priest at St. Ignatius Church in Innsbruck, Austria, and then moved to O'Neill, Nebraska, to become assistant pastor at St. Patrick's Church. In 1913, he became assistant pastor of St. Patrick's Church in Omaha, Nebraska, where he dedicated himself to serving the troubled and underprivileged. He founded the Workingmen's Hotel in 1914 to shelter homeless men and itinerant workers. In 1917, Flanagan borrowed money to open the Home for Homeless Boys. Of the home's first five residents, Omaha's Juvenile Court referred three. The home's population grew quickly, which prompted Flanagan to establish Boys Town, a residential community for troubled boys, in a rural area 11 miles west of Omaha.

Boys Town struggled financially and received little support from the local church or Omahans at large, but Flanagan used clever promotional strategies to gain attention and contributions. When celebrities passed through Omaha, for example, Flanagan would arrange to have the Boys Town band play for them, which often resulted in newspaper coverage. He conducted letter-writing campaigns to solicit donations. He convinced Babe Ruth, one of the era's most famous baseball players, and boxing champion Jack Dempsey, to visit Boys Town. These celebrity visits brought news coverage and helped bring thousands of dollars in donations. Eventually Flanagan convinced the Catholic Church to increase its support, too.

Flanagan did more than attract attention and donations; he revolutionized the treatment and care of troubled youth. Notably, Flanagan did not use corporal punishment. He believed environment and other factors contributed to delinquency and he attacked those. Boys Town tried to undo the effects of parental neglect by offering academic and vocational training and recreational programs. Boys Town residents lived highly structured lives designed to keep them busy and out of trouble. Flanagan and his associates heaped praise on boys who followed the rules and constructive criticism on those who did not. Good behavior brought additional privileges.

Boys Town, non-sectarian and open to boys of all races, also delegated responsibility to residents, who staffed a self-governing city administration. Flanagan hoped that by holding positions such as mayor, council member, or fire chief, to name several examples, boys would build a sense of responsibility and improved self-esteem. As graduates of Boys Town became productive members of society, more positive attention came to the project and to Flanagan. Flanagan's ideas spread to other juvenile institutions, which had often relied only on harsh discipline. Priests visited Boys Town to study its programs, which they used when they opened similar institutions elsewhere in the country. Decades of success inspired Metro-Goldwyn-Mayer to make two films about Flanagan's life. In *Boys Town*, which appeared in 1938, Spencer Tracy played Father Flanagan and Mickey Rooney portrayed a troubled boy. After World War II, Flanagan advised the US attorney general on juvenile delinquency and traveled to Japan, Korea, and Europe to visit and advise child care facilities. Flanagan's revolutionary influence, born of his compassionate Catholicism, put the American West in the vanguard of national and international social reform and showed the region maturing beyond a colony into a trendsetter.

All told, the Catholic Church worked to support its earlier work in the West and to expand its reach. It contributed to the region's social welfare infrastructure and continued its mission work. Church and social welfare development served a variety of constituencies and reflected ethnic tensions, notably between Anglos and Hispanics. Social divisions still held by 1945, but they showed signs of softening.

American Indians and Religion

Catholicism touched many western lives in ways that rarely received the publicity received by Boys Town. In fact, popular culture obscured the religion of one of the West's most famous Catholics, Black Elk (Figure 5.1). Thanks to *Black Elk Speaks*,[4] most know him for being a traditional Lakota medicine man and hardly at all for his Catholicism. That shows how easy it has been for historians and popular culture to leave American Indians and their history in the 1800s. In reality, American Indians didn't disappear. Between 1890 and 1945 American Indians continued to practice traditional beliefs, developed new religious expressions, and saw US government policy become much more accepting of cultural and religious matters.

Black Elk's relationship with Christianity, namely Catholicism, provides a good starting point to investigate American Indians and religion in the early twentieth century. After his 1904 conversion, when he took the name Nicholas Black Elk, he became a devoted member of the Catholic Church at Pine Ridge, South Dakota. He joined the St. Joseph Society and helped the priests as he was able. For their part, the Pine Ridge Jesuits saw him as a valuable ally and made him a catechist. In that role, Black Elk filled in for absent priests by holding Sunday services, leading prayers and hymns, reading passages from the Bible, and teaching, all of which he did in the Lakota language. He also traveled as a Catholic missionary to the Arapahos on the Wind River Reservation in Wyoming and to the Winnebago reservation in Nebraska.

In 1930 Black Elk met John G. Neihardt, the poet laureate of Nebraska, and the two men began a collaboration that would produce arguably the most important book on American Indian spirituality

[4] John G. Neihardt, *Black Elk Speaks* (New York: Morrow, 1932).

Figure 5.1   Nick Black Elk and family, Catholic catechist. Source: The
Denver Public Library, Western History Collection, x-31818.

published in the twentieth century. Black Elk entrusted Neihardt with
details of his early life, including the formative spiritual vision he
received when he was about nine years old and other details of Lakota
life and spirituality. He hoped Neihardt would transmit his vision and
an understanding of Lakota culture to a wide audience. Neihardt published *Black Elk Speaks* in 1932. The book became a widely read classic, especially in the 1960s and 1970s when interest in American
Indian culture spiked, even though critics saw problems in Neihardt's
handling of the material Black Elk provided.

Neihardt took liberties with parts of Black Elk's story, but perhaps his
most controversial decision was to end the book with the Wounded Knee
massacre. In so doing, Neihardt told his readers much about traditional
Lakota spirituality, but he told it as a tale of a static culture in decline and
one that ended tragically at Wounded Knee. In the book, which uses

Black Elk's voice to narrate, one of the last things he says refers to Wounded Knee: "And I can see that something else died there in the bloody mud, and was buried in the blizzard. A people's dream died there. It was a beautiful dream."[5] This narrative reinforced the stereotype of the "noble savage" and fit with "vanishing race" theory (Indians had been in decline and were headed for inevitable extinction) that was popular at the dawn of the twentieth century. It also fit neatly into Turner's frontier hypothesis by depicting a last gasp of "savagery" in the rise and fall of the Ghost Dance and the "triumph" of US civilization in 1890.

Neihardt's formula makes for an emotionally powerful ending, but it denies important truths about Black Elk specifically and American Indians generally. Census figures indeed showed a declining American Indian population through 1900; but, starting with numbers gathered in 1910, the American Indian population climbed, which it continued to do through the twentieth century. Neihardt's ending also obscured the complex, often fluid, world of American Indian religion in which many Indians converted to Christianity, including many who adopted Christianity and practiced it alongside their existing religion. Black Elk lived longer as a Catholic (about 46 years) than he did as a non-Catholic (about 41 years) and he spent about 68 years living on the Pine Ridge Reservation compared to less than 20 years (the first part of his life) in the pre-reservation era. Black Elk's children considered the years after 1904 the most important chapter in their father's life. By his late adult years, Black Elk followed a religious path that reflected both his Lakota and Catholic upbringing. Nonetheless, whatever its shortcomings, *Black Elk Speaks* has been called a "bible of all tribes," "the most important book ever published on American Indian religion."[6] Black Elk, American Indians, and the American West did not disappear or cease to exist in 1890. All three entered the twentieth century as dynamic, innovative entities.

The advent of the Native American Church reinforces the argument that American Indian spirituality and American Indians thrived and

---

[5] Neihardt (1932), 270.

[6] Quotations appear in Vine Deloria, Jr, "Introduction," *Black Elk Speaks, Being the Life Story of a Holy Man of the Oglala Sioux, as told through John G. Neihardt (Flaming Rainbow)* (Lincoln, NB: University of Nebraska Press, 1988), xiii; and, Joel W. Martin, *The Land Looks After Us: A History of Native American Religion* (New York: OxfordUniversity Press, 2001), 97.

innovated in the post-frontier era. The Native American Church originated in a syncretic blend of pre-Columbian peyote usage, tribal religious traditions, and, depending on the practitioner, Christianity. Well before 1492 tribes living along the Gulf Coast of Mexico and in what is now northern Mexico ceremonially ate part of the peyote cactus, which induced visions or hallucinations. According to some stories, the peyote spirit spoke to a man or woman in despair and told them to eat the small cactus that could be found growing under a nearby bush. The peyote, the spirit told them, would provide them strength and wisdom to overcome their hardship.

Peyote use spread north from Mexico and the American Southwest during the nineteenth century as tribes, especially on the Great Plains, adjusted to the realities of US expansion and reservation life. The nation's burgeoning rail network speeded the religion's spread. So did boarding schools, whose enrollments included members of tribes from around the country gathered in one place where they all spoke English and traded ideas, including religious ones involving both Christianity and peyotism. Ceremonial peyote use, adapted to tribal custom by each group that embraced it, became the foundation for a pan-Indian movement institutionalized in the form of the Native American Church. As peyote use spread among Comanches in the 1890s, Quanah Parker, a well-known Comanche leader, developed a major ceremony, which became known as the Half Moon Way, for the new religion (Figure 5.2). At the same time, a Caddo/Delaware named Nishkuntu (and also known as Moonhead or John Wilson) created a variation on the ceremony that became known as the Cross Fire Way or, sometimes, Big Moon as a contrast to the Half Moon Way. These two ceremonies came to dominate Native American Church ritual. Native American Church leaders, known as "road men," using railroads and later highways led services and officiated at thanksgivings, and healings. Their message often centered on how peyote offered a gateway to the spirit world and some worshipers reported speaking with dead ancestors and even with Jesus during rituals.

The rituals spread quickly from the 1890s through World War II despite the efforts of opponents to stop the new religion. The social ethos governing Indian policy still demanded "primitive" Indian religious practices be suppressed or erased and replaced with Christianity. Some American Indians, particularly older religious leaders, objected to the new faith. Gertrude Bonnin, a Sioux Indian rights activist, opposed peyote because she considered its social effects detrimental,

Figure 5.2   Quanah Parker, a Kwahadi Comanche chief. Source: National Archives (111-SC-87722).

similar to those of alcohol. Likewise, Susan La Flesche Picotte, an Omaha and the first Indian woman physician in the United States, opposed peyote for years, although late in her life she became convinced of its benefits and dropped her opposition. Others, especially non-Indians, objected to peyote use for the same reason they opposed consumption of alcoholic beverages and other intoxicants. Attempts to make peyote use illegal date to as early as 1620, when the King of Spain issued an edict banning its use. In the 1880s, US Indian agents lobbied for its prohibition and Oklahoma's territorial legislature passed a law prohibiting its use, although it was repealed in 1908.

Native American Church leaders made a savvy response to these threats by organizing formally and incorporating in Oklahoma as the Native American Church in October 1918. In addition to making clever use of the legal system to gain First Amendment protection of their religious freedom, church leaders such as Frank Eagle, a Ponca who served as the church's first president, invoked the church's Christian ideals. The church, leaders said, aimed to promote Christian belief through sacramental peyote use and to teach members Christian morality and self-respect.

The religion met a number of needs in American Indian communities. Unlike the many traditional ceremonies that had been suppressed during the reservation era, peyote rituals took place quietly and enjoyed some legal protection. As many Indians struggled with alcoholism and poverty, they embraced the Native American Church's prohibition on alcohol and its calls for hard work, which echoed key tenets of evangelical Protestantism. Prohibition and an appeal to what amounted to a variant of the Protestant work ethic symbolized modern components of peyotism. The Native American Church contained other modern elements. Ceremonies could take place anywhere believers gathered, rather than being bound to a sacred site, and the church had its own missionaries. At the same time, the Native American Church appealed to traditional values. The peyote spirit's offer of strength and wisdom proved attractive, as did the comfort provided by the incorporation of traditional practices such as group singing and drumming. Mountain Wolf Woman, a Ho-Chunk (Winnebago) born in 1884, summed up her spiritual journey and preference for the Native American Church this way: "I joined the medicine lodge. I was once a Christian. Then, when we went to Nebraska I ate peyote which is even a Christian way. Three things I did. But peyote alone is the best."[7] In another telling comment, Quanah Parker observed that when in church whites "talk *about* Jesus"

[7] Nancy Oestreich Luri, ed., *Mountain Wolf Woman, Sister of Crashing Thunder: The Autobiography of a Winnnebago Indian* (Ann Arbor, MI: University of Michigan Press, 1961), 91.

while the peyotist "talks *to* Jesus."[8] Black Elk's Catholicism and the rise of
the Native American Church showed American Indians thriving and
engaging in religious innovation in a vibrant, maturing American West.
They found ways to be Christian and Indian, American and Indian,
even if white Americans opposed their efforts.

The Native American Church developed in the 1920s and 1930s
against the backdrop of familiar debates about American Indian
religious freedom. In 1921 the commissioner of Indian Affairs
issued an order sustaining the 1883 prohibition of ceremonial
dances and celebrations, seeking to suppress elements of American
Indian spirituality he considered harmful. Indian rights activists,
including a reformer named John Collier, opposed the commissioner's order and lobbied against it. When Congress considered a bill that
would have made the commissioner's order the law of the land, Collier
and his supporters spearheaded the opposition that defeated it.

President Franklin D. Roosevelt named Collier commissioner of
Indian Affairs in the 1930s. In his new post, Collier advanced his
Indian rights agenda from a position of power and changed the course
of Indian policy. He made it official policy in 1934 that Indians receive
constitutional protection for religious matters and ceremonial expression. Collier dropped compulsory attendance at religious services at
Bureau of Indian Affairs schools and allowed students to return home
to attend traditional ceremonies. Many Christian reformers and
Christian Indians viewed Collier's policies as backward steps. Despite
disagreement and the fact that Indian religious freedoms would be
debated for the rest of the century, Collier extended constitutional
protections enjoyed by other US citizens to American Indians.

American Indians not only survived into the twentieth century and
beyond, but also lived dynamic religious lives. Some continued to
practice age-old religious traditions. Some embraced Christianity, an
established religious tradition "new" to North America. Some welcomed innovative religious expressions such as peyotism. And some
followed a religious path that might be labeled "all of the above."
Considered broadly, the principle characteristics of American
Indians' relationship to religious practice changed little, although
particular developments such as peyotism as practiced by the Native

---

[8] Quoted in William T. Hagan, *Quanah Parker, Comanche Chief* (Norman, OK:
University of Oklahoma Press, 1993), 57.

American Church were new. The US government's new policy marked a significant change. From one perspective, it demonstrated a relaxation in the kind of nation-building that demanded imposition of a Christian monoculture in the West. From another, it signaled a changed nation-building, one in which the Constitution's First Amendment protections of religious freedom had finally arrived in Indian Country and could be used to nurture the Native American Church, a religion the mainstream considered suspect.

Asian Religions and Influence

Asians continued to immigrate to the West from 1890 through 1945, although federal law excluded the Chinese and prejudice discouraged the Japanese. A notable development came with the arrival of significant numbers of Japanese immigrants on the West Coast or North America beginning in the 1890s. There they established an organized religious community, which included close institutional ties to Buddhist organizations in Japan. Religious conflict with Christian America encouraged this close tie. Starting in the late 1870s, Presbyterian and Methodist missionaries targeted the San Francisco-area Japanese community. Those Japanese people had emigrated from regions dominated by Pure Land Buddhism. Ordained representatives of Pure Land Buddhism visited California in 1898 to study the spiritual condition of Japanese immigrants. In response to the Protestant mission efforts among the Japanese, they organized the Young Men's Buddhist Association of San Francisco and helped establish the first Japanese Buddhist temple in the United States in San Francisco. In 1899, the Japanese headquarters dispatched two formal missionaries, Shuye Sonoda and Kakuryo Nishijima, to cultivate Buddhism among Japanese people in California and to teach interested European–Americans.

Sonoda and Nishijima embodied an inverted version of the West's frontier narrative by traveling east to get to the West and also complicated the notion of manifest destiny. Sonoda considered himself a spiritual pioneer spreading the light of truth in the New World. He considered Buddhism ideally suited for expansion and destined to become the universal religion. The United States, with its liberal and tolerant population, made a perfect target for expanding Buddhism.

Sonada, then, used the West as a gateway to a nation he hoped, even expected, to make Buddhist.

By 1906, more than 3000 Japanese Buddhists lived in the continental United States and 12 Pure Land Buddhist temples had been founded along the West Coast, most in California but also in Oregon and Washington. These Japanese Pure Land Buddhism communities came to reflect American and Protestant influences. The Young Men's Buddhist Association, for example, followed the example of the Young Men's Christian Association. Japanese Buddhists began referring to temples as churches, calling Buddhist priests "Reverend," developing Sunday schools, and adopting western architecture for temple construction. These developments reflected the strong bonds between Japanese Pure Land Buddhists and Japan. They also provide a telling and often overlooked detail of the West's religious history, which runs deeper than a march of Americanization and Christianity across the continent. Japanese Pure Land Buddhists pushed back against that march and even employed some of its techniques to resist Christianity and to strengthen an alternate vision of religion and community in the American West.

Asian religious influence could also be seen in the work of religious visionaries such as Katharine Tingley, who saw in the West at the dawn of the twentieth century space to pursue new ideas. Stories of such visionaries would multiply over the course of the twentieth century. Tingley, a Massachusetts native born in 1847, attended a Congregational church early in her life. She became a Theosophist in the 1890s and led the establishment of a utopian Theosophist community on the Point Loma Peninsula in San Diego in 1897.

Theosophy, founded in 1875, embraced an eclectic blend of Asian and occult thought and rejected Christian orthodoxy. Leaders organized an international Theosophical Society, which had its headquarters in India. The American branch declared its independence from the international movement in 1895. Theosophists saw themselves as followers of the essential truths of all the world's religions. They believed that a spark of the divine inhabited every atom of the universe, that women and men both enjoyed access to spiritual authority, and that a form of karma allowed human souls to be born into male or female bodies depending on their immediate needs.

Theosophy typically attracted educated middle- and upper-class women, perhaps because Theosophists gave women and men equal access to spiritual authority and the group had prominent female leaders, whose spiritual and psychic needs went unmet by mainstream Christianity.

Tingley fit that profile, and shortly after becoming a Theosophist she found herself among the leaders of the American section of the movement. Her rise to leadership rested at least in part on her claim to be a medium who channeled messages from beyond the grave, notably the spirit of Helena Blavatsky, a co-founder of Theosophy who had died in 1891. Tingley also dreamed of a utopian community in which Theosophists could unite arts, education, and labor to create a new model for human life. Wealthy patrons purchased land on Point Loma in 1897 and Tingley and her followers settled Lomaland by the turn of the century. Lomaland grew to 500 residents and became a tourist attraction thanks to its pageants, dramas, and concerts. Residents conducted agricultural experiments and contributed to the development of California's citrus and avocado crops. Lomaland's social experiments extended to child rearing. An experimental school placed children in groups of six to 12 with a teacher, who cared for the group around the clock and instructed the children in physical, academic, artistic, and spiritual matters. Children visited their biological parents on Sunday afternoons. This might seem odd, but the Lomaland child-rearing experiment happened at the same time US Indian policy called for children to be removed from their families and for education or re-education in vocational, social, and spiritual matters at boarding schools. Indian children at boarding schools went months without seeing their biological families.

Lomaland showed the world an impressive façade, but the community struggled financially. Leaders sold land to pay debts and by 1928 much of the original estate was gone. The community limped along until World War II, when it moved inland then disbanded. The Lomaland Theosophists passed quickly as a community, a fate they shared with many utopian communities. Their experimental spiritual community showed the diversity of religious paths that developed in the un-churched West, which would see much more innovation, over the course of the twentieth century.

Modernism, Fundamentalism, and
the Spirit of the West

Arguably the most important event of this period on the national religious stage involved a near-civil war within Protestantism. The conflict, between camps most often labeled modernist and fundamentalist, had been brewing for decades. It centered on how to reconcile science with religion, namely, the inerrant (without error) authority of the Bible. The development of Charles Darwin's theory of evolution played a part. How could the biblical creation story exist alongside Darwin's theory? So did the rise of the modern university system. Harvard, Yale, Princeton, and other leading schools once had been relatively small schools centered on religious education. In the 1870s, they diversified and encouraged independent disciplines and specialties. Large state universities also developed at about this time, particularly in the West with the rise of land-grant colleges, and it was often difficult to raise theological questions on public campuses. In a related development, the rise of scientific history encouraged critical evaluation of texts, including the Bible. This led many scholars to consider the Bible as a text assembled by humans who were subject to historical forces. The Word of God might come through the Bible, but the words were assembled by humans subject to human foibles. Rather than take the Bible as the literal, inerrant Word of God, these scholars tried to understand how humans composed it, what accounted for its inner contradictions, and how to determine its true meaning in terms acceptable to modern reason.

These events influenced the development of a modernist theology and a fundamentalist reaction to it. Modernists tried to help their followers maintain their faith and at the same time embrace new science and knowledge with the goal of adapting to the modern world. Fundamentalists held tightly to the Bible's inerrancy and traditional doctrinal statements. Using these, they identified and excluded unacceptable beliefs and people. Modernists looked down on fundamentalists as unsophisticated and primitive. Fundamentalists did not think modernists qualified as Christian. These warring camps caused splits in a number of Protestant denominations and profoundly influenced American religious thought in the twentieth century. The fundamentalist–modernist debate had a strong western component and it shaped many of the best-known and most influential religious figures that came out of the West in this remarkably fertile period.

The decade of the 1890s makes a good starting point for this story. The nation as a whole grappled with anxiety-inducing developments such as a rise in immigration, industrialization, and urbanization. US political and social leaders saw these developments as dire threats to what they would have considered "the American Way." One US historian even called her book about this tumultuous period *Standing at Armageddon* (Nell Irvin Painter, 1989, W.W. Norton). The title refers to a place mentioned in the Book of Revelation where the Messiah will battle and defeat evil and has come to mean any end-of-the-world scenario. Some national leaders also worried about developments in the West. The US Census Bureau had declared the frontier of settlement closed as of 1890 and historian Frederick Jackson Turner claimed the frontier's critical Americanizing effect had been lost. These anxieties can be seen in the West's religious history.

Beginning in the 1890s, Lyman and Milton Stewart used profits from their Los Angeles-based Union Oil Company to support a variety of fundamentalist causes. Lyman Stewart, for example, attacked theological liberals such as Thomas F. Day, a Presbyterian who taught biblical criticism at the San Francisco Theological Seminary. The seminary dismissed Day in 1912 for his liberalism. Stewart also helped found the school that would become the Bible Institute of Los Angeles (BIOLA) to support theological training more to his liking. Perhaps most notably, Stewart paid for publication of *The Fundamentals*, a series of pamphlets that appeared from 1912 through 1916 considered by some as the first shots fired in the fundamentalist–modernist controversy.

Other newcomers brought innovative spiritual ideas with them to southern California. William Seymour, for example, brought with him the seeds of Pentecostalism. Pentecostalism originated in Topeka, Kansas, spread south to Texas, and then traveled west from Houston to Los Angeles with Seymour. "Pentecostal" refers to the day of Pentecost, described in chapters 1 and 2 of the New Testament books of *Acts*, when the Holy Spirit descended on the first Christians, who then "spoke in tongues." Speaking in tongues and faith healing are two characteristics of Pentecostal Christianity, which focuses on emotional, mystical, and supernatural experiences.

In Topeka, Kansas, Charles F. Parham was a former Methodist minister who had gone independent and operated Bethel Bible College. In 1901, speaking in tongues and other ecstatic behavior erupted at Bethel, and Parham claimed these demonstrated a person had been truly baptized in the Holy Spirit. Parham's Apostolic Faith movement gathered momentum in and around Kansas and Parham traveled to spread his message.

When Parham taught a class in Houston, Texas, in 1905, his words found the ears of a black preacher named William Seymour. Because he was black and the course was taught in the South during the Jim Crow era of segregation, Seymour had to sit outside the classroom. According to Parham, Christians had to be baptized both with holy water and the Holy Spirit, which involved speaking in tongues. When Seymour accepted an invitation to visit a Holiness church in Los Angeles, he took with him doctrine gained from Parham's teaching and provided one of the earliest examples of the "Okie" migration stories central to this period.

Seymour began to preach at the Los Angeles church, but its leaders rejected his ideas and barred him. Unfazed, he moved to a private home, where his preaching moved audience members to speak in tongues in April 1906. Seymour's following grew and the group moved its meetings to the former First African Methodist Episcopal Church on Azusa Street. Freshly ordained ministers preached in the streets of Los Angeles to spread the movement's message. Seymour also published a periodical, *Apostolic Faith*, to reach an even greater audience.

Seymour incorporated his ministry as the Azusa Street Apostolic Faith Mission of Los Angeles in 1907. Through the rest of the year and into 1908, Azusa Street welcomed people from all races and ethnic backgrounds as Seymour's movement flourished. The Pentecostal movement has been described as a protest against the stuffy middle class character of mainline Protestant churches. It appealed to the poor, the uprooted, recent immigrants, blacks, Hispanics, and other minorities. It also appealed to people struggling with the transition from living in a preindustrial society to a modern, urban, industrializing society, precisely the transformation happening in the United States in the early twentieth century as the rural agricultural population moved to cities. Los Angeles, a destination for displaced agricultural workers of the Great Plains and Southwest and home to a diverse population, provided a fertile environment for Pentecostalism.

Although the revival at the Azusa Street mission declined rapidly after 1908 thanks to personal issues and racial and theological schisms, Seymour continued to travel the country preaching, mostly to black audiences. His unique message influenced every major form of Pentecostalism. Visitors to Azusa Street during the movement's heyday carried the movement around the nation, in fact around the world, within a few years. Seymour's work and influence show the West's significance in generating new religious movements and fore-shadow the importance of Texas and California as populous and influential western states in the twentieth century.

One of those movements leads us to an often overlooked facet of early twentieth-century US religious history, the rise of Protestantism among Hispanics. Azusa Street reached into the Latino community and reminds us that Protestantism had a foothold among Hispanics by the early 1900s. The Latino Pentecostal movement also strengthens the argument that the twentieth-century West spawned innovative religious movements that spread north and east. This challenges a major narrative in western history in which influence spread from east to west.

Shifting our gaze to the Pacific Northwest, we find another varia-tion on the modernist–fundamentalist controversy and a transplanted southerner who shaped both the religious and secular history of Seattle. Mark Allison Matthews used his position as pastor of Seattle's First Presbyterian Church to build a thriving congregation and to shape the city as it boomed after the Alaskan gold rush of 1897. As one biographer wrote, Matthews and Seattle grew up together.

Mark Matthews' journey to Seattle showed that frontier or not, the demographic phenomenon of westering continued into the twentieth century. A native of Calhoun, Georgia, Matthews spent the first 34 years of his life in the Southeast. He became an ordained minister in the Presbyterian Church of the United States, a regional southern denomination, at age 20. He served as pastor of his hometown church from 1888 to 1893, followed by pastorates in Dalton, Georgia, and Jackson, Tennessee. In Jackson, he studied law, which he saw as a tool he could use alongside religion in his fight against social corruption. Matthews married fundamentalist theology to modern technology and a progressive social agenda.

When in 1902 the First Presbyterian Church of Seattle called Matthews, he answered. Matthews assumed leadership of a young,

debt-laden congregation of 400 in a 50-year-old city that had just hit
an explosive growth spurt thanks to its role as a jumping off point for
the gold fields of Alaska. The church and the city presented a wealth
of opportunities for the ambitious, energetic young reformer.
Matthews pursued an aggressive growth strategy for his church and
for spreading Presbyterianism in Seattle and the region. Soon after his
arrival, he held the first of several evangelistic campaigns. His congregation doubled in the first year and within two years doubled again.
In 1907 First Presbyterian opened a new church building to serve its
members holistically. In addition to a sanctuary large enough to house
the booming congregation, the church included a miniature art gal-
lery, libraries, recreation rooms, and a roof-top track for running and
bicycling. Matthews founded 28 branch churches, several of which
developed into permanent congregations, including the Japanese
Christian Church. He also broadened religious outreach in 1917 by
founding the Bible Institute of Seattle to educate the laity for full-time
Christian work, and in 1922 he played a leading role in establishing
radio station KTW, a pioneer station in the Northwest and among the
first church-owned and operated stations in the nation. Matthews
used KTW not only to preach the Gospel of Jesus Christ, but also to
defend the Constitution of the United States. That approach strongly
suggests that Matthews saw himself as an agent of manifest destiny
and that the notion of settling the continent and making it American
continued past the closing of the frontier and that church and state
continued to have a strong association, at least in some people's eyes.
Matthews' work as a civic reformer and shaper of Seattle also testify to
those links.

Throughout his ministerial career Matthews worked not only in his
church, but also extended his ministry into the community to correct
individual and social problems. For example, he worked to rid Seattle's
notorious Skid Road section of gambling, prostitution, and booze, for
which it was known. He campaigned to recall Seattle's mayor in 1910
for allegedly tolerating those conditions on Skid Road. He also
charged the police chief with bribery and failure to enforce the laws.
On other fronts, Matthews and his congregation founded the Anti-
Tuberculosis Society of Seattle, which grew into a hospital affiliated
with the University of Washington's medical school, the Child's
Welfare and Humane Society, the Voter's League of Washington, and
Seattle's first kindergartens.

Matthews' migration to Seattle shows the continued movement of people into the West after the frontier's closing. He also brought religious influence to bear in shaping both the spiritual and secular communities of a major US city as the West urbanized with the rest of the nation. Seattle's *Post Intelligencer* newspaper credited Matthews with doing more to shape Seattle during the years of his pastorate than any other person. In terms of religious practice, he and other westerners pioneered the development of multifaceted churches and the use of new technology (radio) to spread the Gospel. In 38 years of service, Matthews grew his church's congregation to 9000, which made it the largest Presbyterian Church in the country. That work and his civic engagement made him a celebrity in Seattle and the Pacific Northwest.

World War I and Religion in the West

World War I (1914–1918) ravaged Western Europe and touched religious life in the American West in ways that showed the region's multiple global connections. Most obviously, World War I brought ethnic tension and violence to the West in ways that touched certain religious groups. The war pitted the United States and its allies against the Central Powers, which included Germany. American justifications for fighting included a quasi-religious crusade to make the world safe for democracy. The war encouraged a hyper-patriotism that led to frequently unjustified persecution of German Americans. On the Great Plains, where Lutheran and Catholic churches and parochial schools had helped preserve German cultural identity, persecution could be particularly vivid. For example, in 1918 the Nebraska State Council of Defense, a body formed by the governor to help him coordinate the state's support of the war, pressured churches and parochial schools in the state to stop using German in worship services and lessons. Churches across the state (and elsewhere, thanks to similar pressure across the country) complied to demonstrate their loyalty to the United States. In a sense, this could be seen as a type of Americanization comparable to the Mormon Church's abandonment of plural marriage. Another example involved an unfortunate case of mistaken identity. Angry vigilantes in Iowa burned several Dutch Reformed Churches mistaking them for German churches.

Elsewhere in the West, wartime tensions led hundreds of Mennonites to flee the United States for Canada. Many Mennonites, a Christian denomination that originated in central Europe and known for a commitment to pacifism, had fled militarism in Europe and settled farming communities on the Great Plains. Because many Mennonites were ethnically German *and* pacifists, outsiders questioned their loyalty to the United States. German Americans in general faced persecution during World War I, but Mennonites might have been the most persecuted cultural group in America. Facing both persecution and the prospect of conscription into the US military after the draft was initiated, hundreds of Mennonites in Oklahoma, Kansas, Nebraska, and Minnesota sold their farm equipment and moved to Canada.

The Sunbelt and the Bible Belt

The modernist–fundamentalist conflict continued after World War I and coincided with the rise of the Sunbelt, the region stretching from the Southeast to southern California, to produce a small but powerful cadre of religious leaders who developed a new evangelical creed and contributed to the rise of twentieth-century conservatism. Much of the Sunbelt overlapped with a region called the Bible Belt, which includes much of the former Confederacy. That region developed what religious historian Darren Dochuk calls a "Texas theology," which is practically a synonym for fundamentalism. Its core tenets include the importance of individual conversion, the Bible's inerrancy, and a scriptural command to witness for Christ. The Texas flavor came from a certainty in their correctness, a willingness to fight, and an openness to new methods of spreading the message. Migrants from Texas, Oklahoma, Arkansas, and other places carried these ideas with them to California in the 1930s and 1940s as they left farms and sought jobs in California defense plants. These were the "Okies" (even though they weren't all from Oklahoma) depicted in works such as John Steinbeck's novel *The Grapes of Wrath* and the black and white photos of Farm Security Administration photographers such as Dorothea Lange. Their relocation in the West, especially in California, created a fertile field for the development of an evangelical powerhouse that would fuel the rise of conservative politics and launch Ronald Reagan to the California governor's office (1960s) and then to the White House (1980s). What you're about to read explains not only western religious innovations, but also how religion and politics conspired to form a regional political juggernaut that shaped the nation and the world.

Although southern California dominates this discussion, the interior West also produced major figures such as the "Texas Tornado," J. Frank Norris. In Fort Worth, Norris became one of the nation's most influential fundamentalist evangelists and one whose career rode the rise of the Sunbelt and shaped the region's – and fundamentalism's – association with conservative politics. Norris embodied the "Texas theology" mentioned earlier. His career shared some facets with that of Mark Matthews of Seattle, but violence and vituperation clouded Norris' works and he foreshadowed the work of Sunbelt megachurch pastors who would emerge later in the century.

Like Mark Matthews, Norris was a son of the South born in Dadeville, Alabama. Like Matthews' family, Norris' migrated west, but to Texas. Norris earned a bachelor's degree at Baylor University, a Baptist school, and a master's degree at the Southern Baptist Theological Seminary. Norris' education, incidentally, shows how the educational infrastructure built by the pioneer generation of religious enthusiasts bore fruit that shaped history. In 1905, Norris took over McKinney Avenue Baptist Church in Dallas. He expanded the congregation from about 100 to more than 1000 in three years. He also managed and edited the *Baptist Standard*, the publication of the Southern Baptist Convention in Texas. Norris used the editorial page to campaign against racetrack gambling at the state fair, an example of his social reform agenda. Norris took charge of First Baptist Church in Fort Worth in 1909 and served that congregation until 1952.

From his base in Fort Worth, Norris used publications, radio, and air and rail travel to become one of the most prominent religious voices of his age. From 1917 to 1952, Norris edited his own newspaper. He used it to publish his sermons, provide news of fundamentalist events, and write social commentary. At one point Norris claimed an audience of 80 000 readers. He embraced radio to broadcast his sermons on 27 stations, which allowed him to reach most of the nation. And, from 1934 to 1948 Norris led both First Baptist in Fort Worth and Temple Baptist Church in Detroit. Why Detroit? A large number of southerners had migrated there to work in the automobile industry. Norris' southern

Figure 5.3   J. Frank Norris. Source: Reproduced by permission of
Arlington Baptist College.

style and fundamentalist message appealed to them. He commuted by
train and plane to preach in each city on alternate Sundays. Norris
claimed that between the two congregations he led 25 000 congregants,
the largest number of people led by a single pastor in the world. In
addition to ministering to congregations in Fort Worth and Detroit,
Norris conducted revivals in 46 states (Figure 5.3).

Norris used his influence in attempts to reform society, especially
in Fort Worth. In the course of a 1911 crusade against alcohol, prostitution, and political corruption, Norris delivered a sermon titled
"The Ten Biggest Devils in Fort Worth, Names Given." Only one of
the officials attempted to respond, and he was hooted off the
speaking platform by a pro-Norris audience. Norris criticized Fort
Worth's Catholic mayor in 1926, accusing him of channeling
municipal funds to Catholic institutions and attacked the mayor's
character. When a friend of the mayor confronted Norris in his

study at the church, Norris shot and killed the man. Norris beat a murder charge when his defense attorney convinced a jury that Norris had acted in self-defense. Two years after the shooting, Norris vigorously supported Herbert Hoover, a Protestant, against his Catholic opponent for the presidency, Alfred Smith. After Hoover's victory, the Republican Party honored him for his role in defeating Smith. The shooting brought Norris infamy for the rest of his life and his anti-Catholic actions mirrored sentiment expressed in much of the South and West with the revival of the Ku Klux Klan, which was particularly popular in Texas, Oklahoma, and Oregon.

Norris exhibited an independent streak, a characteristic often associated with the West, in his conflicts with denominations, most notably the Southern Baptist Convention. He clashed with the convention because he believed it interfered with the independence of local churches and because he believed its leadership showed too much tolerance of liberal theology. His strident criticisms led him to be kicked out of an array of organizations in the 1910s and 1920s: the Pastor's Conference in Fort Worth in 1914, the Tarrant County (Fort Worth's county) Baptist Association in 1922, and the Baptist General Convention of Texas in 1924. Norris reveled in the controversies and the attention they generated. Ultimately, he founded his own association of churches. He criticized the theory of evolution and railed against Russian Communism. He regularly visited Los Angeles, which he saw as important to the South and as a vital staging area to launch Sunbelt religion across the Pacific Ocean to Asia. A Norris sermon led a young college student named John Birch to convert and follow Norris to Fort Worth and, eventually, to travel to China as a missionary for the Fort Worth preacher. Birch, who was killed by Chinese Communists on that trip, lent his name to the John Birch Society in the 1950s, a militant anti-Communist organization that accused President Dwight Eisenhower of being a Communist. Norris embodied the fundamentalist response to modernism and provided a vital link in the chain that connected Bible Belt religion to the thriving Sunbelt.

The life and ministry of Francisco Olazábal enriches the story of Sunbelt fundamentalism and illustrates important developments in Latino religion in the early twentieth century. Born into a Catholic family in Mexico in 1886, Olazábal received Protestant influences from his mother, who converted in 1898. Francisco studied Methodist theology in Mexico from 1908 through 1910. He worked as an evangelist during those years in northern Mexico and in the border region of Texas. He – and thousands of other Mexicans – fled into the United States to escape the violence of the Mexican Revolution that started in 1910. Olazábal became the pastor of a Mexican Methodist church in El Paso in 1911.

Olazábal's ties to Methodism began to unravel in 1916 when he ran across old friends who had participated in the Azusa Street revival. Although Olazábal had criticized Pentecostals, his old friends convinced him that Pentecostal tenets including divine healing and speaking in tongues were critical parts of Christian life. Olazábal left the Methodist church and joined the Assemblies of God. He worked among Spanish speakers in California and in El Paso opened a Mexican mission to serve immigrants crossing the border. Despite the Assemblies of God's Mexican outreach, Olazábal eventually left because, as he put it, "the gringos have control."[9]

In 1923, Olazábal and other ministers formed the Interdenominational Mexican Council of Christian Churches, a new Mexican Pentecostal denomination, in Texas. He continued his work in the West, but also took his message to Spanish-speaking communities in New York City and Puerto Rico. When his 30-year ministry ended with a fatal car crash, Olazábal had preached to an estimated 250 000 people and contributed to the origins of denominations in Mexico, Puerto Rico, and the United States. In 1937, the year of his death, his organization claimed 150 churches and 50 000 followers. Francisco Olazábal's career not only enriches our understanding of Latino religion and that of the West, but also establishes the foundation for a boom in Latino Protestantism that would happen in the late twentieth century.

As Norris and Olazábel worked in Texas, southern California produced one of the era's biggest religious stars. Aimee Semple McPherson, who became a household name as "Sister Aimee," provides yet another example of a westering figure who combined religious fervor with innovation. Sister Aimee found freedom and opportunity in the West to develop a unique blend of religion and entertainment. She also found in Los Angeles the infrastructure and inspiration of the movie industry as well as a receptive population of recent migrants from the South and Southwest who were open to, even hungry for, her message and innovations.

[9] Gastón Espinosa, "'El Azteca': Francisco Olazábal and Latino Pentecostal Charisma, Power, and Faith Healing in the Borderlands," *Journal of the American Academy of Religion* 67 (September 1999), 602.

Figure 5.4   Aimee Semple McPherson at a revival. Source: Courtesy of The Bancroft Library, University of California, Berkeley, McPherson, Aimee POR 2.

Born in a small town in Ontario, Canada, the very year the frontier closed, Sister Aimee grew up in the Salvation Army (Figure 5.4). She converted to Pentecostalism at a revival meeting led by Robert James Semple, whom she married and accompanied to China as a missionary. Semple died in 1910 and by 1917 Sister Aimee started her own career as an evangelist and divine healer in the United States. She traveled the country with her mother, who had become her manager, in McPerson's "Gospel Car," one of the new technologies she harnessed for her work. One side of the car had a message that asked, "Where Will You Spend Eternity?" The other side displayed a sign that said, "Jesus Is Coming Soon – Get Ready." In the early part of her career, Sister Aimee could rely on a megaphone to gather a crowd. But, as her fame grew, she began to fill tents, parks, auditoriums, and arenas with audiences numbering in the thousands and, then, the tens of thousands.

She settled in Los Angeles and in 1923 built the Angelus Temple, which had a 5300-seat auditorium and offered wide range of services. LA perfectly suited the theatrical Sister Aimee, who had once aspired to become an actress. She filled her sermons with drama and performed flamboyantly in a trademark white dress and blue cape. Her sermons dealt with the end of the world and Christ's return, but without the fire-and-brimstone themes found in the work of most contemporary revival preachers. Instead, she used familiar stories such as "Little Red Riding Hood" and *Dr. Jekyll and Mr. Hyde* to illustrate her message. Sister Aimee emphasized God's love and the blessedness of heaven. Her services included music, impressively presented by a 200-voice choir, orchestras, and bands. Dramatic interpretations of biblical stories might include camels and macaws onstage, storytelling, healing, and speaking in tongues. Atop the Angelus Temple stood a lighted, rotating cross visible from 50 miles away. Sister Aimee tapped Los Angeles' show-business sensibilities and, quite literally, contributed to the bright lights of the big city and used them as tools in her religious mission.

Sister Aimee called her new creation the Church of the Foursquare Gospel, a reference to a vision recorded in Ezekiel, one of the books of the Hebrew scriptures (the Christian "Old Testament"), which she interpreted as Christ's fourfold role as savior, healer, baptizer in the Holy Spirit, and coming king. Sister Aimee preached 21 times a week from the Temple. Through the Temple, she offered telephone counseling, a 24-hour prayer vigil, and the Lighthouse for International Foursquare Evangelism (LIFE) Bible College, and she ministered to the hungry and homeless.

In 1922, Sister Aimee became the first woman to broadcast a sermon by radio, a new medium she deftly exploited. In 1923, the Angelus Temple began operating a 500-watt AM station known as KFSG (Kalling Foursquare Gospel), which made it an early adopter of this new technology. Audiences gathered in tents in nearby Venice and Pasadena to listen to services broadcast over the radio. Operating in an era before government broadcast regulations, KFSG arbitrarily changed its broadcast frequencies, a practice common at the time. Secretary of Commerce Herbert Hoover complained about this to McPherson. Sister Aimee replied with a characteristically colorful telegram that read, "Please order your minions of Satan to leave my station alone. You cannot expect the Almighty to abide by your wavelength nonsense."[10] Her knack for innovation and the appeal of her

---

[10] Quoted in Hal Erickson, *Religious Radio and Television in the United States, 1921–1991: The Programs and Personalities* (Jefferson, NC: McFarland, 1992), 127.

message proved successful in Los Angeles and far beyond. By the end of the twentieth century, the Church of the Foursquare Gospel had 21 000 churches around the world and claimed membership of more than 2 million.

McPherson became popular across the spectrum of US society. Her admirers included movie star Charlie Chaplin and three-time presidential candidate William Jennings Bryan, who as a high-profile fundamentalist and lawyer prosecuted John Scopes for teaching evolution in a Tennessee high school. Her greatest support, though, came from working class people, especially those who had migrated to California from across the western South, places like Arkansas, Texas, and Oklahoma, also known as the Bible Belt. Many of these people found it troubling that mainline denominations were embracing liberal theology and they left in search of a more comfortable spiritual home. McPherson and other fundamentalists met that need. Although she did not come from the Bible Belt, Sister Aimee provided a rare, prominent female voice in the wave of innovative fundamentalism that thrived in early twentieth-century California.

While McPherson, Norris, and others used radio effectively, Charles Edward Fuller became probably the greatest and most important radio preacher of the era. Fuller, a western fundamentalist evangelist, used the influence he gained through radio to start an influential West Coast seminary that became an enduring influence on religion in the United States. Fuller also led what could be called one of the nation's first megachurches. A native of Los Angeles born in 1887, Fuller grew up as an active member of the Presbyterian Church and personally felt the sting of the modernist–fundamentalist conflicts.

Fuller received his religious calling after working in a gold mine near Sacramento and in nearby orange groves. In the summer of 1917, at a service at the Church of the Open Door in Los Angeles, he had a conversion experience. He lost all desire to succeed in business and to make money and devoted himself to winning souls for God. Fuller attacked his ignorance of the Bible by devoting every spare hour to its study. He organized a Bible class, which grew rapidly. He also received formal education and degrees from the Bible Institute of Los Angeles, where he learned a conservative, fundamentalist theology based on biblical inerrancy, dispensational premillennialism (the belief that

Christ's coming would precede the thousand years of peace and prosperity forecast in the book of Revelation), and a passion for evangelizing.

Fuller continued attending Placentia Presbyterian Church, where he taught the fundamentalist tenets in a Sunday school class that eventually became more popular than the main worship service. Fuller's theology and, maybe, his popularity caused tension in the church. In 1924, Placentia Presbyterian withdrew its sponsorship of Fuller's class, which prompted Fuller to start the independent, fundamentalist Calvary Church. Fuller built Calvary from 50 members to 370 and organized revival meetings throughout the West. He also preached on the radio during the 1920s, but in 1929 a particularly enthusiastic listener response to a sermon he delivered on an Indianapolis station led him to reconsider the new medium's potential and to devote his energy to developing it for his evangelizing.

Fuller became best known for his radio ministry and his seminary. Fuller began radio work in the medium's infancy. He first broadcast in October 1924 when he spoke twice a week for the Bible Institute of Los Angeles. Three years later he received a spiritual call to make radio ministry his life's work. Fuller began broadcasts from Calvary Church in the late 1920s starting with Sunday morning services and later adding Thursday evening broadcasts. His preoccupation with radio ministry fueled growing dissatisfaction among Calvary's congregation.

He left Calvary in 1933 and devoted himself to a new project, the Gospel Broadcasting Association, which depended completely on listener contributions. He tried different formats for his radio show and in 1934 launched the *Radio Revival Hour*, later renamed *Old Fashioned Revival Hour* (*OFRH*), which became a hit. The format captured the feel of a homey, Sunday-evening church service. In an era when President Franklin Roosevelt's fireside chats soothed an anxious Depression-era audience, *OFRH*'s religious broadcasts provided a similar reassurance. Fuller's wife, Grace, read testimonials from listeners. Charles Fuller preached sincerely about human sinfulness, the need for personal conversion, and God's love. A quartet sang familiar gospel tunes and hymns. Listeners, who had seen the economy go to hell, were witnessing dislocations of farmers and massive migrations of people, and who did not care for the liberal bent in mainline religion, loved it.

Fuller's radio ministry grew explosively during the 1930s. About 1935 Fuller added stations in Los Angeles and Hollywood. His relentless campaign of revival meetings served as a publicity machine. To draw a studio audience, Fuller rented the Hollywood Woman's Club. An audience of 50 at his first such broadcast became the seed for the *OFRH*, which 13 stations of the Mutual Broadcasting System aired in January 1937. By the end of 1937, Mutual broadcast Fuller's show nationwide on 65 stations. By 1940, the show's popularity led Fuller to rent the 4400-seat Long Beach Municipal Auditorium to accommodate the studio audience and 150 stations carried the *Old Fashioned Revival Hour*. In 1943 hundreds of stations broadcast the show to an audience of 15 to 20 million people, making it in all likelihood the nation's most popular radio show. By the end of the 1940s, the show had moved to the American Broadcasting Company and had a potential audience of 33 million families. Fuller would eventually be heard on powerful AM stations in Europe, South America, and Asia, taking his California-grown message to much of the world.

In 1943, Fuller established the Fuller Evangelistic Foundation, named for his father, whose estate provided the funds. The foundation supports a wide range of evangelistic work in North America and provided funds for the interdenominational Fuller Theological Seminary, which opened in 1947 and which will be discussed in more detail in the next chapter. Fuller Theological Seminary trained a legion of evangelists and created a new, more open evangelical theology. It enrolled more than a thousand students in its School of Theology and sponsored extension ministries in seven other cities. It also started active black and Hispanic programs.

Through his network radio broadcasts, Charles Fuller made the West Coast a source of cultural innovation and influence that touched the rest of the nation. Likewise, through the seminary he founded, Fuller made Los Angeles (Pasadena) a hotbed of religious intellectual production. Fuller's accomplishments and influence resonate beyond the West's religious history; they also reflect the West's growing influence as a cultural center and trendsetter in the twentieth century.

The fundamentalist–modernist controversy produced a generation of western religious leaders who changed the way people experienced religion. Several developed messages that allowed them to capitalize on California's migration boom. All of them tapped into the spirit of the times and used new technologies effectively to reach wide audiences. Located in every corner of the West, from Seattle to Los Angeles to Fort Worth, they touched the entire region and through print and broadcast reached the nation. Developments in the West changed religion – western religious leaders influenced the nation in ways previous generations could not. The West was coming into its own and becoming a more important part of the nation.

World War II and Religion in the West

World War II (1939–1945), which remade both the world and the American West, makes a good endpoint for this chapter. In contrast to the factionalism produced by World War I, America's participation in World War II produced cooperation and consensus (with an important exception) and spurred developments that reinforced existing religious trends and set conditions for post-war innovations. Japan's attack on Pearl Harbor probably provides the best explanation for the difference. The attack gave the United States a clear and just reason to join the war and provided a cause that united the population. It also explains the anti-Japanese furor that provides the main exception to the era's tone of cooperation.

Japanese Americans and Japanese immigrants faced suspicion and persecution in the aftermath of the Pearl Harbor attack. Since most in these populations lived on the West Coast, the persecution became a western issue. In addition to an ethnic element, the persecution carried religious undertones. US officials feared that ethnic Japanese people might be loyal to Japan and might support additional attacks on the United States. Officials had some good reasons to harbor such suspicions. For example, US policies restricting Japanese immigration and land ownership might have stirred resentment. To cite another example, Shinto, the indigenous religion of Japan had been used for decades as a tool to build national identity and loyalty and included the notion that the emperor was a living god. As US officials scrutinized ethnic Japanese people, community leaders including leaders of Shinto and Buddhist churches received close attention. In 1942 President Franklin Roosevelt ordered all Japanese Americans living on the West Coast to be "relocated" to "internment" camps located in isolated areas of the West. Nationally, religious groups said little or nothing about this unjust policy. On the West Coast, though, some

Protestant, Jewish, and Roman Catholic clergy denounced "internment." Some organized their congregations to help Japanese
Americans with relocation, which often meant leaving homes, farms,
and businesses on very short notice. Church groups also provided
assistance to "internees" during the war and helped them return to
the outside world when the camps closed at the end of the war.

Perhaps the greatest influence World War II had on religion in the
West grew from the changes wrought by the dramatic expansion of the
military–industrial complex. Much of the West grew faster than the rest
of the country in the first decades of the twentieth century, but much of
that growth followed established patterns and came in agriculture,
extractive industries such as mining and lumber, and in commerce.
The war prompted a major change in the West's economy. The military
built a great many new bases in the West (and in the South) and western manufacturing expanded greatly to support the war effort. This
contributed to the rise of new research facilities in the West dedicated
to high-tech industries of the day, notably jet propulsion and atomic
weapons and energy. These developments brought population growth,
an increase in the size of cities and suburbs, and played a role in ending
the Depression. The newly populous, prosperous, and mobile West
provided an atmosphere conducive to an array of religious innovations
as the world entered the Atomic Age.

Conclusion

By 1945 the West looked much different than it did in 1890. Cowboys
still worshipped at camp meetings and an elderly Black Elk held fast
to Roman Catholicism, but much had changed. Westward migration
continued throughout the period and added to the region's population
and influence. Immigration through West Coast ports also contributed to the population boom. Economically, New Deal policies and,
more than anything, defense spending during World War II brought
not only prosperity but economic self-sufficiency to the West. In
terms of religious developments, 1890 through 1945 saw its share of
continuity, but more than anything else it witnessed innovations that
reflected changing times. American Indians practiced traditional ceremonies, participated in new religions with indigenous roots, and
made wholesale conversions to Christianity, to name a few variations

on the religious lives of the West's first peoples in the twentieth century. Perhaps most important, prominent religious leaders continued to serve spiritual communities and to contribute to building infrastructure for larger communities. A handful of preachers embraced new ideas and new technologies to change the way people experienced religion. These trendsetters influenced not only their immediate communities, but far beyond. The power of radio, for instance, allowed Charles Fuller to broadcast his brand of western fundamentalist Protestantism to the nation and to the world. The West had grown into an influential region, it could claim a new batch of religious ideas, and it spread them to inspire the world.

Suggested Reading

Alexander, Thomas G. 1986. *Mormonism in Transition: A History of the Latter-day Saints, 1890–1930*. Urbana, IL: University of Illinois Press.

Arrington, Leonard J. and Davis Bitton. 1992. *The Mormon Experience: A History of the Latter-day Saints*. 2nd edn. Urbana, IL: University of Illinois Press.

Bradley, Martha Sonntag. 1993. *Kidnapped from that Land: The Government Raids on the Short Creek Polygamists*. Salt Lake City, UT: University of Utah Press.

Butler, Anne M. 2012. *Across God's Frontiers: Catholic Sisters in the American West, 1850–1920*. Chapel Hill, NC: University of North Carolina Press.

Butler, Anne M., Michael E. Engh, and Thomas W. Spalding, eds. 1999. *The Frontiers and Catholic Identities*. Maryknoll, NY: Orbis.

Dochuk, Darren. 2011. *From Bible Belt to Sunbelt: Plain-Folk Religion, Grassroots Politics, and the Rise of Evangelical Conservatism*. New York: Norton.

Flake, Kathleen. 2004. *The Politics of American Religious Identity: The Seating of Senator Reed Smoot, Mormon Apostle*. Chapel Hill, NC: University of North Carolina Press.

Guarneri, Carl and David Alvarez, eds. 1987. *Religion in the American West: Historical Essays*. Lanham, MD: University Press of America.

Maroukis, Thomas C. 2012. *The Peyote Road: Religious Freedom and the Native American Church*. Norman, OK: University of Oklahoma Press.

Martínez, Juan Francisco. 2011. *Los Protestantes: An Introduction to Latino Protestantism in the United States*. Santa Barbara, CA: Praeger.

Marty, Martin E. 1984. *Pilgrims in Their Own Land: 500 Years of Religion in America*. Boston, MA: Little, Brown.

Sandoval, Moises. 2006. *On the Move: A History of the Hispanic Church in the United States*. Maryknoll, NY: Orbis.

Stein, Stephen, ed. 2012. *The Cambridge History of Religions in America*, vol. II 1790 to 1945. Cambridge: Cambridge University Press.

Steltenkamp, Michael F. 2009. *Nicholas Black Elk: Medicine Man, Missionary, Mystic*. Norman, OK: University of Oklahoma Press.

Stewart, Omer C. 1987. *Peyote Religion: A History*. Norman, OK: University of Oklahoma Press.

Sutton, Matthew Avery. 2007. *Aimee Semple McPherson and the Resurrection of Christian America*. Cambridge, MA: Harvard University Press.

6

Religion in the Cold War West, 1945–1965

On a Sunday morning in late March 1955, cars pulled into the Orange Drive-In Theater just off the Santa Ana Freeway in Orange County, California. Seventy-five cars eventually made their way onto the lot and pointed toward the screen. Their occupants had responded to a newspaper ad with the catchy slogan, "Worship as you are/In the family car." Atop the refreshment stand stood a 15-foot cross and an altar, both handmade by Robert Schuller, a midwesterner who had been called to California to start a congregation in the Reformed Church of America (RCA), a Protestant denomination founded by Dutch migrants during the colonial era and expanded by immigrants in the nineteenth century. At the appointed hour Schuller clambered on to the roof of the refreshment stand and preached to the drive-in congregation. This new entrepreneurial style of church was destined to be more than a branch of a historic, immigrant-dominated denomination.

Bent on increasing church attendance, Schuller went door-to-door to thousands of homes to build a mailing list. Schuller also invited Norman Vincent Peale, the best-selling author of *The Power of Positive Thinking* (1952, Prentice-Hall) and also a minister in the RCA, to

Inspiration and Innovation: Religion in the American West,
First Edition. Todd M. Kerstetter.
© 2015 John Wiley & Sons, Inc. Published 2015 by John Wiley & Sons, Inc.

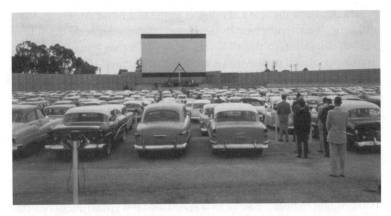

Figure 6.1   Garden Grove Community Church at the Orange Drive-In Theater. Source: Reproduced by permission of Crystal Cathedral Ministries.

speak to his congregation. Peale's sermon focused not on the congregation's sins, but rather on what great people they could become if they let the Holy Spirit fill them. That moment changed Schuller's approach to ministry. As he had abandoned traditional church space in favor of a drive-in theater, he abandoned a preaching style that generated a sense of guilt in his congregants in favor of positive preaching that made people feel good and optimistic (Figure 6.1). Schuller's unconventional church began to grow.

In 1955 Schuller had joined the nation's population shift to the Sunbelt by leaving the Midwest for Orange County, California. Migrants attracted by California's booming economy and pleasant weather filled Orange County in the 1940s, 1950s, and 1960s. Many had cut or lost social and cultural ties that had organized their lives in their previous homes and pursued opportunity and a predominantly secular individualism in the West. Schuller saw opportunity in this booming community of rootless migrants. He also wanted to reach the large number of westerners who, for any number of reasons, did not belong to a church. When it became time to name the church, he chose Garden Grove Community Church. He hoped that name would present an image more attractive and welcoming than anything containing "Reformed Church." Schuller also developed an optimistic theological message focused on the "Dignity of the Person" and aimed at boosting self-esteem with the goal of attracting as large an audience as possible.

Schuller lived the story of religion in the Cold War American West and provides a symbol for its development. Schuller rode the tide of Sunbelt migration in the 1940s through 1960s that remade the West from a peripheral region into a metropolitan center. He brought with him religious ideas and practices that showed continuity with other parts of the country, yet he pioneered developments that helped create a template for the megachurch movement of the late twentieth century. His innovations, rooted in a uniquely western experience, spread from the West to other regions and showed the region's growing importance to the nation's religious culture.

Religious life in the West after 1945 reflected the transformational influences of the Great Depression and World War II, but the Cold War brought to bear a host of new issues. Federal government policies during those years industrialized the region and drew millions of new migrants from other parts of the US and from abroad. Western cities grew dramatically and the West led the nation in suburban sprawl. The region became more powerful politically and economically as it became a core region of the country. For example, western cities such as Los Angeles, San Francisco, Fort Worth-Dallas, Denver, and Seattle came to function much as major cities elsewhere such as Chicago and New York. The West emerged from World War II a more populous and more influential region.

World War II had scarcely ended when the United States and the Soviet Union entered the Cold War. The two superpowers avoided direct armed confrontations with each other, but competed with each other for influence around the globe. At the risk of eliminating any sense of nuance, the Cold War could be boiled down to a set of conflicts rooted in the United States and its allies supporting and spreading capitalism (free markets and private ownership of capital) and the Soviet Union and its allies supporting and spreading Communism (economies and markets planned and controlled by the state).

Many people associate the Cold War with politics and economics, but the conflict touched religion, too. By 1950 both superpowers had nuclear weapons and their combined arsenals soon after had the capacity to inflict massive destruction on the globe. This created enormous anxiety and led the famous evangelist Billy Graham to predict nuclear holocaust. Graham even believed US–Soviet tensions proved that the end times predicted in the Bible's Book of Revelation were near. Furthermore, Graham believed – and was joined by other preachers and politicians of all stripes – that faith provided an important tool with which a Christian or Judeo-Christian America could confront atheistic or "godless" Communism. In a sign of the times, Congress in 1954 added the phrase "under God" to the pledge of allegiance to the US flag.

Western religious life reflected a number of distinctive characteristics during the Cold War years of 1945 to 1965. According to some scholars of religion in the West, the region had no dominant faith. Sub-regions had strong denominational affiliations. The Catholic Southwest and the Mormon corridor of Utah, Arizona, and Idaho provide probably the two best-known examples of regions with strong denominational affiliations. But, as a whole, the West had a religiously diverse society – the region was home to a wide variety of faiths and no single denomination gave the region a recognizable religious personality. This diversity might help to explain why westerners were more comfortable not affiliating with a church than were people in other regions. In measuring church membership as a percentage of total population, the 1950 census reported Oregon dead last among the 48 states (Alaska and Hawaii had not gained statehood yet). A mere 23.7 percent of Oregonians reported church membership. The nation's average stood at 49 percent. The West had the lowest percentage of church membership of any region. These statistics have led scholars to label large portions of the West as "unchurched," which might be the most apt way to describe the region's religious personality in the mid-twentieth century. This characteristic drew the attention of certain religious leaders who saw opportunity in this "problem."

Suburbanization, the creation or expansion of communities adjacent to or near cities, also shaped religion in the West. In the 20 years after World War II the development of American suburbs exploded. The Depression of the 1930s crippled the US economy and World War II (1941–1945 for US involvement) brought restrictions in the form of rationing for food, gasoline, metal, and other materials. Despite these restrictions on the civilian economy, wartime production brought economic recovery and general prosperity. When the war and government restrictions ended, pent-up demand for housing combined with favorable mortgage terms available to military veterans and increased automobile ownership unleashed a torrent of suburbanization. You might think of the suburbs as a new "frontier." As happened with previous waves of new settlement in the West, new settlement in the post-war suburbs meant a boom in church expansion.

Suburbanization affected much of the nation, so what does it have to do with religion in the West? Of the possible answers to that question, maybe the most important involves the "unchurched" character of the West's population. Western suburbs were more than new communities, they were new communities populated by migrants, many drawn west by the lure of jobs during the Great Depression. Others came to assignments at the West's new military bases during World War II, or for jobs supporting the war effort. Many found themselves far from their roots and living in a region known for religious pluralism and for its sizeable population who didn't belong to churches. This is the atmosphere that inspired Robert Schuller to climb onto a concession stand to preach to people sitting in their cars. Schuller and others like him reaching out to new and old westerners alike not only inspired religious innovations but also contributed to the rise of a conservative Sunbelt political movement with its epicenter in Southern California.

The years from 1945 through 1965 also saw westerners face new challenges related to a growing Hispanic presence. Mexican Americans and new immigrants from Mexico and other Latin American countries figured prominently in pushing the Catholic Church to face its attitudes toward race and ethnicity. Protestant denominations saw a significant increase in Hispanic membership in this period. Despite changes by both the Catholic Church and Protestant denominations, by 1965 both groups still had considerable room for improvement with respect to relations with the West's significant and growing Hispanic population.

The West's Mormon population also continued to grow after World War II and issues related to its Mormon past continued to set the West apart from other regions. The Church of Jesus Christ of Latter-day Saints boomed along with the rest of the West. At the edges of American and Mormon society a group that has been labeled "fundamentalist Mormons" found themselves in conflict with mainstream values in yet another battle over polygamy. It should be noted that the Latter-day Saints Church, which abandoned polygamy in 1890, has virtually no connection with the polygamous groups and firmly states the term "Mormon" has been incorrectly applied to such groups.

From 1945 through 1965 the West grappled with a variety of regional religious issues decades or more in the making. The West at once participated in national religious developments and retained distinctive characteristics. Religion continued to inspire westerners and changes on the western scene prompted innovations that would radiate outward. The West became more influential and the inventory in the West's religious catalog expanded.

Religious Innovation

The Cold War era saw in the American West a flowering of religious innovation. I include Buddhism here, even though it has a long history elsewhere in the world and was "new" in this era only inasmuch as it found new adherents in the American West and the United States during the twentieth century. Scientology, a second example, was truly something new. So, too, was an interest in the spiritual possibilities presented by unidentified flying objects (UFOs). The influence and controversy generated by these innovations points to the West's solidifying status as a core region of the United States increasingly capable of exerting cultural influence rather than simply being shaped by outside forces.

Buddhism and the Beats

The 1950s saw a revival of interest in Buddhism. Immigration restrictions virtually stopped the flow of Asians and Asian influences into the United States by the 1920s and the persecution of Japanese Americans during World War II effectively forced Buddhism underground or out of sight during the 1940s. In the 1950s, the Beat generation of writers, who had strong connections to San Francisco and the West Coast, reprised the role played by nineteenth-century Transcendentalists as intellectuals interested in tapping eastern spirituality to inspire their art and to find meaning in life. Writers such as Jack Kerouac, Allen Ginsberg, and Gary Snyder benefitted from access to more and better information about Buddhism than the Transcendentalists had enjoyed. All three became Buddhists and their works contributed to a revival in popular interest in Buddhism in the United States. Their writing reflected Eastern religious traditions such as harmony with nature, rejection of materialism, pacifism, and simplicity. Kerouac's 1958 novel *The Dharma Bums* (1958, The Viking Press), arguably the best-known of these works, told the semi-fictional story of literary Buddhists hitch-hiking around the United States. Beat writers offered an alternative vision for society, including a rejection of mainstream religious institutions and values, which they associated with corrupt values cherished by older generations. These writings inspired idealism in young people and helped provide a philosophical foundation for the counterculture movement of the 1960s.

California's Berkeley Buddhist Temple acted as an important center for Buddhism in the United States. Many students, including Beat writers, learned about Buddhism through the temple's classes and a publication called *Berkeley Bussei*. Kerouac and Snyder even wrote for the *Bussei*. The temple helped sustain the Buddhist Churches of America and trained a generation of Buddhist leaders. Asian immigration and Asian religious influences would boom after immigration reform passed in 1965 and the Beats and the Berkeley Buddhists helped make that possible.

Scientology

While Buddhism was an old religion made new by the Beats, Scientology, a truly new religious movement, was born in the Cold War West and became its most significant contribution in this field. Scientology sprang from the mind of L. Ron Hubbard, a native of Tilden, Nebraska, who was raised in rural Montana. Hubbard had a successful career as a writer, notably of science fiction and fantasy, and served in the US Navy during World War II. Hubbard spent nearly a year hospitalized after being wounded in the South Pacific during the war. In the late 1940s, Hubbard began researching mental health. In 1950, he published *Dianetics, the Modern Science of Mental Health* (1950, Hermitage House), which became a bestseller. Hubbard's system of Dianetics formed the basis for Scientology. Late in 1953, Hubbard established a church corporation in New Jersey and in the following year established the first local church in Los Angeles, where the church also established its international headquarters. Hubbard followed with a second congregation in Auckland, New Zealand, the next year. From its Southern California headquarters, the religion spread rapidly worldwide.

Scientology ranks among the most controversial new religious movements, thanks largely to legal debate over whether it qualifies as a religion. Scientology believes human beings are naturally good, but have fallen into disarray due to an aberrant mental state. The Church teaches and coaches members to train their minds to operate properly. Scientology seeks to correct aberrant mental function, which it believes will lead to freedom from war, pollution, insanity, drugs, and crime. It refers to its thought system as "data" and claims to be the first human attempt to approach spiritual questions using scientific methodology. Critics have claimed that the Church of Scientology charges excessive fees, uses deceptive marketing practices, and intimidates and harasses its critics. These charges led the US government and other governments to take legal action against the church. The church responded with charges of persecution. The church won most of the legal battles. In 1993, the Internal Revenue Service ruled that the church was a charitable religious organization and granted it tax-exempt status. Regardless of the controversy, Scientology stands as an important innovation that radiates influence nationally and internationally from its West Coast headquarters.

Unidentified Flying Objects (UFOs) and religion

Scientology might have only tangential links to the military–industrial complex, but the Atomic Age and the Space Age both had military–industrial roots and sparked new interest in UFOs and the interpretation of alien encounters in terms of philosophy and religion. Southern California and the Roswell, New Mexico, area became centers for this activity. The 1950s brought a flurry of reports that humans had made contact with extraterrestrial beings. Most who reported contact with aliens wrestled with philosophical and religious questions. What did it mean that other life forms existed in the universe and that some claimed to have come to earth to visit "their own"?

George Adamski, a Polish immigrant who worked in a hamburger stand on the slopes of Mt. Palomar in southern California, posed a possible answer to such questions, which seemed particularly acute in an age when nuclear holocaust was a distinct possibility. Adamski claimed that in 1952 he met a spaceman named Orthon. Orthon came from a planet where people lived in harmony and peace and had come to earth as part of a mission to warn humans about the danger of nuclear proliferation. Adamski's story appeared in the 1953 book *Flying Saucers Have Landed* (1953, British Book Centre) and generated a flood of similar contact claims. Adamski reported additional contacts, including trips on UFOs to other inhabited planets. Adamski's stories resonated with thousands of people and he lectured about his experiences and alien philosophy throughout the United States and Europe.

The exploration of extraterrestrial life took a more overtly religious turn in the hands of George Van Tassel, another prominent contactee (person who experienced contact with aliens) who also happened to have worked in southern California aerospace plants in the 1930s and 1940s. Van Tassel, in his 1952 book *I Rode a Flying Saucer!* (1952, New Age Publishing Co.), claimed he had made telepathic contact with extraterrestrials on a mission to improve the human race. Van Tassel, who had founded the Brotherhood of the Cosmic Christ in the late 1940s and the Ministry of Universal Wisdom in 1953, merged extraterrestrial lore with the Bible. He claimed to see evidence in the Bible that humans were a race of extraterrestrials that had been planted on earth for spiritual development. Interference from "negative" space beings led an extraterrestrial Mary to be sent to earth to deliver the historic Jesus, who would aid humanity in its spiritual mission. Van Tassel predicted Jesus would return to earth with a fleet of spaceships in the 1950s to save humans, who, as shown by their obsession with atomic weapons, were still controlled by negative space beings.

In addition to attempting to reconcile extraterrestrials with traditional Christianity, Van Tassel made important contributions to popular UFO religion by sponsoring an annual UFO convention at Giant Rock in the Mojave Desert and by establishing telepathic contact with a spaceman named Ashtar, an intergalactic lawman on a mission to liberate earth from the clutches of the negative space beings. The convention drew tens of thousands of people from 1953 to 1977 and served as a forum for the UFO community. Messages from "Ashtar Command" came not only to Van Tassel but also to a growing group of others who predicted aliens would land on earth and set matters right. As had happened with other religious groups who dared to predict the date of the second coming and failed, Ashtar devotees lost credibility and followers as one after another prediction of the space fleet's arrival failed. The concept of Ashtar had a wide reach in the UFO community at its height, but most groups interested in Ashtar have disbanded. Devotees changed their interpretations of the message, too. Instead of seeing Ashtar Command as offering a global, physical rescue, they began to see the message as a source of personal and metaphysical salvation.

UFO-related religious movements exist outside the American West, but the region has a long history of prominent movements dating to the Cold War era. The movements' links to the rise of the military–industrial complex in the West are difficult to ascertain, but their concern with the nuclear age, which figures prominently in the region's history, are not. At the very least, these movements present a little-considered result of World War II's influence on the region and the world of spirituality. As we will see in the next chapter, these influences outlived the Cold War.

The Fundamentalist Church of Jesus Christ of Latter-day Saints

The Southwest, specifically Arizona and Utah, continued to grapple with the decidedly non-Space Age fallout from the anti-Mormon crusade of the nineteenth century, which remained very much evident in the Cold War era. When The Church of Jesus Christ of Latter-day Saints renounced plural marriage (often called polygamy) in the manifesto of 1890, some Mormons disagreed and continued the practice. Probably the best-known and largest contingent became widely known as the Fundamentalist Church of Jesus Christ of Latter-day Saints (FLDS). It bears repeating that the Latter-day Saints Church disavows any connection and disapproves of labeling this group "Fundamentalist Mormons." As these hardcore polygamists saw it, Latter-day Saints Church leaders were misguided when they abandoned polygamy. The polygamists believed Latter-day Saints Church leaders had acted out of political expediency and had turned their backs on the divine revelation to practice plural marriage. Fundamentalists settled in clusters around the West, but the community of Short Creek, Arizona, gained special notoriety.

Short Creek sits a long way from anyplace else, which probably proved attractive to the polygamists who moved there in 1928. They saw it as a place for Saints (as they called themselves) to gather, similar to how Brigham Young viewed the Salt Lake Valley in the 1840s. The nearest settlement, Hurricane, was 28 miles away and the nearest city, St. George, Utah, was even farther – 50 miles and across the Utah state line. In that kind of isolation, residents could do pretty much as they wished. By 1935, the divine law of plural marriage, "the Principle," distinguished Short Creek and had made it a magnet for other polygamists.

As the community grew, non-polygamous neighbors and the Latter-day Saints Church became concerned and pressed Arizona's Mohave County attorney to act. The neighbors resented the exploding demand for schools and social services that had to be supported by tax payers. The Latter-day Saints Church, which had moved considerably toward the mainstream of US values by the mid-twentieth century, resented the lingering polygamy and the fact that some polygamists had joined local Latter-day Saints stakes, which threatened to tarnish the Latter-day Saints Church's reputation and to cloud its renunciation of polygamy. Short Creek's isolation protected it. A crow flying from the county seat of Kingman to Short Creek would have to cover 90 miles. But a county attorney traveling by automobile would have to drive 425 miles through California, Nevada, and Arizona to reach Short Creek.

In the late summer of 1935, both the state and the Latter-day Saints Church moved against the Short Creek fundamentalists. Using information gathered from welfare applications, Elmo Bollinger, the Mohave County attorney, filed charges against leading members of the community in what would become known as the "polygamy cases." The Latter-day Saints Church authorities went after Short Creek fundamentalists who had joined the local stake. Claude Hirschi, the stake president, presented the fundamentalists a loyalty oath, which included a statement of support for the Church presidency and a denunciation of plural marriage. The fundamentalists refused to sign and the Church excommunicated them. In the civil legal system, two prominent Short Creek polygamists were convicted for violating the state's anti-polygamy law. They served less than a year in the state penitentiary then returned to Short Creek. The raid generated considerable publicity, evoked public interest and a measure of sympathy for the fundamentalists, and, in fact, hardened the convictions of the polygamists and brought new members to the community. As the Church and state saw it, the raid had backfired.

In 1944, federal and state law enforcement officials tried to force a permanent solution to the polygamy problem with a massive regional round up covering communities in Arizona, Utah, and Idaho. The

"Boyden Raid" took its name from US Attorney John S. Boyden (a Mormon), who organized the raid with Utah State Attorney General Brigham E. Roberts, grandson of a polygamous nineteenth-century Church leader. Those arrested in the raids faced a variety of state and federal charges. State charges included unlawful cohabitation and criminal conspiracy. Federal charges included mailing obscene materials, kidnapping, and Mann Act (White Slave Trade Act) violations. The raid and resulting charges set off a complex series of prosecutions. Some charges resulted in convictions and jail sentences, some did not, and some found their way to the US Supreme Court. In the end, the state and federal government spent more than $500 000 prosecuting the cases. Fifteen fundamentalists served sentences in the state penitentiary, which left 15 polygamous families without a head of household.

The fundamentalist colony of Short Creek thrived through the 1950s. The population doubled each decade from 1935 to 1955. Natural increase accounted for much of the growth, but the communal nature of the community also drew new members. In 1953, 39 men, 86 women, and 263 children lived in the community. Businesses included a saw mill, a shingle mill, a cannery, an automobile repair shop, a fruit drier, and a carpentry shop. The thriving community continued to hold the attention of the Mormon Church and Arizona state officials. Outsiders' concerns about the women and children of Short Creek brought a third raid on July 26, 1953. It would devastate the community (Figure 6.2).

Arizona officials kept tabs on Short Creek and by the early 1950s claimed the fundamentalist community created a taxpayer emergency. More and more Short Creek women requested state aid for a growing number of dependent children. Many of the women listed the same man as their husband and some of the women were underage. The growing population of children required schooling and the community petitioned for expanded school facilities. Non-polygamous neighbors who paid taxes resented the burden placed on the social welfare and educational system by the Short Creek polygamists. This resentment contributed to a state investigation that began in 1951.

After more than a year of planning, Arizona law enforcement officials raided Short Creek with arrest warrants for every adult on July 26, 1953. Charges in the warrants included rape, statutory rape, carnal knowledge, polygamous living, cohabitation, bigamy, adultery, and misappropriation of school funds. Court documents filed after

Figure 6.2   Short Creek Residents, 1953. Source: Used by permission, Utah State Historical Society, all rights reserved.

the raid included accusations of adults encouraging underage girls to participate in unlawful conduct. Whatever the legal documents said, officials placed paramount importance on rescuing Short Creek's children. Assistant Attorney General Paul LaPrade, who prepared the case, put it this way, "The principle objective is to rescue these children from a life-time of immoral practices without their ever having had an opportunity to learn of or observe the outside world and its concepts of decent living."[1] The conflict pitted competing visions of family, community, and morality against each other.

In the raid's aftermath, the children taken from Short Creek, regardless of whether they remained with their mothers, became wards of the state. Juvenile cases began entering the state court system

[1] Quoted in Martha Sonntag Bradley, *Kidnapped from that Land: The Governnment Raids on the Short Creek Polygamists* (Salt Lake City, UT: University of Utah Press, 1993), 131.

on July 29. Over the course of the next two years, the legal system found no sufficient evidence to remove the children from their parents. On March 3, 1955, the Superior Court of the State of Arizona ruled all children removed from Short Creek should be returned to their parents. The parents still faced their own legal issues related to their living and marriage arrangements.

Utah, which had not participated in the raid, followed another route in an attempt to protect children of Short Creek fundamentalists living in that state. Arguing that parents who raised children in a polygamous setting had, effectively, neglected their children, the state removed children of a polygamous family for a test case. The court system upheld the removal. The parents regained custody only after signing an oath renouncing their belief in polygamy and testifying that they had ceased to practice it. After the children were returned, the parents returned to their fundamentalist, polygamous lifestyle. The family saw in the experience what they considered the state's loathing of their lifestyle and religious beliefs as well as a willingness to destroy families.

The Short Creek raids occurred against the backdrop of the Cold War and McCarthyism. A conservative, paranoid nation saw threats to the American Way from communism and, at Short Creek, communalism and polygamy. The Short Creek raid generated bad publicity for Utah and Arizona and strengthened the community bonds among the fundamentalists. In the following decades, law enforcement agencies in each state established an informal truce with Short Creek, which after 1962 became known as Colorado City, Arizona, and Hilldale, Utah. The twin communities continued to grow and more than 4500 fundamentalists lived there as of the early 1990s.

In a 1990 interview, Paul Van Dam, Utah's attorney general, explained that law enforcement officers in his state turned a blind eye toward polygamists. To Van Dam, Short Creek demonstrated that fighting polygamy caused enormous social disruption and that taking children of polygamists into state care would be expensive. Furthermore, prosecuting polygamists for illegal cohabitation would open the door to prosecuting every unmarried couple living together. Finally, it had become apparent that prosecuting polygamy would not stop adherents from practicing what they considered a matter of faith. As for the twin communities, one cannot understand them without understanding their theology, which sees the hand of God in everything they do. They

view polygamy and their communal lifestyle as righteous. These episodes reveal the ongoing challenge of church–state relations in the
American West. They demonstrate the significance of religion in shaping family life and social relations. They illustrate how the West, which
in the mid-twentieth century still included vast stretches of remote
territory, could provide refuge for outlaws, in this case religious outlaws. And, they show an ongoing contest over the meaning of religious
freedom and the ability of communities to chart their own courses
within the limits of a national society. Furthermore, the Latter-day Saint
Church's cooperation in the raids demonstrated how it had moved
toward the main stream of US culture and society in the decades since
it abandoned polygamy. In the next chapter, we will see that the legacy
of polygamy extended into the twenty-first century and into Texas,
where another dramatic raid on an FLDS settlement demonstrated
continuity in the West's distinctive religious history, in this case conflict
between the Christian mainstream and fundamentalist Mormon communities. By the middle of the twentieth century, even as members of
The Church of Jesus Christ of Latter-day Saints were becoming more
and more mainstream, so-called fundamentalist Mormons continued
to defy American law and be prosecuted, and perhaps persecuted, for
it, now with mainstream Mormons supporting the prosecution.

The Native American Church

Although polygamy remained outside the law, the sacramental use of
peyote by members of the Native American Church gained important
legal protection thanks to a 1964 ruling by the California Supreme
Court. The case, *People v. Woody*, stemmed from a peyote bust in the
desert outside Needles, California, in 1962. A group of Navajos had
gathered there to conduct a Native American Church ceremony in
which ingestion of peyote played an integral part. Police arrested
several congregants and charged them with violating California law
that prohibited possession of peyote. After being convicted, the defen-
dants appealed.

In overturning the Navajos' convictions, the California Supreme
Court interpreted the First Amendment's free exercise of religion
clause to protect peyote use within the Native American Church.
Recall that the US Supreme Court ruled in the 1879 *Reynolds* decision
that the Mormon practice of polygamy was *not* a practice protected by

the free exercise clause. In that case, the court ruled the state had a compelling social interest in prohibiting polygamy to protect women and families. The court also ruled that practice of polygamy was not central to observing Mormonism. In the peyote case California's attorney general cited the *Reynolds* decision as a precedent for restricting religious practice, but the justices of California's Supreme Court rejected that argument. They wrote that ingestion of peyote constituted a vital component of Native American Church practice – the religion could not be practiced in the absence of peyote. They also ruled that whatever social threat peyote use posed, it did not compare to polygamy's threat to democratic institutions and the morals and well-being of its practitioners. The ruling also struck a note that would echo, especially in the West's religious life, for decades to come: "The varying currents of the subcultures that flow into the mainstream of our national life give it depth and beauty. We preserve a greater value than an ancient tradition when we protect the rights of the Indians who honestly practiced an old religion in using peyote one night at a meeting in a desert Hogan near Needles, California."[2] After 1965 the West would be home to a remarkable array of new religious movements that would flow into the mainstream of national life, give it depth and beauty, and create sharp controversies. As for the Native American Church, it would face more legal battles later in the century, but the *People v. Woody* decision pointed toward a better day for Native Americans.

Hispanics and Religion in the West

The years after World War II brought special problems and opportunities for Hispanics and religion in the West. In the Roman Catholic Church, ethnic divisions and prejudices discussed in earlier chapters continued. One issue involved a shortage of Spanish-speaking priests that was illuminated by the *bracero* (Spanish for manual labor) program and immigration from Mexico. The bracero program started during World War II, and consisted of a series of laws and diplomatic agreements between the United States and Mexico designed to provide temporary Mexican workers in the United States.

[2] *People v. Woody*, 61 Cal.2d 716 (1964).

The war had created a labor shortage and the program aimed to alleviate it, especially in agriculture. The program, which at its peak in 1956 brought 445 197 workers into the United States, continued until 1964. Braceros and non-braceros who entered the United States illegally joined a substantial Spanish-speaking community of Catholics served by very few Spanish-speaking clergy and a church more interested in serving its Anglo constituency than Hispanics.

The church recognized this problem and took steps to address it. The church established the Bishops' Committee for Spanish Speaking in 1945 in an effort to reach out to Spanish-speaking Catholics. That program was, at least in part, a defensive measure to fend off Protestant recruiting of Hispanics, which grew increasingly successful in the post-war decades. Recognizing that most braceros had little or no access to Spanish-speaking priests, the bishop's committee in 1953 brought 24 Mexican priests into the United States to minister to the workers. The program did not endure, though, and the shortage of Spanish-speaking priests and Hispanic representation led civil rights activists to call for changes in the church during the 1960s and 1970s.

The shortage of Spanish-speaking priests was a manifestation of another problem in the Catholic Church: lingering racism. The problem existed nationally, but was especially pronounced in the Southwest, which had a large Mexican American population. Few Hispanics qualified for admission to seminaries in this period. Those few Mexican Americans who graduated from high school, for example, often attended inferior schools (thanks at least in part to inequitable funding and Jim Crow-style segregation in many areas) and struggled to pass seminary entrance exams. Those who qualified found a cold reception waiting at seminary. David Gómez, who ultimately succeeded in becoming a priest, said his Anglo classmates at seminary ignored him. Gómez felt deceived by promises of acceptance and equality he had been given. Denver's archbishop said, "The reason I don't have Mexican seminarians is that they just don't meet my standards."[3] The archbishop's comment reflected the belief that Hispanics had weak faith and were not suited for the priesthood. A corollary belief, usually left unspoken, held that Hispanics were inferior and that the priesthood was for whites.

---

[3] Quoted in Moises Sandoval, *On the Move: A History of the Hispanic Church in the United States* (Maryknoll, NY: Orbis, 2006), 78.

Whatever prejudices existed, the Catholic Church in the West increased its outreach to Hispanics in the 1950s and 1960s. Motivation for this outreach came from several sources, including the pope, who in 1947 issued a call to Catholics to work harder in fighting social injustice. On the local level, priests and nuns wished to engage youths, to increase religious participation by men, and to improve the lives of migrant workers.

The church reached out to urban Hispanics with one set of programs. For youths, the church sponsored organizations such as the Catholic Youth Organization (CYO). The CYO taught church doctrine to members and also organized athletic competitions and provided chaperoned meeting places. In east Los Angeles, the CYO sponsored two car clubs with the hope of engaging young males swept up in the post-war automobile culture. The *cursillo* ("little course") movement aimed to engage older men. The movement started in Texas in 1958 and spread to California. *Cursillos* used a program of self-reflection to inspire men to become more active in church activities and to engage in social service. Activist César Chávez, whose rise to prominence in the 1960s will be discussed later, provides the best-known example of someone inspired by a *cursillo* to fight for social justice. Women could find a similar experience in groups called *Guadalupanas*, which originated to celebrate the feast day of Our Lady of Guadalupe and sometimes grew into community action groups. Salt Lake City provides a good example. Hispanic Catholic women there began meeting with their priest in 1962 to discuss issues in their neighborhood. These discussions led to the creation of a Catholic credit union, a cooperative food market, and adult literacy classes.

Hispanic Protestants faced issues similar to those of their Catholic counterparts, but some Protestant denominations addressed the problems earlier and successfully. In the decades after World War II mainline Protestant denominations such as Methodists and Presbyterians either lost Hispanic members or saw the growth in their Hispanic membership decline. The Methodist Houchen Settlement in El Paso illustrates how mainline Protestants reached out to Hispanic populations but in a way that might have alienated the community. Houchen, modeled after settlement houses such as Jane Addams's Hull House in Chicago and designed to help immigrants adjust to life in American cities, provided medical services, child care, arts and crafts classes, and other services. It also emphasized Americanization and tried to convert its users to Methodism. Or, as one historian put it, Houchen offered a bilingual environment but not a bicultural one. That started to change in 1959, though, when Houchen's leaders de-emphasized conversion and focused on serving families and the neighborhood.

At the same time, Baptists and Pentecostals saw their Hispanic membership grow rapidly. The divergent growth patterns can be traced to several factors. One example comes from the nature of church leadership. Both Methodists and Presbyterians expected pastors to obtain a seminary degree before ordination. That educational standard made it difficult for Hispanics (and others, for that matter) who lacked formal education, the ability to study in English, and the means to pay seminary tuition to obtain seminary training. In this sense, the mainline Protestant denominations exercised an educational elitism similar to that of the Catholic Church. On the other hand, Pentecostal and Baptist churches held ordination expectations that were easier to meet. Potential pastors could train on the job or attend short-term Bible institutes that might offer classes in Spanish and specialize in ministry among Hispanics. These factors help us understand why Catholic leaders might have been worried about Protestant proselytizing in the decades after World War II. They also help explain why, despite their head start with mission work in Texas, the Methodists and Presbyterians have each had fewer than 100 congregations in 2010 while later arriving Baptists had nearly 1500 Hispanic congregations and Assemblies of God had more than 400.

Evangelicals and the Sunbelt West

With respect to evangelical Protestantism, the West after World War II saw both innovation and a renewed effort to convert the unchurched. Both reflected the region's ongoing development and the latter echoed earlier efforts to "civilize" the frontier. The "Texas theology" that had developed earlier in the century (described in the previous chapter) combined with the dynamic development of suburbs in Southern California to create a "Sunbelt creed," a new religious culture that would change the West and the nation. The Sunbelt creed featured entrepreneurialism, experimentation, and engagement. Entrepreneurial pastors and denominations started new churches and adopted new tactics to win followers. They also experimented with new worship styles and messages. For example, a new generation of religious leaders carried on the tradition of mixing religion and show-business that brought Sister Aimee success. Some, but not all, sought greater engagement with their communities and current events. Possibly the most important example involved preachers becoming partners in a new conservative movement that would gain strength through the end of the century. The West and religion in the West were becoming more influential within the national arena.

Post-World War II evangelical influence in the Sunbelt rode on momentum built by pioneers discussed in the previous chapter. Charles E. Fuller, in particular, enjoyed ongoing success and his contributions provide a bridge into the post-war period. In 1947 he founded the Fuller Theological Seminary in Pasadena, California. Fuller dreamed of an institution that would not only train ministers and missionaries, but also produce conservative Protestant scholarship. He hoped the seminary would be "a Cal Tech of the evangelical world," giving them the intellectual firepower they needed to critique cultural and intellectual movements that threatened Biblical authority and orthodox doctrine. The school attracted prominent scholars and became the largest interdenominational evangelical seminary in the world. In the 1960s it added schools of psychology and missions. As the school developed, many faculty members pursued a "progressive" conservative form of Christian faith they considered open-minded and intellectually defensible and orthodox. Some fundamentalists, who had supported Fuller and the seminary, criticized these efforts, the seminary, and Fuller himself. The seminary trained a legion of evangelists and created a new, more open evangelical theology. The new movement associated with Fuller became known as neo-evangelicalism: conservative but not fundamentalist. Aside from institutions in the Fort Worth-Dallas metroplex, Fuller had little competition in the West. The seminary enrolled more than a thousand students in its School of Theology and sponsored extension ministries in seven other cities. It also started active black and Hispanic programs. The establishment of an influential evangelical seminary in southern California demonstrates how the West was growing into a more powerful role.

Just two years after Fuller opened his seminary, a remarkable revival called the Christ for Greater Los Angeles Campaign signaled the arrival of a new era for Sunbelt evangelicalism. The revival turned a promising young preacher, Billy Graham, into a national star who would become an adviser to every twentieth-century president starting with Eisenhower. More important, Graham brought together religion and politics in a way that would shape a new conservative movement.

Graham's revival commenced in September 1949 days after the world learned that the Soviet Union had exploded its own atomic bomb. The possibility that the Soviet Union could use nuclear weapons on the United States dramatically heightened Cold War tensions and anxiety. That anxiety appeared in Graham's sermons. "Communism is not only an economic interpretation of life – Communism is a religion that is inspired, directed, and motivated by the Devil himself who has declared war against Almighty God," Graham told his audience. "In this moment I can see the judgment hand of God over Los Angeles. I can see judgment about to fall."[4] But Graham preached more than fire and nuclear brimstone, he also preached about the Lord's mercy. The revival drew crowds numbering in the thousands. When a local celebrity converted, even more people came. Organizers extended the revival's run by five weeks. National news magazines *Time*, *Newsweek*, and *Life* reported on the revival. Drumming the perils of communism and the rewards of Christ, Graham emerged from his Los Angeles revival a national celebrity.

After Graham packed up his tent a new generation of preachers in Southern California picked up where he had left off and none did it better than J. Vernon McGee. Born in Hillsboro, Texas, and educated at Dallas Theological Seminary, among other places, McGee embodied the "Texas theology" discussed in the previous chapter, and he took it with him when he moved to Pasadena, California, in the early 1940s to lead Lincoln Avenue Presbyterian Church. In 1949 he accepted the senior pastorship at the 3300-member Church of the Open Door. His embrace of radio ministry helped him build the congregation to 4400 by 1965 and made him a star with a broad audience. McGee's star power gave his message a long reach and his message shows how religion and politics mixed to support a movement.

---

[4] Quoted in Darren Dochuk, *From Bible Belt to Sunbelt: Plain-Folk Religion, Grassroots Politics, and the Rise of Evangelical Conservatism* (New York: Norton, 2011), 139.

McGee preached to an audience primed to hear his message. His audience overlapped with the electorate that put Richard Nixon into the House of Representatives in 1946. Named to the House Un-American Activities Committee (HUAC), Nixon became a star of the anticommunist movement by investigating reports of "Reds" (communists) in the motion picture industry, among other things, and making Southern California a hub of anticommunist activity. McGee's audience also included residents of Southern California's prosperous, booming suburbs. In the mid-1950s about a thousand people a day moved into California and most of those headed for the suburbs of Southern California. Those newcomers prospered by finding work in a variety of sectors, but in the years from 1952 through 1962 a substantial 38 percent of Southern California's manufacturing jobs were tied to the defense industry. In short, many of the Californians McGee reached not only disliked communism but also enjoyed a comfortable suburban lifestyle because of massive government spending to fight communism. In the binary Cold War fight between godless communism and capitalism, they saw God's blessings in democracy and post-World War II prosperity.

McGee attacked communism, but he also attacked what he identified as related trends. These included, in no particular order, collectivism, socialism, secularism, and liberalism, any and all of which threatened to undermine America's social fabric and interfered with an ideal society populated by a community of autonomous individuals bound by common religious beliefs and commitment to liberty. For example, McGee disliked Franklin Delano Roosevelt's New Deal, which saw the federal government regulate the economy and institute work and other programs to assist individuals struggling through the Depression. He saw the New Deal as a step toward communism. McGee also criticized the United Nations (UN), which had been established after World War II as an attempt to promote world peace. McGee and other evangelical preachers saw the UN as a step toward one-world government discussed in the Book of Revelation that indicated the apocalypse was near. They saw the UN as a political tool for the Antichrist. McGee and his followers do not represent a universal trend in southern California, but they do offer insight into how religion in the West incorporated post-World War II social, political, and economic influences and moved in new directions.

The Great Plains states also contributed to the post-war invigoration of evangelicalism. At roughly the same time as Charles Fuller and Billy Graham transformed evangelical ministry in California, the more populist, charismatic Oral Roberts experimented on the southern plains. Roberts, born outside Ada, Oklahoma, in 1918, was among the first to use television in ministry and became known as the patriarch of prosperity gospel, which claims those who pray and donate with sufficient fervor will receive good health, wealth, and happiness. Oral Roberts' works, like those of Charles Fuller, contributed to the West's importance as a source of religious innovation.

Roberts felt the call to ministry in 1935 and spent the next 12 years in general evangelical work and as pastor to several churches. In 1947 Roberts' entrepreneurial side emerged as he became a traveling evangelist in order to reach as many people as possible. Roberts founded Healing Waters, Inc., which later became the Oral Roberts Evangelical Association, Inc., in Tulsa to support his work. By 1955, Roberts' traveling ministry boasted $240 000 worth of equipment, including a "cathedral tent" with seating for 14 000. In 1954 he used filmed tent services as the foundation for his move into television ministry. Roberts also developed a publishing business and a radio ministry. Starting in 1957 he broadcast sermons via short-wave radio into the Soviet Union contributing in his own way to the United States' Cold War fight against godless communism. Roberts expanded his evangelical reach through Oral Roberts University, founded in Tulsa in 1963.

Despite the migration of many mainstream Christians to the West to find work in wartime industries and the florescence of institutions such as Fuller Theological Seminary, some religious leaders saw a region needing salvation and a more developed religious infrastructure. In 1952, the Southern Baptist Convention (SBC) voted to expand into eight western states it termed "pagan land": California, Arizona, Colorado, Wyoming, Montana, Oregon, Washington, and Nevada. In September 1952, 1500 Southern Baptist ministers met in Dallas to promote expansion. Dr W.A. Crisswell of the First Baptist Church of Dallas told the gathering that he had recently visited Oregon and been able to drive an entire day without spotting a single church. Another minister claimed that millions in the West had never heard a genuine Gospel sermon. The Southern Baptists at the Dallas convention decided to abandon a longstanding agreement with the American (Northern) Baptist Convention that left the West to the latter group.

The Southern Baptists believed their northern counterparts had failed to establish a significant presence in the West and they set out to right the situation. The SBC moved aggressively into the West with the slogan "a million more in '54." The Southern Baptists saw the "unchurched" West as a spiritual frontier to be won for Christ.

The Rev. Robert Schuller, subject of this chapter's opening vignette, also reflects these themes, although his work fits better in the West's legacy of innovation and reflects its new status as a core region. Schuller's work embodied both an entrepreneurial approach and a willingness to experiment with worship form and message. Schuller aimed to get the unchurched excited about spirituality in general and about Christianity in particular. Schuller essentially disguised the RCA, the denomination in which he received his training, in an effort to get marginally interested people into his drive-in church. Schuller argued that self-respect or self-esteem is the most basic of human desires. People lacking self-esteem suffer not from humility, but from shame. As he saw it, churches that remind people of their sinful nature reinforce a sense of shame. Instead of emphasizing sin, Schuller taught that awareness of God's love allows a person to enjoy healthy self-esteem. Only that, not power, money, fame, sex, or any material item can produce fulfillment. The next chapter will discuss the maturation of Schuller's efforts in the period after 1965. For the period up to 1965, suffice it to say that Schuller changed traditional Reformed Christianity to make it more appealing to migrants newly arrived in the West and to the unchurched living in automobile-centric southern California. A magazine article on Schuller colorfully reported, "His critics contend that Schuller has done for Jesus what Colonel Sanders has done for chicken, that he offers a kind of fast-food franchise salvation bearing the same relationship to the Christ of the Cross that the plastic automaton Abraham Lincoln at Disneyland does to the American Civil War."[5] Maybe the reporter should have used McDonald's, which, like Disneyland (an especially apt comparison given its proximity), had its origins in the post-World War II consumer culture of southern California. Whatever critics thought of his message, many grudgingly acknowledged Schuller's success in reaching the unchurched and bringing them closer to the Bible. No one did it better. Until, that is, pastors using strategies similar to Schuller's, built megachurches even larger than his. They, too, will be discussed in the next chapter.

[5] T. D. Allman, "Jesus in Tomorrowland," *New Republic*, November 27, 1976: 7–9.

Conclusion

The Cold War saw the West come into its own economically, politically, socially, and culturally. Thanks largely to economic and population growth unleashed by World War II, the region moved from periphery to core and became more influential nationally and internationally. The region's religious history reflected those changes and suggested that the transition was not complete. Robert Schuller and the Southern Baptists both acted as pioneers to a region they saw as a kind of frontier awaiting development. The legal battles over plural marriage indicated that mainstream US social and religious values had not been completely imposed on the West. At the same time, the establishment of institutions such as the Fuller Theological Seminary and Oral Roberts University marked a kind of maturity. The development of a strong neo-evangelical movement and the maturation of the Texas theology planted across the Sunbelt contributed to a strong conservative movement that would change religion and politics nationally. Even as the West showed clear signs of having come into its own and as westerners lived more and more like people in other parts of the United States, the region retained a distinctive flavor. Its location on the Pacific Rim made it a natural location for Asian religions to flourish. The presence of the military–industrial complex influenced new religious movements. Its open spaces and fluid, dynamic demographics made it a refuge and suitable home for groups outside the mainstream. These themes would continue to influence the region's religious history for the duration of the Cold War and beyond.

Suggested Reading

Aponte, Edwin Aponte. 2012. *¡Santo!: Varieties of Latino/a Spirituality*. Maryknoll, NY: Orbis.

Gallagher, Eugene V. and W. Michael Ashcraft, eds. 2006a. *Introduction to New and Alternative Religions in America: Volume 4: Asian Traditions*. Westport, CT: Greenwood Press.

Gallagher, Eugene and W. Michael Ashcraft, eds. 2006b. *Introduction to New and Alternative Religions in America: Volume 5: African Diaspora traditions and Other American Innovations*. Westport, CT: Greenwood Press.

Lewis, James R., ed. 2000. *UFOs and Popular Culture: An Encyclopedia of Contemporary Myth.* Santa Barbara, CA: ABC-CLIO.

Martínez, Juan Francisco. 2011. *Los Protestantes: An Introduction to Latino Protestantism in the United States.* Santa Barbara, CA: Praeger.

People v. Jack Woody, 61 Cal.2d 716 (1964).

Stein, Stephen J., ed. 2012. *The Cambridge History of Religions in America,* Vol. III *1945 to the Present.* Cambridge: Cambridge University Press.

Szasz, Ferenc Morton. 2000. *Religion in the Modern American West.* Tucson, AZ: University of Arizona Press.

7

Creativity and Controversy after 1965

"We're going to rock today," promised Victoria Osteen. "This place has been rocked a lot of times, but it's never been rocked for Jesus."[1] Sixteen thousand Sunday worshippers, passions and spirits aroused by a live performance of the up-tempo gospel song "Better than Life" broadcast over three Jumbotrons, cheered the announcement by Osteen, wife of Joel Osteen, senior pastor of Lakewood Church in Houston, Texas. Lakewood Church had just moved into the Compaq Center, former home of the National Basketball Association's Houston Rockets, late in 2003 to accommodate the massive crowds that attend its services. "We love it. We don't miss a Sunday," said Annette Ramirez, sitting in the arena's front row with her husband, Joe. "The message is always very positive and the music is great."[2]

[1] Kris Axtman, "The Rise of the American Megachurch," *Christian Science Monitor*, 30 December 2003, 1.
[2] Kris Axtman, "The Rise of the American Megachurch," *Christian Science Monitor*, 30 December 2003, 1.

Inspiration and Innovation: Religion in the American West,
First Edition. Todd M. Kerstetter.

Originally known as The Summit, the arena *had* rocked. It opened in 1975 with a concert by The Who, played host to two National Basketball Association championships won by the Rockets, and closed its career as a secular facility with a concert by the local rock group ZZ Top in 2003. Church member Regina Blancas remembers bopping to the Go-Go's (another rock band) and cheering the Rockets in the building during those years before Osteen's church bought it. At the dawn of 2004, Lakewood Church stood poised to spend $95 million to transform the Compaq Center into one of the nation's largest churches. Lakewood needed an arena-sized venue to accommodate a congregation that had exploded from about 6000 to 30 000 in less than five years. That put the church squarely in the world of the megachurch, defined as a Protestant Christian congregation with an average weekly attendance of at least 2000. In fact, Lakewood ranked as the nation's largest megachurch, which made it the nation's largest church period. Religion was alive and well in the twenty-first-century West.

The enthusiasm shown in churches such as Lakewood (Figure 7.1) contrasts starkly with the West's reputation for being "unchurched." Figures dating to at least the 1890 census show the West as less religious than the rest of the nation. A century later, researchers

Figure 7.1   Lakewood Church in Houston. Source: © Timothy Fadek/Corbis.

undertook the largest-ever national survey on religion in American life, which showed that respondents in the West were twice as likely to indicate "no religion" than any other sector of the nation. Nine of the ten highest "no religion" states were in the West. Yet a preponderance of the nation's largest and most influential megachurches reside in the West, namely in Texas and California. This seeming contradiction barely scratches the surface of the region's complex religious life.

The years after 1965 saw the West continue to develop along paths established during and immediately after World War II. A demographic shift had brought new waves of settlers into the West and that trend would continue bringing large numbers of people to the Sunbelt (from Florida to southern California), much of which falls in the West. The Metropolitan West that emerged in the second half of the twentieth century had many features in common with the rest of the nation. Suburbs continued to boom and the advent of the Internet added a new facet to mass communication that expanded or enhanced the reach made possible by radio and television. Immigration patterns and laws changed. All of these developments reshaped life in the nation and especially in the West. Western religious life after 1965 reflected and participated in many of the changes that reshaped the West. Plots established in earlier chapters with Mormons and American Indians at their center continued to develop. The lifting of immigration restrictions in 1965 brought demographic changes that led to dramatic increases in the number of Latinos and Asians, who raised the profile of Asian religions in the West and changed the face of Christianity in the United States. Countercultural movements drew migrants to the West and inspired religious creativity. The work of previous religious pioneers bore new results ranging from glorious spiritual achievements to ghastly tragedies. The West's unique atmosphere made it home to some of the nation's most intense religious conflicts in this period and it made headlines for negative events involving "sects," "cults," and "new religions" that proliferated in the region. In short, the West's religious history after 1965 saw a burst of innovation and outbursts of violence that showed the legacy of previous events could not be escaped.

Immigration Reform and Asian Religions in the West

After 1965, Asian religions enjoyed a friendlier reception and occupied a more prominent place in US society and culture. The Immigration and Nationality Act of 1965, also known as the Hart-Celler Act, ended immigration quotas that had been in place since 1924 and opened the way for vastly increased immigration from Asia and Latin America. The counterculture movement of the 1960s encouraged experimentation with drugs, sex, and ideas including eastern religions. These two developments rank among the most important in opening the way for the expansion of Asian religions in both numbers and influence in the US after 1965. The friendlier atmosphere also came from US military personnel returning from service in Asia during World War II, Korea, and Vietnam. Their experiences abroad made them more receptive to Asian culture, perhaps none more so than those who returned to the United States with Asian spouses. The West, thanks to its proximity to Asia and San Francisco's role as an epicenter of counter-culturalism, played an outsized role in the rise of Asian religions in the United States.

Before considering Asian religious traditions, we should note that many Asians who arrived in the United States after 1965 practiced Christianity. Some Asian immigrants came from countries such as the Philippines that have strong Christian traditions. Other Asian nations such as Vietnam and Korea have large Christian minorities. Cities along the West Coast from Los Angeles to Vancouver, British Columbia, have Asian communities served by a variety of Christian churches with ethnic labels such as Chinese Pentecostal or Korean Baptist. In the US Korean community, Christians outnumber Buddhists by a wide margin.

Among Asian religions, Buddhism surged in the West and no event affected Buddhism more profoundly in the 1960s, maybe in the entire twentieth century, than the Immigration Act of 1965. The law ended racist immigration restrictions and allowed a new wave of Asian immigrants to enter the United States. Chinese, Japanese, Koreans, Sri Lankans, Vietnamese, and others came to the United States. They not only swelled the ranks of Buddhist groups already established, but also brought with them new forms of Buddhism to add to the array of religions in the United States. Virtually every form of Buddhism exists in the United States, and Los Angeles might be the most diverse Buddhist city in history. "Los Angeles is the only place in the world that you can find all forms of Buddhism," religious scholar J. Gordon Melton noted. "Not even Asian countries have all forms of Buddhism."[3]

---

[3] Quoted in Gustav Niebuhr, "Land of Religious Freedom Has Universe of Spirituality," *New York Times*, March 30, 1997.

Possibly the largest Chinese Buddhist movement in the United States, Fo Kuang Buddhism, arrived with the Chinese immigration boom of recent decades. Founded in Taiwan in 1967 by Master Hsing Yun, Fo Kuang, or the International Buddhist Progress Society as it is known in the United States, has been described as a "humanistic Buddhism" with an optimistic agenda to improve human society. In particular, Master Hsing Yun shaped traditional elements of Chinese Buddhism to help followers cope with the demands of living in a consumer-driven, urban, industrial society. The movement built an extensive monastic compound in the Los Angeles area to serve as its American headquarters. The Hsi Lai ("Coming to the West," as in western hemisphere, not American West) temple serves affiliates in San Francisco, San Diego, Dallas, Houston, Austin, Las Vegas, Kansas City, and New York. The movement's choice of Los Angeles for its headquarters illustrates how the American West received immigrants, especially Asians, at the West Coast and how the American West has become a source or distribution point for ideas spreading to the rest of the nation.

The US defeat in Vietnam and the fall of Saigon in 1975 loosed a torrent of Vietnamese immigration to the United States. More than 500 000 Vietnamese, some Roman Catholic and many Buddhist, found their way to the United States and most settled in California. The story of the Thanh Cat temple illustrates the role of religion in the late twentieth-century Vietnamese–American Buddhist community. Thich Giac Minh, the temple's abbot, arrived in California shortly after the Vietnam War ended. He worked as a licensed acupuncturist and donated his earnings to help Vietnamese refugees come to the United States. Others in the community followed his example. Again and again the community delayed building a temple, choosing instead to use their money to help their countrymen emigrate. When the refugee situation stabilized, the community shifted its priorities and its money to building Thanh Cat temple, which opened in 1983. Thanh Cat provided a worship center, but it also provided a social center. One member remarked, "We come here to feel anchored. We share news about our lives and we support each other."[4] The temple also became the headquarters and training center for monks and nuns of

---

[4] Quoted in Richard Hughes Seager, *Buddhism in America* (New York: Columbia University Press, 1999), 176.

the Vietnamese Buddhists of America, a network of about 100 Vietnamese Buddhist temples throughout the United States. Again, one can see a religious development unique to the American West largely influenced by the region's proximity to the Pacific Rim and evidence of the West radiating religious influence to other parts of the nation.

Buddhism's influence continued to grow in the 1980s and 1990s. Vietnamese monk Thich Nhat Hanh established the Community of Mindful Living in Berkeley in 1983. Hanh emphasized simplicity and everyday applications of Buddhist teachings, and spawned a national network of meditation groups. Hollywood helped make Buddhism trendy again in the 1990s. Films such as *Little Buddha* and *Kundun* had Buddhist themes. Well-known Tibetan Buddhist actors such as Richard Gere and Steven Seagal set an example followed by other celebrities and fans across the country. The story of Buddhism in California shows the West's continuing religious diversity, even among forms of Buddhism. It also offers insight into how Hollywood's influence radiated to the nation and the world, which supports the argument that the West had become an influential cultural force by the late twentieth century.

The International Society for Krishna Consciousness (ISKCON), more popularly known as the Hare Krishna movement, also entered the US during this period and made its way to the West Coast. ISKCON is the missionary form of devotional Hinduism which teaches that all people can attain their spiritual goals through love and devotion to the Hindu deity Krishna. A.C. Bhaktivedanta Swami Prabhupada founded the Hare Krishna movement in Bengal, India, and brought it to the United States in 1965. During a brief stay in New York City, Bhaktivedanta initiated 19 disciples and established ISKCON as a nonprofit, tax-exempt religious organization.

In January 1967, Bhaktivedanta moved the organization to the heart of the Haight-Ashbury section of San Francisco where the movement flourished with a temple at the heart of the counterculture. Underneath a large sign bearing "Hare Krishna" a smaller sign said, "Stay High All the Time, Discover Eternal Bliss." ISKCON gained 150–200 converts in its first two years in the Haight. Many of the hippies in the Haight had just arrived from somewhere else, and the temple offered a stable home. Bhadktivedanta demanded those living in the temple complex abstain from meat, intoxicants, gambling, and illicit sex, and that they chant and attend worship services.

The San Francisco phase produced a model used by missionaries deployed across North America. In each area targeted for attention, the exclusive communal structure took on an appropriate local flavor. In Los Angeles, for example, where recruiting in public places brought poor results, Hare Krishnas located in a middle class residential area and focused their recruiting on friends and relatives of people already in the movement. ISKCON started the Bhaktivedanta Book Trust in Los Angeles in 1971, making southern California the movement's publishing headquarters. In 1976, ISKCON distributed more than 18 000 religious tracts each week in the United States and Canada. Hare Krishnas gave away more than 5000 books each week at Los Angeles International Airport alone.

These examples show how increased immigration from Asia changed the face of religion in the western United States. Increased international movement and the West's proximity to the Pacific Rim invigorated existing Christian and Buddhist communities and brought new people and ideas into the region. These events also remind us that the West's location on the Pacific Rim has made it a gateway for Asian immigration and a borderland more complex than the Spanish borderland that so often comes to mind and which also changed after 1965 thanks to immigration reform.

Religion in the Hispanic West

The 1965 immigration law also increased immigration from Latin America. Combined with substantial and growing Hispanic communities already in the United States, increased legal migration and continued illegal migration produced a rapidly growing Hispanic population and one that contributed unique elements to the West's religious landscape after 1965.

Religion, for example, played a prominent role in the Mexican American civil rights movement and in the life of its most important activist, César Chávez. Many of the movement's signature events happened in the West and Chávez, an Arizona native and devout Roman Catholic, was a westerner, which make this relevant to the region's history. His reputation rests largely on unionizing Chicano farmworkers, but his appeal to moral values and his wide-ranging inclusion of religious principles qualify Chávez as a spiritual leader, too.

Chávez knew first-hand the struggles of migrant farmworkers in the West. His parents lost their farm during the Depression and moved to California to look for agricultural work. Thanks to his family's constant relocations, Chávez attended dozens of elementary schools and never graduated from high school. His family's experiences motivated him to work passionately to help farmworkers. Chávez worked for 10 years as an organizer for the Community Service Organization, a Latino civil rights group. In 1962 he helped found the National Farm Workers Association, which eventually became the United Farm Workers (UFW). To call attention to low wages for farmworkers, Chávez organized workers' marches to the state capitals of California and Texas. He also called for a national boycott of grapes to put pressure on growers to pay better wages and to provide better working conditions.

These tactics had much in common with other labor organizations, but Chávez imbued his work with spiritual elements. In this respect, he echoed clergyman Martin Luther King, Jr's tactics of nonviolent confrontation in the African American civil rights movement. For example, in 1968 in the midst of the grape boycott some impatient UFW members began to advocate violent tactics. Chávez responded with a 25-day "spiritual fast" to remind his followers of their dedication to nonviolence in the tradition of Mahatma Gandhi and Martin Luther King, Jr. This led the *New York Times* to describe the UFW's agenda as a "quasi-religious cause."[5] Chávez put it more bluntly when he explained his fast was "not intended as a pressure on anyone but only as an expression of my own deep feelings and my own need to do penance and to be in prayer."[6] The fasts produced mystical experiences that shaped his leadership of the UFW.

In addition to following King and Gandhi, he included other religious traditions by worshipping with and organizing with Pentecostals, consulting traditional Mexican healers, and tapping popular Catholicism by often carrying the symbol of the Virgin of Guadalupe (a Mexican version of the Virgin Mary) on protest marches. In short, Chávez brought strong spiritual and religious connections to his quest for social justice in the West.

---

[5] Dick Meister, "'La Huelga' Becomes 'La Causa,'" *New York Times*, November 17, 1968.
[6] Quoted in Luís D. León, "César Chávez and Mexican American Civil Religion," in *Latino Religions and Civic Activism in the United States*, Gastón Espinosa, Virgilio Elizondo, and Jesse Miranda, eds (New York: Oxford, 2005), 59.

At roughly the same time, "liberation theology" migrated north from Latin America into the West. Liberation theology originated with a group of Latin American bishops who met in 1968 in Colombia to discuss responses to the suffering that plagued huge numbers of poor people in Latin America. The bishops believed that the Bible must be read as a document about the poor and oppressed. The historical Jesus, according to the doctrine, was crucified for sedition against the Roman Empire and should be seen as a revolutionary who fought the evils of colonialism. Liberation theologians believed the Catholic Church should continue that fight and assist the poor and oppressed in fighting social inequality.

The West's population of rigorously worked and often poorly paid Hispanic laborers made it fertile ground for an idea like liberation theology in the early 1970s. A group of Chicano priests organized PADRES (Padres Asociadas para los Derechos Religiosos, Educativos, y Sociales, or Fathers associated for religious, educational, and social rights) in 1970. In 1971 a group of Hispanic nuns formed Las Hermanas (The sisters). Both PADRES and Las Hermanas were national groups, but they had particularly important influence on Hispanic Catholicism in Los Angeles. PADRES led the charge in calling for the appointment of a Chicano bishop and pushed for greater church assistance to the poor. Las Hermanas pushed a similar agenda and brought the Hispanic civil rights movement into the Catholic Church.

Liberation theology also shaped the ecumenical sanctuary movement that spread through the US borderlands in the 1980s and 1990s. Political turmoil and violence in much of Central America during these years led thousands of people to flee their home countries to seek political asylum in the United States. The Reagan administration, though, refused to grant asylum to refugees from Guatemala and El Salvador as the regimes in those countries were friendly to the United States. Beginning in Arizona and California, churches began responding to the situation by declaring themselves sanctuaries for those fleeing from violence and persecution. These churches offered food, shelter, and legal protection to refugees. The example started by a handful of churches spread to include more than 400 churches, two states, and 28 cities. The movement of liberation theology into the West shows that more than people crossed the US border with Mexico: so, too, did ideas such as this novel adaptation of Christianity.

New Religious Movements

A number of factors in the late 1960s led to a boom in "new religions" or "new religious movements" originating in or finding homes in the West. The increased immigration from Asia and Latin America, for example, included the religious leaders discussed above as well as leaders of new movements. Interest among baby boomers in psychoactive drugs such as LSD, marijuana, and peyote, to name three examples, coincided with increasing meditation and spiritual exploration. Although these trends spread across the nation, western cities such as San Francisco and Boulder, Colorado, held especially prominent roles in the countercultural movement and in attracting seekers of many stripes, including religious seekers.

The American West functioned as an aerospace-age borderland in more esoteric ways with respect to some of the new religious movements that appeared in the region. Links between outer space, extraterrestrials, and religion continued to develop in the West in the last decades of the twentieth century. Rumors of UFO abductions of humans for medical experimentation escalated during the 1960s. In 1969 Erich von Däniken's *Chariots of the Gods: Unresolved Mysteries of the Past* (1969, G.P. Outnam's Sons) popularized the idea that ancient astronauts had visited the earth and that religious texts and images recorded their visits. The rise of the US space program, which has a significant presence in western cities such as Houston and contributed to the aerospace industry, also likely fueled interest in space and the implications of space travel. In addition to the continuation of phenomena discussed in the previous chapter, interest in extraterrestrials brought forth two new religious movements after 1965, each of which had implications for the West.

The first had its start with a Presbyterian minister's son named Marshall Herff Applewhite. Born in Spur, Texas, in 1932, Applewhite found himself hospitalized in Houston in 1972 for a heart condition. In the hospital, Applewhite met nurse Bonnie Lu Nettles by accident. Together they would lead Heaven's Gate, one of the most infamous of the West's late-twentieth century new religious movements.

"Bonnie" and "Herff" bonded over a shared an interest in the Book of Revelation and the occult. They quickly became convinced that God had brought them together for a special purpose. They left Houston in 1973 on a journey of discovery that led them to a campsite on the Rogue River in Oregon. There they realized they had known each other in past lives and that they were the modern incarnation of two witnesses referred to in Revelation 11:3–13. These two witnesses are instructed to prophesy and are then killed. After enemies gloat over their bodies, God revives them and transports them to heaven in a cloud. Bonnie and Herff decided they would ascend to heaven not in a cloud, but in a spaceship, and that they were destined to update antiquated Biblical language for modern sensibilities. As they told potential followers, Herff and Bonnie, acting as shepherds to be called Bo and Peep, would lead their flock aboard UFOs bound not for heaven, but for "The Evolutionary Level Above Human" or TELAH.

Intentionally or coincidentally, the group maintained a western association for the duration of its existence. Bo and Peep sent members of their flock out to spread their message. The messengers traveled extensively, but mostly in the West. Bo and Peep, too, spread their message in public talks in Los Angeles, Denver, and Chicago. Their presentations drew negative media coverage, much inspired by claims that a spaceship would pick them up in Waldport, Oregon. Bo and Peep compared their followers to astronauts in training as they prepared for life at the "Next Level." The group settled in New Mexico by the mid-1990s. They preferred locations in the Southwest because of its history of alleged UFO activity. Two significant developments marked this stage of their history. First, members capitalized on the high-tech boom by learning computer languages, including HTML and Web design. They began an Internet consulting business and built their own Web site. Second, they had debates over how to reach the Next Level. They expected to go as a group and they began to wonder how necessary their bodies, their "human vehicles," were for the journey. The group began to consider "shedding their vehicles" by committing suicide. In 1996 the group's Web site flashed this message: "Last Chance to Evacuate Earth – Before It's Recycled."

The group sold all its possessions in 1996, moved to a San Diego suburb, and rented a seven-bedroom, seven-bath mansion. News that the Hale–Bopp comet would travel near the earth in 1997 struck the group as a sign that a spaceship from TELAH was coming for them. They prepared to depart, to commit mass suicide, in late March when the comet came nearest to earth. Thirty-nine Heaven's Gate members committed suicide in the San Diego mansion and, over the next several days, three other members killed themselves elsewhere. The 42 people who presumably believed they had shed their vehicles to depart for TELAH marked the largest mass suicide (as most outsiders saw it) in the United States to that date.

Many discussions of Heaven's Gate label the group's religious sensibilities dangerous and bizarre. That overlooks an important point, that they incorporated extraterrestrials, spaceships, and UFOs into their belief system to modernize and update an essentially biblical narrative. Their links to the space age, the high-tech industry, and UFOs also lent them a western character insofar as those phenomena have associations with the western economy and society built on World War II and Cold War militarization. During the group's formative years, it found isolation in the West's open spaces, which, perhaps, contributed to the group's ability to survive and develop innovative ideas. To the extent the group shared its beliefs with outsiders, it seems to have found a tolerant atmosphere in the West.

UFO religion in the West assumed an international and more sophisticated incarnation in Chen Tao, a Taiwanese movement that gathered in suburban Dallas and that many feared might produce a repeat of the Heaven's Gate experience. *Chen* (or *zhen*) translates to "right" or "true" and *tao* (or *dao*) means "way." The movement originated in the mid-twentieth century in southern Taiwan. The group used technological devices to identify, measure, and cultivate spiritual light energy in partnership with precepts of Buddhism and Taoism. A sociology professor named Honming Chen assumed prophetic leadership of the group in 1995. Professor Chen claimed throughout his life to have seen spheres of golden light, which he interpreted as God the Heavenly Father telling him that he had a mission to criticize degraded popular religion and to prepare the world for the return of Christ.

Professor Chen's message added Christian elements to the group's Buddhist–Taoist origins. Namely, he stated that collective negative karma of all living beings (Buddhist–Taoist influence) would bring the Endtime (prophesied in the Book of Revelation). The degradation of civilization and damage to the environment pointed to the late 1990s as the last days. Christ, he said, would arrive soon in God's spacecraft. Chen and about 150 others left Taiwan for San Dimas, California, in 1995. A prophecy led Chen to identify Garland, Texas, a Dallas suburb, as the site of salvation. According to Chen, when pronounced quickly Garland sounds like "God's Land." He moved there in 1997 with as many as 160 followers. Group members dressed in white to symbolize purity. After moving to Texas, many wore cowboy boots and white cowboy hats.

Professor Chen predicted Heavenly Father would arrive in late March 1998. News organizations reported on the prediction and speculated that Chen Tao might be another Heaven's Gate in the making. When March ended with no otherworldly events, the news media lost interest and many followers returned to Taiwan. Some devotees, though, moved to New York State to continue to wait for the saucer salvation, which had been postponed to late 1999.

Chen Tao passed quickly through the West, but the group touched themes important in the region's history. For one thing, they remind us that the story of the West is more complicated than the stereotypical tale of westward expansion with a frontier moving from east to west. Newcomers to the Americas for centuries have entered via the West Coast. Chen Tao believers, like so many others who headed for the West, saw great hope. Even though it stemmed from an accident of enunciation, the notion that Texas held "God Land" echoed a familiar theme. The region failed them, like it did so many others, and they moved on. In this case, the disappointed Chen Taoists continued their eastward journey and moved to New York, thus providing an exact opposite of the stereotypical narrative of westward expansion.

Other unusual religious movements found expression in the West thanks to the region's links to the rise of countercultural movements in the 1960s, especially in and around San Francisco. For example, the "New Age" had critical origins at the Esalen Institute in Big Sur on the California coast south of San Francisco. Founded in 1962, Esalen annually sponsors hundreds of workshops that aim to help people develop their potential. Workshop leaders have included philosophers, psychologists, artists, musicians, and religious thinkers. Many of the early workshops challenged the status quo in many areas, including religion, at the same time as the counterculture movement took off in the Bay area.

New Age traditions mean different things to different people. New Agers often identify themselves as spiritual, but not religious (it's notable that many Christians say the same, suggesting that people tend to view others as merely religious, while their beliefs and practices are personally held and authentic). They also tend to be eclectic, and New Agers pursue spiritual development through a variety of avenues that range from elements of eastern religion and philosophy to appropriating elements of American Indian religion to the use of crystals to the belief in areas that hold special vortices of spiritual power. Psychiatrist Fritz Perls, who led workshops at Esalen on Group Gestalt Therapy, which stressed the importance of immediate, authentic experience, contributed to New Agers' quest for spiritual advancement through experience. Perls viewed the mind and body as a holistic organism and the New Age beliefs that followed from his teaching expected that if enough people could make enough spiritual progress, the entire population of earth would enjoy a significantly enhanced collective consciousness. The goal of transforming consciousness provides possibly the one unifying element of New Age thought.

New Age sensibilities, immigration from Asia, and the wide open spaces of the West contributed to one of the most sensational religious developments in the late-twentieth century: the boom and bust of the Rajneeshpuram community in rural eastern Oregon. The story began in India with Chandra Mohan Jain, whose family called him Rajneesh. He graduated from college in 1955, earned a master's degree in philosophy, and began a university teaching career before delivering a controversial series of lectures in the early 1960s. In the lectures, he criticized Gandhi, denounced Hinduism, and sang the praises of capitalism, technology, and birth control. He argued for the divinity of sexual energy and that sexuality should be expressed freely. Religion, he taught, should show people how to enjoy life. The lectures earned much attention and brought him many followers, especially wealthy business patrons.

Rajneesh fused a variety of teachings into his own method of meditation. From Tantric techniques he borrowed the notion of channeling sexual energy for spiritual illumination. From post-Freudian psychologist Wilhelm Reich he borrowed "bioenergetics" bodywork. From Sufism (a mystical Islamic tradition) and others he adopted ecstatic dancing. These techniques and others went into "dynamic meditation," in which participants laughed, shouted, screamed, and took off their clothes.

One of his wealthy followers provided funds for the Bhagwan (a title meaning "god" he adopted in 1970) to open a meditation center near Poona, India. The center attracted wealthy seekers from around the world. By the early 1980s more than 30 000 people visited the center each year. A number of visitors brought with them psychological problems, drug habits, or both and landed in local jails and hospitals. The resulting bad publicity and increasing local hostility led an American follower, Mo Anand Sheela, to lead the community to the United States.

The Rajneeshees wanted a place to be alone, "a desert kind of land ... a place which was our own," according to one, where the Bhagwan could develop his vision.[7] They found such a place in the American West, which had long been associated with such refuges and continued to be in the 1980s. In August 1981, Sheela bought Big Muddy Ranch, a 64 000-acre spread in eastern Oregon, to provide a new home for the Bhagwan's followers. Through Bureau of Land Management leases, "Rancho Rajneesh" expanded its land base to nearly 85 000 acres. By 1985 the community boasted excellent roads, schools, banks, office buildings, and even an airport.

Rancho Rajneesh did not just change the landscape, its members revolutionized the area's population, society, and culture. Into sparsely inhabited, politically conservative eastern Oregon came thousands of highly educated, well-funded, free-loving spiritual pioneers. Huge "celebrations" between 1982 and 1984 brought 7000 to 15 000 annual visitors. Many remained. The residents hoped to build a city of 10 000 united in following the Bhagwan's vision. The Bhagwan's followers saw themselves as living a philosophy and the Bhagwan denied that he had founded a religion. Neighbors saw a cult whose lifestyle conflicted with established local social and cultural standards, and whose ballooning population threatened to take over the community.

Rajneeshpuram appeared to mix church and state, and local opposition came from both church and state. A nearby conservative Baptist congregation criticized Rajneeshpuram's "immoral" display of wealth. The Bhagwan's fleet of more than 80 Rolls Royces served as one example. The Baptists also criticized the community's ultra-liberal attitudes toward sexuality. Area ranchers worried that establishing a community with thousands of new residents in arid eastern Oregon would require new wells that would irreparably lower the water table. Ultimately, local bureaucrats and federal judges effectively hemmed

---

[7] Quoted in Carl Abbott, "Utopia and Bureaucracy: The Fall of Rajneeshpuram, Oregon," *Pacific Historical Review*, LIX (February 1990): 100.

in, then dismantled, the community. Land-use planners halted Rajneeshpuram's development ideas, which violated local regulations. In December 1985, a federal judge ruled Rajneeshpuram's incorporation illegal because it violated constitutional separation of church and state. The Bhagwan called the move to America a "mistake" and told his followers to leave Oregon. Many of the housing units and furnishings ended up at another controversial religious settlement in Montana – the Royal Teton Ranch of the Church Universal and Triumphant.

The Church Universal and Triumphant (CUT), another movement with roots in New Age thought, made its home in the West starting in 1966. The aptly named Mark L. Prophet started the movement in Washington, DC, in 1958 as Summit Lighthouse. Prophet followed the lead of groups that sought to publish hidden teachings from higher planes of existence to help humans cope with what Prophet and others perceived as a critical moment in history. Prophet claimed to be a messenger for "ascended masters," beings similar to the Buddha who had achieved "enlightenment," whose revealed wisdom would guide human spiritual progress.

As Prophet saw it, an ascended master named Saint Germain had sponsored the United States since its origins granting it an exceptional place in achieving the New Age. But, as of the 1960s, Prophet claimed "fallen ones" threatened to weaken the United States and its special place. Prophet associated so-called fallen ones with any number of things that posed a threat to the social fabric including socialism, jazz, rock and roll, tobacco, alcohol, gambling, and abortion. Summit Lighthouse cast its followers as a spiritual army that would fight such threats. This orientation displayed a new spiritual approach, but a socially conservative one that supported a patriotism, or even hyperpatriotism among followers. As it happened, it also contributed to an increasing paranoia that would threaten to destroy the group by the early 1990s.

Prophet moved the group to Colorado Springs, Colorado, in 1966. The group became increasingly popular with young people conditioned by countercultural movements to experiment with new or novel lifestyles and it began to grow. From Colorado Springs, the group reached out to the rest of the nation. Outreach included starting Ascended Master University in 1972 to teach new members about the movement.

When Prophet died in 1973, his wife, Elizabeth Claire Prophet, took over the movement. She renamed the movement Church Universal and Triumphant and, in 1976, moved it to southern California. From her new California base, Elizabeth Claire Prophet continued to establish study groups and teaching centers nationwide. By the 1970s, CUT claimed it was the true church of ascended masters Gautama Buddha and Jesus Christ. Prophet became a nationally known figure in the New Age movement and continued to promote a conservative social agenda and to support strong national defense, which provided more evidence of CUT's patriotism.

A lawsuit filed by a disgruntled ex-member and a rash of bad publicity led Prophet to move the church's headquarters in 1986 once again, this time to southern Montana. Fears of earthquakes, fear of a nuclear attack by the Soviet Union, and zoning conflicts with neighbors also motivated the move to an isolated stronghold in the interior West. Prophet saw CUT's new home, the Royal Teton Ranch (partially furnished with items bought from the liquidated Rancho Rajneesh), as a haven in which her followers could follow teachings of ascended masters to help usher the planet into the Age of Aquarius.

In the late 1980s, ascended masters warned of a possible nuclear war with the Soviet Union between 1989 and 1991. This sent CUT into a period of heightened anxiety and paranoia, and sparked frenzied construction of fallout shelters at the ranch. CUT called its members to assemble in Montana for the nuclear apocalypse it feared was imminent. When the predicted events did not happen, CUT entered a different crisis, one of confidence. A mass exodus of disillusioned, maybe even disappointed, members forced CUT to reduce operations in Montana. By the mid-1990s, CUT began to sell property to pay expenses. CUT appointed a management consultant as president in 1996 and began a wholesale reorganization. The church distanced itself from its apocalypticism and hyperpatriotism and focused, instead, on promoting Mark and Elizabeth Claire Prophet's less controversial New Age teachings and presenting itself as a mainstream church. Elizabeth Claire Prophet, suffering from Alzheimer's disease, relinquished all CUT duties in July 1999.

Although it originated in the East, CUT had a critical relationship with the West. Its moves to Colorado Springs and to southern California allowed CUT to tap freewheeling elements of the counter-culture, while at the same time it reacted against what it perceived as detrimental effects of the counterculture that threatened mainstream social values. CUT benefitted from its move to a region not dominated by a religious mainstream. In Montana, CUT found space its members considered protective and an escape from constricting neighbors.

The San Francisco Bay area's thriving counterculture scene in the mid- and late 1960s included religious groups that reacted against the status quo and that tapped the spirit behind the Summer of Love in 1967. Probably the most radical reaction against the status quo religiously speaking came from the Church of Satan, which should not be confused with Satanism. Satanism has been used to refer to religious practices including worship of the diabolical described in the Bible to various new religious movements, Mormonism, Roman Catholicism, and the Church of Satan. The Church of Satan, founded by Anton LaVey, has a distinctive set of practices and beliefs that do not often reconcile with what is widely feared about and assumed to be Satanism.

LaVey founded the Church of Satan in San Francisco, where he had lived since boyhood, on April 30, 1966. He intended the new church to challenge the status quo, especially established religion and, most of all, Christianity. Rather than celebrate selflessness and spirituality, LaVey emphasized gratification, the individual, and the material. In its outline, this message shared ground with the prosperity gospel advocated by some of the broadcast evangelists and megachurch pastors discussed in earlier chapters as well as later in this chapter. As he saw it, the Church of Satan would accept humans as they are and satisfy their natural instincts. LaVey's Satan symbolized opposition, an "adversary" to challenge religious and social conventions.

LaVey considered mainstream religions, especially Christianity, guilty of misleading followers and infringing on personal liberty. He wanted to eliminate those constraints. He also wanted his followers to cultivate a strong sense of self. LaVey summarized his approach in "Nine Satanic Statements." Satan represents indulgence instead of abstinence; undefiled wisdom instead of hypocritical self-deceit; kindness to those who deserve it instead of love wasted on ingrates; and vengeance instead of turning the other cheek, to name several examples. In short, LaVey believed mainstream religions mislead humans by repressing their animal nature, rather than acknowledging, celebrating, and encouraging it. He aimed to

liberate people, not repress them. The San Francisco counterculture created an atmosphere in which a figure like LaVey could
become something of a celebrity. It also allowed for a robust marketplace of ideas, including religious ones as far out as LaVey's
counter-Christianity.

Other, less shocking new religious movements also found the Bay
Area welcoming. James Warren Jones, a progressive religious leader
from Indiana for example, brought his followers to northern California
in 1965 thinking the environment would welcome and sustain his
agenda to promote socialism and racial integration. Jones had become
a faith healer and a self-proclaimed preacher at age 20. His sermons
and speeches reflected influences of Communism, liberal Methodist
social thought, and elements of Pentecostalism, including emotional
preaching and worship styles and millenarianism. In mid-1950s
Indianapolis, he founded a church that would become known as the
People's Temple. He used it to promote racial integration and the
social gospel. The church started a nursing home for the elderly and
adopted African American children and children orphaned by the
Korean War. By 1960, the People's Temple had become affiliated with
the Christian Church (Disciples of Christ), which ordained Jones
despite his lack of theological training.

Jones assumed a prophetic role. He preached racial equality and
harmony. He also predicted an apocalyptic end of the world involving
race war, genocide, and nuclear war. Jones' opposition to segregation
led to conflict with Indianapolis society. To escape the friction and to
find a haven from nuclear destruction, he lived briefly in British
Guyana and for two years in Brazil in the early 1960s. Jones returned
to Indiana, but by 1965 Jones decided to abandon Indianapolis and
led about 70 families, half of them black and the other half white, to
Ukiah in northern California.

The People's Temple, continued its social missions by ministering
to the elderly and to juvenile delinquents. Jones started a radio
ministry and, by the early 1970s, had established branches in San
Francisco (located in the largely African American Fillmore district)
and Los Angeles, and amassed thousands of followers. In 1975, the
group established a multiracial agricultural mission in Jonestown
(named after Jim Jones), Guyana. The Jonestown mission aimed to be
a utopian community that would eliminate racism, sexism, ageism,
and classism.

Meanwhile, Jones organized the church such that he held complete power. He used allegedly spiritual techniques to monitor members and gather information. Jones resorted to humiliation, emotional abuse, and physical punishment to silence critics and to maintain absolute power. Jones also became involved in local and national politics. He supported San Francisco Mayor George Moscone, which earned Jones an appointment to the City Housing Commission. Jones also met with First Lady Rosalyn Carter, California Governor Jerry Brown, and vice-presidential candidate Walter Mondale.

Trouble began to find the People's Temple in the mid-1970s. A group of "apostates" from the core leadership defected in 1975 and 1976 and publicly aired their grievances with Jones and the institution. Reports emerged that Jones had become authoritarian, that he punished wrongdoers with paddlings, that he had sex with male and female followers, that he insisted followers relinquish all property to the church, and more. Complaints from relatives of Jones' followers, lawsuits, and other negative publicity brought the attention of anti-cult activists and the promise of a government investigation. In the summer of 1977, Jones fled with more than a thousand followers to Jonestown in the "Promised Land" of Guyana, where the People's Temple had leased nearly 4000 acres from the nation's Marxist government

Charges of abusive practices in Jonestown led California Congressman Leo Ryan to investigate. Ryan, who represented a Bay Area district, had friends and constituents affected by the Temple. In his capacity as chairman of a congressional subcommittee concerned with US citizens living abroad, Ryan led an investigative entourage to Jonestown in November 1978 that initiated the group's stunningly tragic demise. Jones' followers ambushed and killed Ryan and three members of his party. Jones immediately ordered his followers to dismantle the community. The leadership distributed Flavor Aid (a soft drink similar to Kool-Aid) laced with tranquilizers and cyanide to the members. All told, 914 people died in a mass murder or mass suicide. About 75 percent of the victims were black; about two-thirds were women; almost 300 were under the age of 18.

Although the tragedy happened in Guyana, the story of the People's Temple is largely American and one in which the West figures prominently. The People's Temple originated in Indiana, but it did not flourish until it moved to California. There, it thrived in the currents of the Bay Area's counterculture and atmosphere of openness. From its West Coast headquarters, the People's Temple projected its influence internationally. As historian of religion Ferenc Szasz put it, the People's Temple is best understood as a religious movement and one that needed 1970s San Francisco to succeed.

Arguably the dominant and most controversial story of religion in the West in the 1990s, possibly for the entire era after 1965, came from the conflict between the Branch Davidians and the US government outside Waco, Texas, in 1993. The Branch Davidians trace their roots to a group that split from the Seventh-day Adventist Church in 1935. Victor Houteff, a Bulgarian immigrant who converted to Seventh-day Adventism and settled in Los Angeles, began a movement to, as he saw it, purify the church from within. Church leaders did not appreciate Houteff's efforts and removed him from the church roll. Houteff led his followers to a site outside Waco, Texas, where they established the Mount Carmel commune. The group's leadership and name changed over the decades. In the late 1980s a young man named Vernon Howell joined what had become known as the Branch Davidians. Howell changed his name to David Koresh in 1990 and took control of the group. Koresh derived much of his power from charismatic teaching and interpretation of the Bible, especially the Revelation of St. John. He depicted himself as a Christ figure and claimed to speak the words of God.

The group enjoyed more or less amicable relations with their neighbors for decades. But, by the early 1990s a public sensitized by the Jonestown tragedy, the events at Rancho Rajneesh, and heightened activity by anti-cult activists looked warily at groups such as the Branch Davidians. Also, disturbing reports about the Branch Davidians began to surface. Two reporters from the *Waco Tribune-Herald* investigated the Branch Davidians for eight months to prepare a seven-part exposé titled "The Sinful Messiah." The series relied heavily on ex-members of the group and anti-cult experts. The articles vilified Koresh and portrayed his followers as dupes brainwashed by the charismatic Koresh. The series also contained troubling allegations of firearms stockpiling, illegal manufacture of automatic weapons, reports that Koresh had marital relations with multiple female members, and that Koresh had married his legal wife when she was 14.

At the same time the *Tribune-Herald* was investigating the Branch Davidians, so, too, was the Bureau of Alcohol, Tobacco, and Firearms (BATF). By early 1993, the BATF had gathered enough information to obtain search and arrest warrants. On February 28, BATF agents stormed the Branch Davidian residence to serve the warrants. Alerted to the action, the Branch Davidians prepared to defend themselves against what they perceived as an assault. A firefight erupted. Four BATF agents and at least two Branch Davidians died as a result. The raid initiated a 51-day standoff that ended on April 19 when the Federal Bureau of Investigation (FBI) used armored vehicles to insert CS gas (a type of tear gas) into the Branch Davidians' residence. Fires ignited during the gas insertion and quickly destroyed the building. More than 70 Branch Davidians, including women and children, perished. Autopsies revealed or suggested that victims died by a variety of means ranging from gunshot and stab wounds to injuries sustained from the building's collapse to possible poisoning or asphyxiation. Whatever the causes, the horror of the outcome cannot be denied.

What roles did religion and region play in the Branch Davidian tragedy? Religion ran throughout the episode, sometimes subtly and other times not. Religion brought the Branch Davidians to Mount Carmel and paved the way for Koresh to dominate the group. Koresh's religious vision organized life at Mount Carmel and provided the rationale for virtually everything the group did. And religion permeated outsiders' responses to the group and its actions. Reporters from the *Tribune-Herald* recognized the Branch Davidians' religious affinity in referring to Koresh as a "doomsday prophet," "a deranged, violent megalomaniac with a messiah complex," and "false prophet." The paper also called Koresh "a classic sociopath."[8] *Christian Century* called Koresh a "religious fanatic."[9] *Time* called him "the mad messiah of Waco."[10] The Branch Davidians lived what they perceived to be righteous, religious lives. Mainstream society perceived them as a religious group. The conflicts between the two revolved around dramatically different interpretations and applications of what can ultimately be traced to religious principles. The Branch Davidians sought space in the West to develop their system

---

[8] "FBI: Howell Cares Only for His Own Life," *Waco Tribune-Herald*, March 28, 1993; "Making Koresh a Kind of Hero," *Waco Tribune-Herald*, April 4, 1993; "'Visitor' Leaves Cult Compound," *Waco Tribune-Herald*, April 18, 1993; and, "Family Uneasy about 'Flea Market,'" *Waco Tribune-Herald*, August 1, 1993.

[9] James M. Wall, "Eager for the End," *Christian Century* 110 (May 5, 1993): 475–476.

[10] Sophronia Scott Gregory, "Children of a Lesser God," *Time*, 17 May, 1993, 54.

and for decades did that. But in 1993, the Branch Davidians and mainstream society both found the bloody boundaries of tolerance and religious freedom.

The groups discussed in this section, even with all their followers combined, represent a tiny portion of the West's population and to many readers their beliefs will seem extreme or even bizarre, yet they deserve a place in this discussion. The kinds of "new religions" discussed here proliferated globally in this period, not just in the United States. But, in the United States the largest, best known, and most infamous such groups resided on the West Coast, isolated areas between the Rocky Mountains and the Sierra Nevada, and in Texas. These groups show the complexity of western religious life after 1965. That complexity traces to legacies of immigration changes, World War II and the Cold War military and economic development, continued population shifts into the West and the Sunbelt, the West's open spaces, and the West's relatively tolerant "unchurched" society.

Religion and the Internet in the West

The Information Technology (IT) revolution of the late twentieth century provides another example of how the Cold War touched religion in the West. Government spending on research and development for the military played a significant role not only in the aerospace industry, but also in computer technology including networking systems that would become the Internet. Although not strictly a western phenomenon, western universities and cities played central roles in the IT revolution and the "high-tech" industries that allowed western religious organizations to democratize religion and to obliterate the obstacle of space in organization and service.

One California church that innovatively lowered the bar for ordination of its clergy in the 1960s used the Internet to make ordination even easier. In 1962, Kirby Hensley founded the Universal Life Church in his garage in Modesto, California. Hensley started the church as an act of protest against the tax exemptions granted to churches. The church has no traditional doctrine and simply advocates doing "that which is right." In addition to that, Hensley preached a message of freedom from taxes and sold $5 mail-order clergy ordination certificates to anyone who could pay. As of this writing, interested parties can become ordained online for no charge and almost instantly. A 2009 article in the *Modesto Bee* reported that the church claimed 15 000 active congregations internationally, that it issues 8500 to 10 000 ordination certificates monthly, and has ordained about 20 million people worldwide since 1962. As it has with information generally, the Internet allowed Universal Life Church to speed and democratize religious participation.

A church founded on the Great Plains in the midst of the dotcom boom used the Internet to expand and enhance its ministry in ways earlier churches used radio or television and then some. Life Covenant Church, also known as Life Church and LifeChurch.tv, uses the Internet as an innovative tool to pursue Christianity. As a part of the Evangelical Covenant Church, Life Church follows core Christian beliefs, although it allows adherents considerable latitude in inter-preting issues not clearly presented in scripture. Founded in 1996 in Edmond, Oklahoma, Life Church has grown to include at this writing 15 campuses (11 in Oklahoma, and one each in New York, Florida, Tennessee, and Texas). Life Church also lists "Church Online" among its campuses. Each campus offers live, casual services supplemented with teaching from founder and Senior Pastor Craig Groeschel or another Life Church teaching pastor delivered by video. People who live in remote areas, who are homebound, or for whatever reason cannot attend a physical campus can participate in an interactive online service. In this way and others, Life Church has used new tech-nology to obliterate space that is a particular problem for people who live in remote areas of the rural West.

The LifeChurch.tv Web site includes beautifully designed content for a Web-savvy audience. Groeschel and his colleagues designed Life Church, both the physical and online versions, in response to market research conducted with non-churchgoers (people who would qualify as "unchurched") in the Edmond area in the mid-1990s. "They said churches were full of hypocrites and were boring," Groeschel told *Businessweek* for a 2005 cover story on evangelical churches using business techniques.[11] He designed lively multimedia services presented in a setting that crosses rock concert with coffee shop in an effort to attract participants. The "jobs" page at the Web

---

[11] Quoted in William C. Symonds, "Earthly Empires: How Evangelical Churches Are Borrowing from the Business Playbook," *Businessweek* (May 23, 2005): 87.

site includes a video showing employees and work settings that might have come straight from a new high-tech company in Silicon Valley. The church developed a Bible application for mobile phones. The online church features a live chat, an opportunity to connect with a volunteer for live prayer, and links to Facebook and Twitter, and is available as a Podcast. These developments led *Outreach* magazine to name Life Church as the most innovative church in the country in 2007. By 2011, Life Church claimed weekly attendance of 38 000, placing it in the ranks of megachurches. Life Church shares character-istics with a number of other megachurches, which have become a prominent feature of the West's – and the world's – religious landscape.

The Megachurch Boom

As this and previous chapters have shown, the West saw the creation of large churches and congregations, and clergy using radio effec-tively to build large regional, national, and international audiences. As with the IT revolution and the high-tech industry, these devel-opments were not exclusively of the West; but, the West seems to have played an outsized role in their development and to hold a disproportionate number of examples when compared to other regions. Timing and space appear influential. Twentieth-century migrations into the West, including those by religious leaders seek-ing to build new communities and congregations, coincided with the arrival of new technologies such as radio in the early twentieth century. In the late twentieth century, some of those churches served as prototypes for truly massive institutions and for evange-lists who would use not only radio, but also television and the Internet to achieve spectacular reach in the era of the Sunbelt.

Large churches have existed in the United States for a very long time, but the megachurch (Protestant Christian congregration with weekly total attendance of at least 2000) phenomenon of the late twentieth century and early twenty-first century is different. The rapid spread, the large number, and the role of these megachurches in shaping new models of religious life chart new territory for mega-churches in the United States. For much of the twentieth century the United States had maybe 10 to 20 congregations that would qualify as megachurches. By 1970 about 50 megachurches existed. The number climbed dramatically through 2000: 150 megachurches in 1980, 310 in 1990, and at least 600 by 2000. The number hit 1210 in 2005 and had reached 1350 by 2009. With respect to location, megachurches thrived in the Sunbelt (about 67%) and in the suburbs (about 80%). The largest and arguably the most influential megachurches can be found in the West.

Oral Roberts, whose pioneering efforts in large-scale evangelicalism came to light in the previous chapter, expanded his religious empire into healthcare and pushed his message to extreme lengths in the decades after 1965. In 1981 he expanded his mission into healthcare by opening the City of Faith Medical Center in Tulsa. By the mid-1980s, Roberts' evangelical operations and university employed more than 2300 people and drew $110 million in revenue.

Roberts' fundraising tactics created high-profile controversy in the late 1980s. In a January 1987 televised service Roberts told his audience he needed to raise $4.5 million to support his financially troubled medical center. "I'm asking you to help extend my life," he said. "We're at the point where God could call Oral Roberts home in March." Religious leaders and comedians mocked the tactic, but Roberts eventually claimed to have raised $8 million dollars. The campaign succeeded, but the medical center closed in 1989.

Despite this episode, Roberts became an enormously influential religious figure of the twentieth century and provided evidence of religious innovation and influence in the West. According to estimates provided by Oral Roberts University, Roberts laid hands on more than 1.5 million people, reached more than 500 million on radio and television, and counseled or prayed with presidents John F. Kennedy, Richard M. Nixon, and Jimmy Carter. In so doing, he elevated Pentecostal theology, which focuses on emotional, mystical, and supernatural experiences and was discussed in more detail in Chapter 5, and practice to the mainstream and helped make the Pentecostal and charismatic movements the fastest-growing Christian movements in the United States in the 1980s and 1990s. He trained and mentored several generations of prosperity gospel (believers will enjoy health and wealth) preachers who went on to create television and multimedia empires of their own. Roberts' success in bringing respectability and visibility to Pentecostalism shows the Plains states, too, had enduring influence on religion and the roots of the megachurch movement in this case, through the twentieth century.

Another western evangelical pioneer introduced in the previous chapter, the Rev. Robert H. Schuller, also continued to expand his influence through the late twentieth century and into the twenty-first century. Schuller's drive-in church might not suggest it, but he believed in the spiritual power of architecture. Schuller collaborated with southern California architect Richard Neutra to design his first church building. The church connected congregants with the outdoors and natural elements such as flowers, trees, and pools of water, which provided a spiritual oasis amidst suburban sprawl. When Schuller later decided to construct an even more elaborate cathedral, he hired renowned architect Philip Johnson to design a glass structure that would seat 4000. The $20 million Crystal Cathedral opened in 1980. *Newsweek* called it "one of the most spectacular religious edifices in the world" and another observer wrote it was "the kind of church God would build – if he could afford it."[12]

By the late 1990s, Schuller had written more than 30 books and his "Hour of Power" television program had been reaching millions of viewers worldwide for more than 25 years. Schuller had gained international renown not only for his words, but also for his actions. His Crystal Cathedral made a bold architectural statement and a bold statement of inclusiveness through its multicultural staff and far-reaching services that included support group classes, telephone crisis counseling, singles and divorce recovery programs, a youth ministry, a senior ministry, and counseling centers as well as worship services. Congregants could improve their physical health in a gym and a workout facility. Schuller's influence even reached the White House. President Clinton invited Schuller to attend the 1997 State of the Union speech, where Schuller sat in a position of honor next to First Lady Hillary Rodham Clinton. As it turned out, Schuller had been advising President Clinton for years and had prayed with him in the Lincoln Bedroom. Even Schuller's critics respected Schuller's ability to reach the unchurched, an important achievement in diverse southern California. By carefully crafting his message, Schuller has been able to draw them closer to the Bible. That, Schuller would note, has been his aim all along. No one did it better. Until, that is, pastors using strategies strikingly similar to Schuller's, built megachurches even larger than his.

---

[12] Quoted in Dennis Voskuil, *Mountains into Goldmines: Robert Schuller and the Gospel of Success* (Grand Rapids, MI: William B. Eerdmans, 1983), 34.

Among the most famous and influential of those who built the
megachurch movement, Rick Warren came from a family of evangelists and was raised in northern California's rural Mendocino County.
The Warren family helped build dozens of churches around the world
and at home kept a large vegetable garden so they would have food to
give away to the needy. Warren earned a bachelor's degree at California
Baptist University and a master of divinity degree at Southwest Baptist
Theological Seminary in Fort Worth, Texas.

Warren and other graduates showed the success of those institutions, planted by pioneer religionists to develop spiritual life in the
West. While in Fort Worth, Warren began researching and planning a
pioneer church of his own. He learned that his native California
ranked among the states with the fewest churches per capita. He also
learned that Lake Forest, in Orange County south of Los Angeles, was
one of the nation's fastest growing communities. Seeing opportunity
in suburban LA, Warren moved his family to Lake Forest to establish
a Southern Baptist church.

For his first three months in Lake Forest, Warren researched the
community. He went door-to-door and asked people, especially
non-churchgoers, what in a church might appeal to them. Their
answers helped Warren to develop "Saddleback Sam," a composite
potential congregant he named after a nearby mountain. Saddleback
Sam was a 35-year-old man, educated and middle class who preferred
casual to formal and was skeptical of organized religion as more
dedicated to money than to the everyday concerns of regular people.
Warren then designed services to attract Sam to church. Put another
way, Warren modified religion to cater to the famously unchurched
westerner.

Saddleback Valley Community Church had its first service on
Easter Sunday in 1980 at Laguna Hills High School. Two hundred
people attended and heard Warren give a sermon laden with references to present-day situations and very little theological vocabulary.
Warren dressed casually, replaced traditional Christian music with
contemporary music, and asked congregants to call him Rick.
Critics, including some evangelicals, viewed this approach as pan-
dering, if not flirting with heresy. Warren defended his approach
in an interview in 1995: "Today, in America, the church must learn
the culture and language of the 1990s to communicate. Now that
may be a marketing principle, but it's also just a biblical principle

that says: Start where people are. Jesus started where people were, not where he wanted them to be."[13]

Saddleback's congregation grew steadily over the next 15 years. The church held services in schools, recreation centers, restaurants, and theaters – nearly 80 different buildings overall. In the 1990s, when the congregation had surpassed 10 000, Warren began planning construction of a home that focused on the needs of his followers. On its 120-acre compound, Saddleback built two worship spaces, seating 4800 and 2800, two 32 000-square-foot educational buildings, three athletic fields, a gym, and a cafeteria. In these facilities Saddleback offers weekend services and 79 weekly programs ranging from Bible study to child care and weight loss.

Warren's success made him a guru of the megachurch movement. Pastors from around the country visited Saddleback to learn from Warren how to increase the sizes of their own churches. Warren lectured around the country, drawing audiences ranging from seminary students to corporate executives. In 1995 Warren published *The Purpose-Driven Church* (1995, Zondervan), a manual for building churches. The book sold well in religious circles and crossed over to achieve success in non-religious audiences. The book sold more than a million copies and proceeds allowed him to pay off much of the debt he incurred building Saddleback. In 2002, Warren took a sabbatical from Saddleback to write *The Purpose-Driven Life: What on Earth Am I Here For?* (2002, Zondervan). In 40 chapters, meant to be read in 40 consecutive days, the book tells its reader how to find a sense of purpose according to God's plan. *The Purpose-Driven Life* has sold more than 30 million copies, has been translated into 20 languages, and helped make Warren an influential public figure who has been invited to address the World Economic Forum, the Council on Foreign Relations, and the UN, and who is sought by national political candidates and leaders as a counselor. Warren, born of the West and its religious institutions, became one of his generation's great religious entrepreneurs and an example of western influence radiating to the rest of the nation and world.

---

[13] Quoted in Barbara Bradley, "Marketing that New-Time Religion: Methodology, Not Theology, is the Secret Behind the Latest Boom in the Church Business," *Los Angeles Times* December 10, 1995, A1.

Figure 7.2   Bishop T. D. Jakes. Source: © Mike Fuentes/AP/Corbis.

In Texas, another evangelical pioneer used religious entrepreneurship to minister to African Americans, primarily, in one of the West's largest urban areas. In South Dallas, one of the state's most economically depressed places, T.D. Jakes founded in 1996 a high-tech house of worship called the Potter's House (Figure 7.2). Jakes drew the name from the biblical story of Jeremiah, whose experiences with a potter's wheel made him realize damaged vessels could be restored to objects of beauty. Jakes has been called "the shepherd of the shattered" for his efforts to restore damaged human vessels including prostitutes, drug addicts, alcoholics, the homeless, and the illiterate. The Potter's House donated satellite dishes to hundreds of prisons in 29 states so Jakes could get his message to inmates. Jakes found a receptive audience. In its first year, the Potter's House drew 7000 members. It grew to 17 000 in its second year and counted 21 000 members by its third, making it one of the largest churches in Texas and the West.

A native of South Charleston, West Virginia, Jakes founded his first church, Greater Emanuel Temple of Faith, in Montgomery, West Virginia, in 1980. Jakes rapidly expanded the church's membership from 10, but kept his day job. Jakes used radio and television broadcasts to spread his message and expand his flock, which eventually grew large enough to support him as a full-time preacher. Jakes' diverse congregation included 40 percent white membership, an unusually high number for a church led by an African American pastor.

Accompanied by 50 families, Jakes moved his ministry to Dallas' Oak Cliff neighborhood in 1996. Jakes' services reflect musical influences ranging from Broadway musicals to funk and soul. In fact, Jakes turned one of his best-known sermons into a musical. "Woman Thou Art Loosed!," based on the book of Genesis, sought to help women who had been abused or disrespected, played to large audiences across the nation. Its success led to a million-selling book that paved the way for other best-sellers. Jakes expanded into the music business by issuing successful gospel CDs that earned him a Grammy nomination. Jakes' multimedia reach extended into greeting cards in 2001 when Mahogany Cards, a division of Hallmark dedicated to African American buyers, issued a line of cards based on Jakes' writings and sermons. Jakes' multimedia empire spreads his influence from Dallas to a national, if not international, audience and shows the growing cultural power of the metropolitan West.

Success brought wealth to Jakes and his conspicuous consumption has inspired criticism. Jakes wears expensive, tailor-made suits, drives expensive cars, and lives in a home valued at more than a million dollars. Critics say this promotion of consumerism does a disservice to the African American community. Jakes defends his lifestyle. Young African Americans can see him as a role model, someone who has become prosperous without breaking the law. "Once they see a black man who is successful, who has written several books and been celebrated [across] the country and overseas, and he's not selling drugs but he's driving the same kind of car the pimp or drug dealer is, and he's not illegal and he's not immoral, it encourages young men," Jakes told a newspaper reporter.[14] To Jakes, his success supports his ministry's message of economic empowerment by demonstrating what can be had through hard work and a spiritual life. Furthermore, Jakes' life shows that the mythical dream of going west to find success endures into the twenty-first century, and the Potter's House reminds us to consider the presence and importance of African Americans in the West's religious history.

[14] Quoted in Bill Broadway, "From His Pulpit, Messages on Prosperity, Pain," *Washington Post*, July 26, 1997, B07.

A few hours' drive from the Potter's House, Lakewood Church in Houston, Texas, during the first decade of the twenty-first century became the largest church in America and transformed the religious marketplace under the dynamic leadership of its pastor, Joel Osteen. As of 2010 more than 47 000 attend Lakewood services each week. In January 1999, John Osteen, Joel's father, Lakewood's founder and, at the time its pastor, telephoned Joel from a hospital bed to ask his son to preach the Sunday sermon at Lakewood. Joel had never preached. His lack of experience made him pause, but Joel accepted the invitation. Within a week, John Osteen died of a heart attack. By the end of that year Joel had become Lakewood's senior pastor. Over the next six years, Joel Osteen turned Lakewood into the fastest-growing, largest, and most ethnically diverse megachurch in the United States.

Joel Osteen, born in 1963, has no formal theological education. In 1982 he urged his father to televise sermons. Joel wanted to use television to reach a bigger audience and his father agreed under the condition that they not petition viewers for money. Joel left Oral Roberts University, where he was an undergraduate, and began producing and directing broadcasts of Lakewood services. By the mid-1980s Lakewood's sermons appeared nationally on the Family Channel. Television brought more people into the church, which moved into a newly built facility in 1987 to accommodate its 6000-member congregation.

Under Joel Osteen since 1999, Lakewood aims to create a better Houston by helping its congregants discover God's plan for their lives. Lakewood also uses Houston as a base for world-wide Christian outreach. In pursuing those goals and in seeking new congregants, Lakewood has taken a kind of "market mentality" when it comes to practice. To compete in a wide-open religious marketplace, churches strived to attract members. Few have succeeded like Lakewood.

Osteen acts as much a guide as he does a shepherd. In Houston, an international gateway to the United States, the American West, and the American Dream, he promises to lead the way to freedom and prosperity. Osteen often invokes freedom in his sermons using the expression "beacon of hope," a reference to the Statue of Liberty. Osteen sometimes embodies the symbolism by raising his right arm, Bible in hand, over his head. Visually, the Bible replaces the torch held by the Statue of Liberty. Those with the determination, he preaches, can go from rags to riches. His own life proves it and he regularly encourages his congregation to "dream big dreams." This approach and a midday Spanish-language sermon on Sundays contribute to Lakewood's wide appeal. Blacks, Hispanics, and whites populate Lakewood's congregation in roughly equal numbers.

The sanctuary at Lakewood reflects the church's market mentality in its absence of overt religious symbolism. The entry resembles a mall or an office building more than a church. Congregants sit in stadium seating rather than pews. A rotating globe depicting the world illuminated with gold light stands where many churches would, instead, have a cross. Award-winning musicians perform and lead singing as part of worship services. Giant television screens project the services for easy viewing by the thousands in the audience. Two waterfalls, a café, and other amenities help attract and hold congregants' attention. In short, Lakewood aims at a wide audience and communicates its Christian message through top-quality entertainment and spectacle.

Spectacular success brought the means and the need to move Lakewood into a former basketball arena, the former Compaq Center. The new building not only had enough seats for the booming congregation, but also sat in a much more car-friendly location. "Everybody in Houston has been to the Compaq Center," Osteen said in 2007, "so instead of 'I don't know where it is,' it's 'I know how to get there.' And the parking! There are nine thousand covered spaces."[15] According to Osteen, the new centralized location produced an immediate increase of 10 000 at each week's services.

Osteen parlayed Lakewood's success into a multimedia empire and a role as an international religious leader. His influence originates in and radiates from Houston via television, the Internet, and other media. Osteen reaches more than 200 million US households and 100 countries around the world. His book, *Your Best Life Now* (2004, FaithWords), has sold about five million copies and reached number one on the *New York Times* bestseller list. Simon and Schuster paid Osteen a $13 million advance for his 2007 book, *Become a Better You* and printed three million copies, the largest first printing of a book ever at the time of its publication. Meanwhile, Lakewood's weekly attendance surpasses 47 000.

---

[15] Quoted in Evan Smith, "Joel Osteen: Can Joel Osteen Get an 'Amen'?" *Texas Monthly*, November 2007, http://www.texasmonthly.com/content/joel-osteen (accessed July 20, 2014).

Osteen, Jakes, Warren, and other religious entrepreneurs refined evangelical models pioneered during the twentieth century, notably in the West. They built enormous churches that catered to the needs of people in the booming metropolitan western Sunbelt. With the aid of multimedia outreach, these western religious leaders spread their message and methods to the nation and beyond.

Religion in the Native West

Little that is coherent can be said about religion among the West's Native Americans during the late twentieth century because of the variety of practices and because faith traditions frequently overlap and coexist. Many thousands of Indians practice Christianity, some exclusively. In New Mexico, residents of San Ildefonso Pueblo favor Roman Catholicism, but many still participate in the ancient ceremonies of the kiva societies. At the Pine Ridge Reservation in South Dakota, site of the Ghost Danced-related Wounded Knee tragedy of 1890, a Lakota might practice Christianity, participate in Native American Church peyote rituals, and participate in any number of rites associated with "traditional" Lakota spirituality. Similar patterns can be found across Indian Country. Perhaps most important, many American Indian beliefs and practices survived concerted attempts at eradication to enjoy a surge of interest after 1965 and the legal protections for Indian religious practices experienced continued negotiation. These developments showed that matters associated with the nineteenth-century conquest of the West remained decidedly unsettled and influential in the twenty-first.

By the 1960s, American Indian beliefs that had survived enjoyed a revival of interest among Indians and non-Indians, alike. Currents that inspired movements to advance civil rights of US minority groups also touched American Indians. As the Black Power movement celebrated African American culture, so the Red Power movement celebrated American Indian culture. Books about American Indian spirituality found wide audiences in the years after 1965. *Black Elk Speaks*, first printed in the 1930s, enjoyed a revival. It provided a touchstone for non-Indians in the counterculture and served as an important source for a generation of American Indians seeking to reconnect with their heritage. *Lame Deer, Seeker of Visions*, published in 1972 by a Lakota from the Rosebud Reservation, criticized Christian churches among his people, offered insight into Lakota spirituality, and found a wide audience (1972, Simon and Schuster). One of the most popular American Indian writers of the period, Vine Deloria, Jr, wrote from the perspective of a Standing Rock Sioux descended from two generations of missionaries and someone who held a master's degree from the Lutheran School of Theology and a law degree from the University of Colorado. Deloria wrote more than 20 books and two of the best-known have religious themes. *Custer Died for Your Sins: An Indian Manifesto*, published in 1969, made Deloria a national figure (1969, University of Oklahoma Press). In *God Is Red*, published in 1973 (1973, Putnam), Deloria argued that American Indian spiritual traditions were more suited to the planet's needs than Christianity, which facilitated imperialism and disregard for ecology. These works showed the enduring significance of Lakota religion in the 1960s and 1970s. Furthermore, they demonstrate what Patricia Limerick would call the unsettled and complex legacies of the conquest of the West. Indian people were still very much evident in the West, including a university-educated Lutheran Sioux lawyer who wrote a best-selling critique of Christianity.

Congress reflected the general warming toward American Indian religious practices when in 1978 it passed the American Indian Religious Freedom Act (AIRFA). AIRFA stated Congress' belief that native religious rights should be respected. The weak law, though, did little to protect those rights. Sacred sites, for example, found little protection. In *Lyng v. Northwest Indian Cemetery Protective Association* (1988), the US Supreme Court ruled members of the Yurok, Karok, and Tolowa tribes of Northern California could not stop the US Forest Service from building a road through a site considered sacred by the tribes despite evidence that the road threatened to make it impossible for the tribes to practice their religion, which would therefore destroy the religion. As described in Chapter 1, place plays a critical role in American Indian spirituality. The *Lyng* ruling showed that principle still at work in the late twentieth century and the Court unwilling or unable to recognize it. In the end, property rights trumped religious rights.

Two years later, *Employment Division, Department of Human Resources of Oregon v. Smith* (1990) saw the Court undercut legal protection for sacramental peyote use by the Native American Church. The California Supreme Court extended protection to peyotists in its *Woody* decision (see Chapter 6). *Smith* brought a similar question to the Supreme Court. Two members of the Native American Church had been fired from their jobs for sacramental peyote use (Oregon law prohibited peyote use) and the state denied the workers unemployment benefits. The peyotists sued to challenge that denial, but the Court's majority upheld it. This effectively subjected peyotists to state drug laws. The ruling outraged the public and Congress, offering further evidence of the era's embrace of Indian spirituality.

Congress responded to *Smith* (and *Lyng*) by passing the Religious Freedom Restoration Act (RFRA) in 1993. This act aimed to expand free exercise of religion protections to protect peyotists and others. For good measure, Congress also amended AIRFA in 1994 to provide specific protection for peyotists. That extra measure turned out to have been a good idea, as the Court later struck down part of the RFRA. With the Native American Graves Protection and Repatriation Act of 1990, Congress protected graves found on federal or tribal lands and provided for the return of human remains, sacred objects, and other cultural items obtained illegally.

This era also witnessed tension and tragedy related to the appropriation of American Indian religious practices by spiritual seekers or entrepreneurs associated with the New Age. Arguably the grossest of these involved the deaths of three participants in a sweat lodge ceremony based on rituals found in a range of traditional Indian cultures but run by James Arthur Ray, a nationally known New Age guru, at a retreat near Sedona, Arizona, in 2009. Ray charged $9695 for a "spiritual warrior" experience that included a vision quest (36 hours in the desert with neither food nor water) followed by a session in a sweat lodge. Ray intended the lodge, basically a tent turned into a sauna by heated rocks and steam, as a tool to break mental and spiritual blocks. This session left 21 participants hospitalized and three dead. The episode prompted Arvol Looking Horse, a Lakota spiritual leader known as Keeper of the Sacred White Buffalo Calf Pipe Bundle, to decry the commercialization and misinterpretation of the ceremony. In November 2009, Ray received a two-year prison sentence and was ordered to pay $57 000 in restitution to the families of the three victims.

Paths to the Present in Mormon Wests

The history of the Mormon West after 1965 looks similar in some ways to that of Indian Country. The rich legacy of Mormon pioneers and the polygamy controversy settled in 1890 seem safely locked away in the Old West of the nineteenth century. The Reed Smoot investigation covered in Chapter 5 and the Short Creek raid discussed in Chapter 6 showed that's simply not the case. Yet another high-profile raid on persistent polygamists, this one in Texas in 2008, and the nomination in 2012 of Mitt Romney as the Republican presidential candidate showed varied legacies of the Mormon past shaping the West and the nation in the twenty-first century.

After decades of quiet coexistence, the Fundamentalist Church of Jesus Christ of Latter-day Saints (FLDS) and mainstream US society clashed again in the West. By the first decade of the twenty-first century the FLDS counted about 10 000 members. Fall-out from the 1953 Short Creek raid by Arizona state police and national guardsmen to enforce anti-polygamy laws led state authorities to tolerate polygamists for more than five decades.

Shortly after the turn of the twenty-first century the FLDS expanded its presence by moving into rural west Texas. A company named YFZ LLC bought land near Eldorado, Texas, in 2003. YFZ suggested it planned to build a corporate retreat on the property. When the true nature of the development became known in the spring of 2008, the local newspaper reported that residents were surprised to learn that the corporate hunting retreat was an FLDS compound complete with a temple (Figure 7.3). YFZ, it turned out, stood for Yearning for Zion and the company was a creation of the FLDS community. Local residents had no objection to a corporate hunting retreat. A religious compound suggested something else altogether, especially with the Branch Davidian tragedy a fresh memory.

Conflict erupted at the YFZ Ranch at about midnight on April 3, 2008. Texas Child Protective Service investigators accompanied by law enforcement agents raided the ranch to investigate charges of child abuse based on an anonymous tip. The state removed more than 400 children, the largest removal of children in US history, first placing them and their mothers in shelters then placing the children into foster care. According to a spokesman for the Texas Department of Family and Protective Services, the state believed all children living at the YFZ

Figure 7.3   Members of the Fundamentalist Church of Jesus Christ of Latter-day Saints Leave the Tom Green County Courthouse in San Angelo, Texas. Source: © Eric Gay/AP/Corbis.

Ranch had been abused or were at risk of abuse, and neither religion nor lifestyle influenced the raid. But, Harvey Hilderbran, Eldorado's state representative, told a *New York Times* reporter that authorities had been looking for a way to fight FLDS polygamy. Officials worried especially about accusations that FLDS men were marrying underage women.

The raid quickly drew scrutiny. Within six weeks of the raid, the action's cost exceeded $7 million. The state contracted with at least two faith-based organizations, the Salvation Army and Baptist Child and Family Services, for assistance in the action. Texas lawmakers suggested seizing FLDS assets to cover costs associated with the action. The raid's origins also drew attention. An anonymous phone caller claiming to be a pregnant, abused 16 year old married to a 50-year-old FLDS member sparked the investigation. The state's alliance with "acceptable" faith organizations and the concept of seizing FLDS assets showed little had changed since the federal government's nineteenth-century crusade against the Latter-day Saints Church.

As the raid came under scrutiny, Texas Governor Rick Perry expressed his support. "The governor is very proud of the work being done by [Child Protective Services]," a Perry spokeswoman said.[16] About a week after Perry's endorsement, the Third Court of Appeals revoked the state's custody over the children of 38 mothers citing lack of evidence that they faced immediate danger of abuse. The ruling eventually extended to virtually all the seized children. The unanimous ruling said removing children from their home was "an extreme measure" and could be justified only in cases of immediate danger. The state had taken the position that the FLDS "belief system" condoned underage marriage and pregnancy and treated the entire YFZ Ranch as a household. The appeals court found no evidence of widespread abuse and said the district judge had approved the removal without sufficient evidence. The state appealed the ruling, but the Texas Supreme Court agreed with the appeals court's decision, paving the way for the children to go home, which most did by early June.

The YFZ conflict reflected recurring themes in the religious history of the American West involving different manifestations of family and social organization. The 2008 Texas raid on YFZ Ranch aimed to bring its FLDS residents into line with mainstream social and family values. The Child Protective Services raid and its aftermath brought the FLDS close to the same place the Latter-day Saints Church reached in the 1890 manifesto that renounced polygamy. In early June, shortly after the children returned, a FLDS spokesman read this statement to clarify the group's position: "In the future, the church commits that it will not preside over the marriage of any woman under the age of legal consent in the jurisdiction in which the marriage takes place. The church will counsel families that they neither request nor consent to any under-age marriages. This policy will apply churchwide."[17] The Texas raid yielded criminal charges related to alleged underage marriages against a dozen FLDS men. At least six have been convicted of felonies and sentenced to prison terms of up to 75 years. Polygamists have followed a path from the nineteenth century to the present that has repeated cycles of conflict with mainstream society and has kept them marginalized.

[16] Quoted in Bill Hanna and John Moritz, "Gov. Perry Praises CPS' Handling of Polygamist Sect Cases," *Fort Worth Star-Telegram*, May 15, 2008.

[17] Quoted in Kirk Johnson and Gretel Kovach, "Daughter of Sect Leader Gets Additional Protection," *New York Times*, June 4, 2008.

The Latter-day Saints Church followed a completely different path, a smoother one that led from the margins to the mainstream. As the turmoil of the 1960s and Vietnam War era and their challenges to traditional cultural and social values passed, the Saints' emphasis on morality and family values fit more comfortably in mainstream America. The Church opened the priesthood to African Americans in the late 1970s and in the early 1980s added "another testimony to the Gospel of Jesus Christ" as a subtitle to *The Book of Mormon*. Mormon support of mainstream lifestyles, conservative politics, and regular church attendance give them much in common with evangelicals. These measures showed the Church moving toward the center of American society and Christianity. In addition to social and lifestyle matters, Mormon success has probably contributed to familiarity. The Church counted about 1.5 million members worldwide in 1960. That number jumped to about 11 million by 2000, with 5 million Mormons living in the United States. A vigorous mission program helped build that population, as did a high birthrate (twice the national rate) among Mormons in the West. The Latter-day Saints Church dominates Utah and Idaho and is the second-largest religious organization in Arizona, California, Hawaii, Nevada, Oregon, Washington, and Wyoming. The Mormon region, centered in Utah, provides the greatest exception to the "unchurched" character of most of the West.

Cultural and political developments of the early twenty-first century indicate unprecedented acceptance of Mormonism. On Broadway, a musical called *The Book of Mormon* became a smash hit that spawned a best-selling soundtrack recording and successful touring productions. Although the satire mocks both organized religion and musical theater, the use of Mormonism and Mormon missionaries as a vehicle requires a certain level of understanding on the part of the audience. At roughly the same time, cable television network HBO aired several seasons of the drama *Big Love*, which told the story of a family from a polygamous compound trying to blend in with life in mainstream Utah. In politics, Mitt Romney, a successful Mormon businessman who served a term as Massachusetts governor, pursued the Republican nomination for president in 2008 and 2012. Romney fell short in 2008, but won the nomination in 2012. His success in Massachusetts, his embrace by a national party, and his ability to win more than 59 million votes (47.8 percent of the popular vote) suggested that much of America had put aside whatever stigmas it had attached to Mormonism. That a candidate who is a devout member of what was once a despised sect could come that close to winning the presidency shows the nation and Mormonism had both come a long way from their religious battles of the nineteenth century.

Conclusion

The decades since 1965 have seen the West thrive. The region attracted capital and people and "matured" into an economic and cultural powerhouse that exerts influence on the rest of the nation and the world. The high-technology industry of Silicon Valley, the television and movie industries in the Los Angeles area, and the grunge rock phenomenon associated with Seattle all provide examples. Something similar happened in the religious realm. New immigration patterns brought new peoples and new ideas. The West's reputation, especially San Francisco's reputation, as a center of the counterculture drew religious seekers looking for acceptance outside the mainstream. Religious motives inspired some to make the move and for some the move inspired innovation. Charles Fuller, Oral Roberts, Robert Schuller, Rick Warren, T.D. Jakes, and Joel Osteen moved mass religion in new directions in the West. The exact relationship of region to religion remains difficult to pinpoint, but there can be no doubt that as these men built religious empires their influence radiated from the region and demonstrated the West's growing importance to the nation and the world. For some groups, though, new times brought more of old conflicts. The region's historic links to American Indians and Mormons continued to shape its religious and social discourse into the twenty-first century.

Suggested Reading

Chidester, David. 2003. *Salvation and Suicide: Jim Jones, The Peoples Temple, and Jonestown*, revised edition. Bloomington, IN: Indiana University Press.

Deloria, Jr, Vine. 1973. *God Is Red*. New York: Putnam.

Dochuk, Darren. 2011. *From Bible Belt to Sunbelt: Plain-Folk Religion, Grassroots Politics, and the Rise of Evangelical Conservatism*. New York: Norton.

Ellingson, Stephen. 2007. *The Megachurch and the Mainline: Remaking Religious Tradition in the Twenty-first Century*. Chicago, IL: University of Chicago Press.

Employment Division, Department of Human Resources of Oregon v. Smith, 494 U.S. 872 (1990).

Espinosa, Gastón and Mario T. García, eds. 2008. *Mexican American Religions: Spirituality, Activism, and Culture.* Durham, NC: Duke University Press.

Jenkins, Philip. 2007. *The Next Christendom: The Coming of Global Christianity.* New York: Oxford University Press.

Kerstetter, Todd M. 2006. *God's Country, Uncle Sam's Land: Faith and Conflict in the American West.* Urbana and Chicago, IL: University of Illinois Press.

Lyng v. Northwest Indian Cemetery Protective Association, 485 U.S. 439 (1988).

Marsden, George. 1987. *Reforming Fundamentalism: Fuller Seminary and the New Evangelism.* Grand Rapids, MI: Eerdmans.

Nowicki, Sue. 2009. "Universal Life Goes On." *The Modesto (California) Bee.* March 6.

Partridge, Christopher, ed. 2004. *New Religions: A Guide.* New York: Oxford University Press.

Phan, Peter C. 2003. *Christianity with an Asian Face: Asian American Theology in the Making.* Maryknoll, NY: Orbis.

Sandoval, Moises. 2006. *On the Move: A History of the Hispanic Church in the United States,* rev. 2nd edn. Maryknoll, NY: Orbis.

Stein, Stephen J. ed. 2012. *The Cambridge History of Religions in America,* Vol. III *1945 to the Present.* Cambridge: Cambridge University Press.

Strelley, Kate with Robert D. San Souci. 1987. *The Ultimate Game: The Rise and Fall of Bhagwan Shree Rajneesh.* San Francisco, CA: Harper & Row.

Symonds, William C. 2005. "Earthly Empires: How Evangelical Churches Are Borrowing from the Business Playbook." *Businessweek* (May 23, 2005): 78–88.

Szasz, Ferenc Morton. 2000. *Religion in the Modern American West.* Tucson, AZ: University of Arizona Press.

Tabor, James D. and Eugene V. Gallagher. 1995. *Why Waco?: Cults and the Battle for Religious Freedom in America.* Berkeley, CA: University of California Press.

Tan, Jonathan Y. 2008. *Introducing Asian American Theologies.* Maryknoll, NY: Orbis.

"The Sinful Messiah," [seven-part series] *Waco (Texas) Tribune-Herald,* February -March 1, 1993.

Thumma, Scott and Dave Travis. 2007. *Beyond Megachurch Myths: What We Can Learn from America's Largest Churches.* San Francisco, CA: Jossey-Bass.

Conclusion

The Frontier that Wouldn't Close

Early in the twenty-first century a reality television star brought the West's religious history into federal court and showed that matters once considered settled were anything but. Kody Brown, the polygamous star of the reality show *Sister Wives* and a member of the Apostolic United Brethren Church, a fundamentalist offshoot of the Mormon Church, brought the suit. Brown's lawyer argued that Utah's ban on cohabitation violated his rights to privacy and religious freedom. He won.

In December 2013 a federal judge struck down parts of the Utah anti-polygamy law in question as unconstitutional. The law prohibited "cohabitation," a technique used by mainstream US society since the nineteenth century to limit polygamous relationships. The 1879 *Reynolds v. United States*[1] ruling by the United States Supreme Court stamped the nation's approval on such restrictions. But Judge Clark Waddoups of the United States District Court in Utah ruled that the law's ban on cohabitation violated the First Amendment guarantee of

---

[1] *Reynolds v. United States*, 98 U.S. 145 (1879).

Inspiration and Innovation: Religion in the American West,
First Edition. Todd M. Kerstetter.
© 2015 John Wiley & Sons, Inc. Published 2015 by John Wiley & Sons, Inc.

free exercise of religion. Judge Waddoups noted in his decision that the nation's attitude about government regulation of personal affairs and unpopular groups has changed significantly in the last century. The Supreme Court has become "less inclined to allow majoritarian coercion of unpopular or disliked minority groups," Judge Waddoups noted, especially through legislation motivated by "religious prejudice" or other constitutionally suspect motives. Kody Brown said he hoped "that in time all of our neighbors and fellow citizens will come to respect our own choices as part of this wonderful country of different faiths and beliefs."[2] The *New York Times* reported that in terms of recognizing relationships once prohibited by law, the Utah case "could open a new frontier."[3]

The *Times*' "frontier" had nothing to do with the settlement line that the Census Bureau said became indiscernible in 1890, or with Frederick Jackson Turner's dynamic meeting point of savagery and civilization. Or did it? It wasn't just the settlement line that went away in 1890. So did the Mormon Church's official sanction of plural marriage. So did the lives of hundreds of Ghost Dancers and with them a considerable amount of their religion's vitality. Turner and others can be forgiven for seeing a watershed in 1890, a watershed that included key events in the religious history of the American West. But, as the *Times*' article suggests, it isn't that simple. Many recent historians of the West would agree, although some might blanch at the use of the "f-word" to make the point. As I bring this book to a close, the Brown case helps to make a critical point: The West's religious history continues to unfold and all the stuff you've read to this point *matters*.

The very first people who lived in the West held religious beliefs that ordered their lives and were deeply, inextricably linked to place. Those beliefs inspired them in any number of ways including ways we'll never be able to fully recover or understand. Over centuries people innovated to create new versions of those beliefs and completely new beliefs. The legacy of those beliefs lives in the twenty-first century.

[2] Quoted in John Schwartz, "A Utah Law Prohibiting Polygamy Is Weakened," *New York Times*, December 14, 2013.

[3] Quoted in John Schwartz, "A Utah Law Prohibiting Polygamy Is Weakened," *New York Times*, December 14, 2013.

As we draw closer to the present, we know more about people who lived in the West and their relationships with religion. Religion inspired many of the first non-Indians to come to the West. Spanish, French, Russian, and American newcomers sought material gain, but they also sought to spread their religious beliefs to people who didn't already hold them. Furthermore, religion provided an integral component of the social order they sought to impose on a landscape they viewed as a blank slate. These people planted churches and lived in societies governed or strongly influenced by values derived from religion. Their worldview led them to miss, to misunderstand, and to disrespect indigenous religions. Even as they shared or forced their religion on American Indians, they sought to eradicate indigenous religions. These people saw the West as a wilderness inhabited by savage heathens. They saw opportunities to bestow the civilizing gift of Christianity. They also might have seen a virgin land, a blank slate upon which they could write the story of a new, Christian society organized around transplanted religious institutions and ideas. That plot dominated much of the West's religious history in the eighteenth and nineteenth centuries and its legacies can still be seen as plainly as the churches named for St. Peter the Martyr (the Aleut) in Minot, Calgary, and Lake Havasu City.

But, some unexpected things happened on the way to establishing civilizing Christianity in the West. American Indians maintained their religious beliefs. Some converted to Christianity. Some did both. Still others participated in innovative new religious movements such as the Ghost Dance or the Native American Church. Perhaps nowhere can one see the nuances and complications of the West's religious history better than in the many indigenous communities in the region's cities and reservations.

As it turned out, the desire to spread religion in the West was complicated and contested. Mormons went west to escape persecution suffered in the United States and set out to establish a kingdom of God on earth in the valley of the Great Salt Lake. Jews moved to the West and brought their religion with them. Judaism inspired separatist communal settlements as well as social order and infrastructure for Jewish communities in major western cities. Japanese Buddhist missionaries arrived in the West from the Far East with the intention of spreading civilizing religion in the United States. I found that the most eye-opening revelation of this entire project. It expanded my understanding of the West's diverse religious history and population. Better yet, it fed my interest in the West's complex and often oversimplified history. As much as I appreciate Frederick Jackson Turner's frontier hypothesis, I enjoy seeing it challenged. What better to do that than the arrival on the West Coast of Japanese Buddhists, who viewed the United States as a wide-open frontier for Buddhism and who set out to spread it *eastward from a beachhead in the West*? That kind of evidence flips the Turnerian frontier on its head and reminds us to think about the West much more expansively. The famous arch in St. Louis marks a gateway to the West, but we should remember that San Francisco served as a gateway to the West that opened eastward. El Paso served as a gateway to the West as *el Norte*. From the perspectives of the Alaska coast and Canada, the gateway to the West opened south.

Things got even more complicated in the twentieth century. For most of the first half of the century, the echoes of the nineteenth century seemed to ring loudly. People continued to move into the West and much of the region seemed to be catching up to other regions in terms of population, economic development, and infrastructure. People brought religious ideas with them from other places and planted them in the West or worked to build on religious foundations established earlier. But something else was happening. Sister Aimee might have come to the West from eastern Canada, but in Los Angeles she built something new that capitalized on a unique time and place. Texas theology grew up and grew successful in the Sunbelt. These innovations came from the region, they shaped the region, and they extended to shape the nation and, in some cases, other nations. These events suggest that the West retained a uniquely regional character worth study past the supposed close of the frontier in 1890. They also showed how the region became more powerful, transitioned away from being a colony of the rest of the country, and began exerting more and more influence on the rest of the country and the world.

After 1945, innovation and diversity hit new highs in the West's religious history and conflict, sometimes spectacular, continued to mar the story. All manner of religions made their mark on the West, often in relation to regional developments such as the high-tech industry, the large presence of the military–industrial complex, the availability of land and an atmosphere of tolerance. UFOs and extraterrestrial beings inspired religious innovations, as did the Internet. The San Francisco Bay Area played an outsized role in the period. The Bay Area's diverse and wide-open society sustained the Church of Satan, the People's Temple, Beats and Buddhists, and more. Nearby Silicon Valley contributed to the rise of the Internet, which allowed the Universal Life Church to democratize ordination and provided the tools for Oklahoma's Lifechurch.tv to reach broad audiences and overcome space and distance, both of which had often dictated terms of life in the West in previous generations. During the same decades, megachurches built on prototypes established early in the century provided a new delivery vehicle for religion that capitalized on automobile culture and suburban sprawl. Ongoing immigration brought new faces, new religions, and variations on existing religions into the West, increasing the region's religious diversity.

The post-war years also, sadly, saw tragic religious conflicts. Perhaps the most tragic involved the Branch Davidian standoff against the US government in 1993. Another involved the raid on the FLDS polygamists at the Yearning for Zion ranch in 2008. The raid pointed out the controversial living conditions inspired by religious belief inside the FLDS community as well as the disruption of religiously organized FLDS families by state law enforcement and welfare agencies. These events point out the still-contested nature of society in the West. They also push us to ask questions about bedrock assumptions about the West and what it means to be American. To what extent can freedom be found in the West? To what extent should freedom be allowed in the West, or anywhere for that matter? As the Kody Brown test case, which originated in the West's legacy of conquest suggests, those questions and the exact meaning of First Amendment guarantees of religious freedom are open to interpretation and subject to change.

The West has changed since I rode my bicycle across it in 1989 and it will have changed even more by the time you read this. I thought about religion very little that summer, but I gained an intimate knowledge of the narrow strip of the West I could see from my saddle. This book rides through the West and from its saddle you can see a narrow strip of its history revealed by religion. You don't see everything, but I hope the book has been a good guide and broadened your understanding of a region that holds an important place in the nation's history and in the American mind. Religion has shaped the West and the American mind as well as the relationship between the two. From the beginning of the story until the time you read this, religion has inspired people to be in the West, to come to the West, and to live in the West, often in some very innovative ways.

Index

Inspiration and Innovation: Religion in the American West,
First Edition. Todd M. Kerstetter.
© 2015 John Wiley & Sons, Inc. Published 2015 by John Wiley & Sons, Inc.